Peace

of

Mind

To John,
with love on
your 45th birthday.
All my love,
Ali

Peace

of

Mind

Daily Meditations for
Easing Stress

AMY E. DEAN

BANTAM BOOKS
New York Toronto London Sydney Auckland

To Sonja Dean

PEACE OF MIND

A Bantam Book / March 1995

Library of Congress Cataloging-in-Publication Data

Dean, Amy.
   Peace of mind : daily meditations for easing stress / Amy E. Dean.
      p.   cm.
   Includes index.
   ISBN 0-553-35454-X
   1. Peace of mind—Religious aspects—Meditations.   2. Stress
(Psychology)—Religious aspects—Meditations.   3. Devotional
calendars.   I. Title.
BL624.2.D439   1995
158'.12—dc20   94-21563
                                                                      CIP

Published simultaneously in the United States and Canada

Bantam Books are published by Bantam Books, a division of Bantam
Doubleday Dell Publishing Group, Inc. Its trademark, consisting of the
words "Bantam Books" and the portrayal of a rooster, is Registered in
U.S. Patent and Trademark Office and in other countries. Marca
Registrada. Bantam Books, 1540 Broadway, New York, New York
10036.

PRINTED IN THE UNITED STATES OF AMERICA

FFG   0 9 8 7 6 5

Introduction

Imagine sitting at a desk, facing an IN basket and an OUT basket. The IN basket collects your thoughts and feelings about the people, places, and things around you; the OUT basket takes these thoughts and feelings and responds to them with either a calm, clear action or a distressed one.

If your IN basket is filled with stressful thoughts and feelings—tension, anger, frustration, negativity, or fear—there is the tendency to react in stressful ways. Mentally, you may feel overwhelmed, pressured, incapable of concentrating, or ready to snap. Physically, your muscles may tighten, your heart race, your jaw clench, and your breathing may be quick and shallow. Spiritually, you may feel alone, fearful, hopeless, or find it hard to believe in a power greater than yourself.

However, if your IN basket is filled with peaceful thoughts and feelings—calmness, creativity, capability, optimism, and confidence—then you will be able to act in more peaceful ways. Inner peace instills outer peace.

Even though you may feel as if there are hundreds of tasks you have to accomplish today, you can still experience a peace of mind. Each of the following meditations is designed to help you look at one of your many daily duties, responsibilities, interactions, or circumstances. Let them pass through your mind slowly and evenly, like the grains of sand passing through the narrow neck of an hourglass. They will help you reflect on ways to ease your stress and develop peace of mind.

You might like to read and reflect on each day's

meditation in the morning, before the hustle and bustle of the day begins. Or you might like to read and reflect on the meditation at times that are particularly stressful for you, such as before an important meeting or during your commute home from work. Or perhaps you'll want to save the meditation as a closure for the day, to read and reflect on while taking a bath or before going to sleep.

Each meditation can provide you with the opportunity to find a few minutes of peace each day by reminding you that there's a calm and positive person inside you who *can* respond effectively to stress. As you become reacquainted with this person through your daily readings and reflections, you will gradually find yourself more capable of managing the stresses in your life. And since each daily meditation suggests positive, healthy ways to respond to stress, you will also begin to experience a physical, emotional, and spiritual healing as you employ these methods in your life.

Even though your days may be filled with difficult people, hectic schedules, or challenging problems, this book shows you that you have a choice as to how to handle the stresses: You can be like an amoeba and suck up surrounding stressful moods, or you can learn how to step back from each situation, reflect on other ways of looking at it, and then act in ways that help you maintain your inner peace.

Your most important issue each day is not what's happening around you; it's what's happening within you. By remaining calm and serene in the face of any stress, you can achieve peace of mind.

To return to the root is to find peace. To find peace is to fulfill one's destiny. To fulfill one's destiny is to be constant. To know the Constant is called Insight.

—TAO

*For a long time it seemed to me that real life was about
to begin, but there was always some obstacle in the way.
Something had to be got through first, some unfinished
business. . . .Then life would begin. At last it dawned on
me that these obstacles were my life.*
                                                    —BETTE HOWLAND

Do you begin a new year by creating a list of things
you think will turn your life around and take away all
the obstacles that keep you from truly enjoying each
day? Perhaps your New Year's resolutions involve exercising, dieting, putting in fewer hours at the office,
becoming more patient with your children, or setting
aside time to spend with your partner. But do you really think that making and sticking to such New Year's
resolutions will bring you total happiness?

People sometimes believe their New Year's resolutions will make everything better, that by following the
guidelines made by a resolving statement, obstacles
will magically be removed that prevent them from feeling better about themselves, their job, their family,
their partner, and their life. People give their resolutions much more significance than they deserve and
don't recognize resolutions for what they really are:
simple goals that can improve small parts of their life.

Before you make your New Year's resolutions, keep
in mind that real life is full of obstacles, difficulties,
and things you'd like to change. Simply resolve today
to do the best you can this coming year.

*I'll take it easy on myself this new year by making res-
olutions that will help me be more gentle and kind to
myself.*

*Too often, our minds are locked on one track. We are
looking for red—so we overlook blue. Many Nobel
Prizes have been washed down the drain because someone did not expect the unexpected.*
                                        —JOHN D. TURNER

A mountain stream that flows down a majestic peak
often has to alter its course from year to year. Fallen
tree branches, clumps of dead leaves, and dislodged
rocks can make the mountain terrain change from season to season. So each season the water must forge a
different path on its journey to the valley.

How like the stream are you? Think of this day as the
terrain on the mountainside of your life. You are the
stream. If you had a choice, would you seek out the path
that keeps you entrenched in familiar and ineffective
ways of doing things? Or would you be willing to flow
down a new path—one that holds unpredictable twists
and turns that may encourage you to approach things
differently?

Like nature, life involves change. So the possibility
of doing things the same way over and over again is
nearly impossible. While the Predictable Path may feel
more comfortable, it goes against the nature of change
and growth. The Unpredictable Path, however, flows
with nature, as it guides you to an outlook that's focused on flexibility rather than resistance.

*Today, I can choose to be as fluid and flexible as water.
I'll be much more willing to explore the Unpredictable
Path.*

All the thoughts of a turtle are turtles . . .
           —RALPH WALDO EMERSON

Do you define yourself by the professional role you assume each day? Do you think of yourself as a small-business owner, a mother, a salesperson, or an office worker? From the moment you wake up, do you view the day ahead solely as it relates to your particular role? Do you think, *I'm a mother, so I'd better get the kids ready for school.* Or *I'm a salesperson, so I'd better make my quota.* Or *I'm an office manager, so I'd better keep the office running smoothly*?

Thinking of yourself primarily in terms of the professional role you play can be stressful as well as limiting, for what role do you then fulfill when your workday is done? On weekends? Over holidays and vacations?

Your professional role is just a small part of what you do and who you are. There are other roles in your life you also fulfill—parent, friend, lover, caretaker, volunteer, and many more. Before you automatically lock in to your professional role today, think about other roles you can play. What things interest you? Perhaps you enjoy watching movies, writing poetry, playing a competitive sport, or trying out new recipes. You can explore these interests by taking on a new role—of movie critic, poet, athlete, or chef, for example. Set aside an hour today, then try out your different role.

Today, I won't cast myself in one role. I'll try out a new and different role to explore the range of my talents and capabilities.

In far too many conflicts ... people become so busy blaming others and defending their egos that they forget to solve the problem.

—DIANE DREHER

To be human is to experience conflict. Whether personal, societal, or global, conflict is a part of healthy living. But most people don't act when conflicts arise; they *react*. Rather than resolve the conflict, reaction only serves to escalate it.

Responding emotionally to a conflict with feelings such as anger, distrust, defensiveness, scorn, resentment, or fear makes it hard to communicate or work toward compromise. Yet because these emotions exist, it may be helpful to face the conflict they create in you before you attempt to resolve the conflict with someone else.

To work through your reactions, ask yourself, *What's the basis of this conflict? Why am I so upset about it?* Next, strive to resolve your reactions by talking to someone removed from the conflict or by writing how you feel in a journal or in a letter that you don't intend to mail.

Then ask yourself, *What's the best way for me to act in this situation? How can I contribute in a positive way to resolving this conflict?* By getting your reactions out of the way first, you can seek a more rational, satisfactory, and lasting approach to the problem.

Today, I'll keep in mind resolution, not revolution, when resolving conflicts with others.

Preconceived notions are the locks on the door to wisdom.

—MERRY BROWNE

Do you think you know the outcome of events? Do you believe some people or situations will never change? Do you think it's a waste of time to try new things because you know they won't work? Do you give up easily?

Attitudes based on what you *think* will happen can prevent you from letting events and actions run their course. Preconceived ideas show you the impossibilities rather than the possibilities, the limitations rather than the potentials, the thorns instead of the roses.

When you live each day as if it were new and treat each person in your life as if you had just met, you can see the world and others in a more relaxed and accepting way. Today, take a few moments to look at your reflection in a mirror. Notice something different about yourself. Then extend this same outlook to the events of the day and people with whom you interact. With no preconceived ideas in mind, you may be able to see all the things that *can* happen instead of all the things that can't.

Today, I'll stop projecting outcomes. Instead, I'll focus on the possibility and potential in everything I do.

Plenty of folks are so contrary that if they should fall into the river, they would insist upon floating upstream.
—JOSH BILLINGS

Interacting with people who want their own way isn't easy. Whether a client, boss, or family member, such people can raise your blood pressure, push your anger button, and have you running around in circles trying to give them exactly what they want.

While giving in to them can be very nice, generous, and giving *of* you, it isn't very nice, generous, or giving *to* you. People who want their own way demand, take, and order—they're not concerned about your needs or feelings.

So what's the most effective way to deal with such people? If possible, limit your interactions with them or associate with them only when you feel their controlling behaviors won't bother you. If you often take a passive position to "keep the peace," you might try to be less submissive to their desires. Or, if you often find yourself drawn into "control battles" with them, refuse to react or be defensive when they fire their demands at you.

By letting controlling people expend their energy while you save yours, you'll have more energy to devote to the truly important activities and people in your life. And you'll be the one in control!

I can assert my beliefs to the controlling people in my life without surrendering my self-respect.

Life is made up of interruptions.

—W. S. GILBERT

There are some who might say that life without interruptions would be pretty boring. But there are others who believe that life with fewer interruptions would be a lot easier to handle. While some interruptions can be pleasant, those that occur when tasks need to be accomplished can add more stress to pressure-filled situations.

A time-management study showed that, on the average, people are interrupted every ten minutes. That means it's nearly impossible to have continuous thinking, planning, or working time. How can you get around this? At home, you can talk to those who live with you to agree on an uninterrupted period of quiet time. At work, you can close the door to your office or meet with coworkers to let them know that when you place a sign outside your work space—"Genius at Work . . . Do Not Disturb" or a red flag to show you're under the pressure of a deadline—you don't want to be interrupted. Or, when away from home or the office, you can go for a walk alone or during off-peak times so the interruptions will be kept to a minimum.

Today, I'll reduce outside stimulation so I can set aside time when I won't be interrupted.

Mental health is the ability to love, the ability to work, the ability to play, and the ability to use your mind soundly.

—ASHLEY MONTAGU

Everyone needs balance in their lives, a give-and-take that allows time for work, relaxation, socialization, and pursuing outside interests. Allowing equal space for each of these areas can bring diversity and depth to daily living, provide outlets for creativity and enjoyment, and create opportunities for relaxation and rejuvenation.

Do you remember playing on a seesaw and trying to achieve a balance with you and your friend sitting on opposite ends of the board, suspended in the air, without the board moving up or down? When you did this, that meant the weight on either end of the board was equally distributed. But if you or your friend hopped off, the board quickly became imbalanced.

A life that's imbalanced has too much emphasis in one area and not enough in others. So if you live for your work, spend each night in front of the television, or book your calendar solid with social activities, other areas will be ignored.

While it may be impossible to give equal time to every area, it is possible to make cutbacks in activities that receive more attention than others. Even cutting one hour from work each week and redistributing it to relaxing, socializing, or enjoying a hobby can make a big difference in your mental health.

I'll imagine the areas in my life as equal parts of a pie so I can give time to each area today.

Using order to deal with the disorderly, using calm to deal with the clamorous, is mastering the heart.
                                                        —SUN TZU

Chinese warrior-philosopher Sun Tzu compiled his book on strategy, *The Art of War,* nearly two thousand years ago. Yet it's still perhaps the most influential book on strategy today, for it describes how to achieve success with humanity, alacrity, and simplicity. Whether in the midst of an armed struggle or during times of disorder, Tzu counsels to handle all people and things calmly and without confusion and to face great and unexpected difficulties without upset.

Can you interact with the difficult people in your life with empathy or view the upsetting situations in your life with serenity? One way to do so is to stop obsessing about what you can do to change another person or situation and think instead about what help you can enlist to improve the circumstances. So instead of asking, *What do I need to do to get along better with so-and-so? How am I going to cope in this situation? Where will I find the time to handle such-and-such?* you can ask, *What can we do together to make us get along better? How are we going to cope in the situation? Where will we find the time?* Getting others to share in resolving difficulties can allow everyone to remain open and receptive to one another and capable of seeking harmonious resolution.

Today, I'll be less concerned with how I alone can make the situations in my life better. I'll be more accepting of the belief, "Together, we can make it better."

*I think we fall in love with people who have something
to teach us. And sometimes that is a hard lesson and
sometimes it's a safe and loving lesson.*
                                        —MARY BRADISH

Love is not always an easy emotion to handle. Sometimes it can make you feel strong and sure; other times
it can make you feel weak and vulnerable. It can create
an atmosphere of trust and honesty, as well as one of
mistrust and dishonesty. You may wish that love's good
feelings of security, warmth, openness, and together-
ness never gave way to anxiety, indecision, anger, or
separation. Yet it's important to learn that love, like life,
has something to teach you.

When love hurts you or goes away, you have a
choice. You can become upset and chase after it—or
you can remain calm and serene while you think, *What
do I need to learn from what I'm feeling right now?*

Even though love's emotional expression may
change from time to time, the existence of love won't.
Love is a constant, no matter what form it takes in your
life. Just as the sun rises and sets, so too does love
come and go. And, like the sun, love will always reap-
pear.

*Today, I'll understand and accept love not only during
the easy times, but also in the hard times.*

Every day, in every way, I am getting better and better.
—EMILE COUÉ

Do you find it hard to relax? Is it a struggle for you not to feel edgy, nervous, or tense? Do you tell yourself to calm down, but find you can't?

Around the turn of the century, French pharmacist Emile Coué proposed using affirmative thinking for the treatment of stress. It was his belief that the power of a positive thought far exceeds that of the will.

Today, many people find that repeating phrases or statements that emphasize positive, soothing thoughts can help them relax. This repetition firmly implants the uplifting and serene sentiments in the mind.

Think about an affirmation that would help you relax. Keep your statement short, clear, and focused on a positive action that will have a relaxing effect on you. For example, *No matter what my mood, I can show my children love and attention; I'm in no rush to complete this project;* or *My muscles feel as loose and limp as a rag doll's.* Then imagine how different your life could be if you truly believed your affirmation and that every day, in every way, you *were* getting better and better!

Today, I'll create an affirmation and repeat it five times throughout the day.

I like the dreams of the future better than the history of the past.

—THOMAS JEFFERSON

Do you always see each day as a new beginning—one that's fresh and clean and full of possibilities—or do you sometimes wake up and look back at yesterday, thinking about all the things you could have or should have done differently?

Beginning a new day with thoughts about the previous one is like writing on a chalkboard that hasn't been washed since the start of a school year. Your new message is going to be hard to distinguish among all the other faded messages on the dusty surface. Chalky, ghostly images of minutes, hours, and days gone by make it hard to focus on the activities of the present or to look ahead to the future.

The best way to start any day is to treat it like it's a clean slate. First tell yourself, *There's nothing I can do today that will change the course of yesterday.* Then sit at your desk or kitchen table and compile a list titled "Just for Today." These are your goals for the next twenty-four hours. At the end of the day, throw this list away so you can begin a new one tomorrow!

I have no idea what's in store for me today, but I'll never know unless I keep my attention focused fully on the present.

Someone recently gave me the definition of boredom: "unenthusiastic hostility." Well, I was so unenthusiastically hostile about all the time wasted making movies that I finally went into my trailer and said, "I think I'll write a book."

—SHIRLEY MACLAINE

Why can't you just take it easy for a while? is an often-proposed suggestion for those who complain about how busy they are or who can't seem to slow down. But doing nothing can be as stressful as doing everything when doing nothing is boring, unsatisfying, or unfulfilling. It's a rare person who can do absolutely nothing and enjoy it.

Have you observed children who are stuck indoors during bad weather? At first they amuse themselves with toys, books, and other distractions. But after a while, they become restless, edgy, and cranky. Their whining and fussing express their frustration with having nothing to do that interests them, excites them, or makes them happy.

Slowing down your pace or taking it easy doesn't mean doing nothing. It means taking a break from your pressures by involving yourself in an enjoyable activity. So exercise, read a good book, meditate, talk to a friend, prepare a special dessert, or watch the birds at your backyard feeders. Enjoy your life, rather than be bored by it!

Being bored is stressful! Today, I'll pursue at least one activity that makes me happy.

"I'll soon be dead," the candle said, "I inch by inch decline, but I make light of my sad plight, for while I live, I shine."

—"OLE IRV"

Think about a light bulb. It has an average life of thousands of hours, so it can shine brightly for months. But eventually it's going to burn out.

Human burnout is the gradual dimming of what once was bright—the lost excitement and energy you once felt for a job, a cause you once believed in, or a relationship you were in. Burnout is the overwhelming sense of fatigue and frustration you feel when you don't get what you want or expect from the things in your life, when you don't know how to get what you want, or when you feel trapped or pressured to stay in unsatisfying or unrewarding situations.

Avoiding burnout is a lot like installing a new light bulb. Examine any dimmed "light bulbs" in your life by asking the question, *What in my life is wearing me down?* Perhaps your job isn't as challenging as it used to be, going back to school isn't holding your interest, or a relationship isn't as exciting as it once was. You can then ask, *What will it take to make me feel excited again?* A simple change such as taking on a new project, joining a study group, or having a candlelit dinner with a loved one may be all you need to brighten your bulb.

Today, I'll think about ways I can renew and recharge the interest I once had in things in my life.

Pessimism is in fashion these days. With recession at home, unrest overseas, and all the other bad news around us—optimists are suspect.
—Dr. Martin E. P. Seligman

It's been estimated that ten times as many people suffer from severe depression today as did fifty years ago. But is that such a surprising statistic? With businesses failing, inflation rising, unemployment lines growing, and the number of violent crimes soaring, it's often hard to find positive people and uplifting topics of conversation. Pessimism is all around us.

Think about the conversations you have with people. Do you prefer to talk about the problems and stresses in your life, or do you focus on personal achievements and lighthearted, entertaining anecdotes? Do you find yourself drawn to those people who discuss tragic topics and personal crises, or do you prefer to listen to those who make you laugh or who have something exciting to share?

The other side of pessimism is optimism. Optimism, though not in vogue, fights depression, assists personal achievement, eases the symptoms of stress, and results in better physical and mental health.

Today you have a choice: Will you be an optimist or a pessimist?

Today, I'll choose to associate with smiling, upbeat people—not those who are worried or negative.

I figured I'd have the baby, stay at home for three months, then go back to work. No questions asked, no big deal. Boy, did I figure wrong.

—DENISE HAYNES

It has been estimated that 1.8 million women in the United States go back to work when their babies are less than a year old. Many have no choice, either because they're single parents, they fear being "mommy-tracked," or their household needs two incomes.

For the mother who returns to work because she has to, that pressure—combined with the added strain of arranging for a day-care provider and separating from her baby—can cause great anxiety. Even the most career-oriented mothers who have the freedom to choose whether to return to work can have ambivalent feelings about leaving their babies.

You may be faced with a similar situation in your life: your aged parents need considerable care, your children are sick, or one of your close friends has lost a loved one. How can you handle the practical matter of working while caring for the needs of others?

The key is to remember that you can't take on everything yourself. If possible, explain your situation to your boss and ask for flexibility for a period of time. Simply knowing it's okay to show up for work ten minutes late can ease your stress considerably.

No matter what's going on in my personal life, it doesn't have to create stress in my professional life. I can ask for help.

Don't believe that you work best under pressure—no-body does . . .

—ALEC MACKENZIE

Do you like working at your job when the heat is on? You know the scenario: your future is on the line . . . the boss is screaming at you to finish the project by deadline . . . hours of work loom ahead . . . your stomach growls because it hasn't been fed since the coffee and donut you gulped for breakfast . . . your heart is pounding and you feel flushed . . .

You may claim you do your best work under such intense conditions. Perhaps you're right—what you accomplish when you meet deadlines may be outstanding and even result in a promotion or a big raise. But, over time, working in extremely challenging physical and emotional conditions can wreak havoc on your health. You may experience headaches, peptic ulcers, high blood pressure, and rapid heartbeat. You may have difficulty relaxing or sleeping at night. You may have no time for exercise and even less time for eating well, so you consume high-fat, high-sodium fast foods that leave you feeling sluggish. You may be so exhausted at the end of long workdays that you have no time to socialize or connect with loved ones.

It's okay to work under the pressure of an occasional deadline. But working under constant deadline pressure does not bring out the best in you. In fact, over time it can result in the *worst.*

I need to remember what the first four letters in the word "deadline" spell. Today, I'll make sure I don't work myself to death.

The first thing I had to conquer was fear. I realized what a debilitating thing fear is. It can render you absolutely helpless.

—BYRON JANIS

Feelings of fear can often escalate into full-blown panic attacks, particularly during periods of high stress. When you're feeling edgy, nervous, worried, or tense, and don't think that things are going to get better, a panic attack isn't an unexpected or unusual reaction.

How do you heed the warning of a panic attack? First breathe deeply. When you're in a panicky state your breathing is often quick and shallow. Deep breathing involves taking air slowly into your belly, then gently blowing air out through your mouth. You may wish to feel your pulse as you do this, noticing how it gradually slows as you continue deep breathing.

Then, when you're more relaxed, ask: *What might I be feeling stressed out about?* Think about work pressures, family obligations, interactions with others, your upcoming schedule, events over the past few days, and so on. While you may not figure out *the* reason for your panic attack, you'll get a good idea of the stresses that could be contributing to it. And that knowledge can help you work on reducing those sources of stress so you can prevent future attacks.

I can treat feelings of fear and panic as my friends. They're only trying to help me, so I'll pay attention to them.

Managing is about coping with complexity.
                                        —JOHN KOTTER

Think about who and what you need to manage in a day. First there's yourself: you need to manage your time so you can arrange your schedule to meet your obligations; you need to manage your money so you can pay bills and balance what you earn with what you spend; and you need to manage your health and well-being.

Then there may be others you need to manage: employees, students, children, committee members, and your spouse, to name just a few. Finally, there may be things that come up from time to time that need your management: a home renovation, a relocation, a family crisis, and so on.

Being a constant personal, professional, or family and household manager can be highly stressful. You may never feel as if you have any "down time"—time when you're not managing something or someone.

Yet part of being a good manager is being a good delegator. For example, you don't always have to be the one to clean the house; you can ask your roommates, children, or partner to pitch in or take turns. Asking for help and sharing some of the burden with others are ways you can divide up your managerial responsibilities. Then you can have some time to be an off-duty, rather than always being an on-duty, manager.

I can't manage everything and everybody all the time. Today, I'll share my management responsibilities with others.

I have a dream . . .
　　　　　　　　　　　　—MARTIN LUTHER KING, JR.

When you were younger, was there someone who encouraged you to believe in your dreams? Perhaps your grandparents' journey to America from a distant homeland showed you how persistence and determination could help you achieve your dreams. Perhaps your mother or father showed you the meaning of unconditional love by the support they gave you no matter whether you succeeded or failed. Or perhaps those who had far less than you were able to achieve greatness through their hard work.

But as you grew older, it may have been easy to forget your dreams or put them on hold as you got caught up in the whirlwind of daily activities and the pressure of commitments and obligations. Your dreams may have even faded away.

Martin Luther King, Jr., believed in his dreams and gave African-Americans a wonderful image to carry with them all through their lives. So, too, can you hold on to your ideals. "Keeping the dream alive" means thinking today about one small step you can take toward making it come true. Whether it's putting five dollars into a savings account for a future home, writing your dream in a journal, or taping a picture of something you long for on your bathroom mirror, you can do things today to keep your dreams alive.

My dreams aren't impossible. Today, I'll do something to move me closer to making one of them a reality.

I'm up in the Wisconsin woods, and there are elves in the woods. So when they see me leave, they come into my office and solve all the problems I'm having.
                                              —SEYMOUR CRAY

How many times have you reached an impasse in your life—in your work, in a relationship, or in a hobby or project—and haven't known how to proceed? How did you work through it? Most people, when faced with a seemingly insurmountable problem, keep struggling until they reach a point of exasperation or exhaustion and give up.

However, Seymour Cray, the founder of Cray Research and a designer of high-speed computers, has a unique way of coming up with solutions for problems that stump him. Whenever he can't move ahead in his work, he leaves his desk and goes to an underground tunnel he's digging below his Chippewa Falls house. It's there, in the tunnel and away from his desk, that some of his greatest inspirations come to him.

Taking time away from problems can actually help solve them. It's often easier to find a solution when you're not thinking about one. Diverting your energy to something unrelated—playing a video game, flipping through a mail-order catalogue, or going for a run or brisk walk—can relax your mind and refresh your perspective. Instead of forcing a solution, you may then find that it becomes clear on its own.

A fresh perspective will make me more capable of working through any problems or difficulties I encounter today.

To wait for someone else, or to expect someone else to make my life richer, or fuller, or more satisfying, puts me in a constant state of suspension.
　　　　　　　　　　—KATHLEEN TIERNEY ANDRUS

Do you give away your power to be happy? You do this with thoughts like: *Once my husband finishes grad school, we'll be able to focus on what I want; I know I'll get a raise if I juggle my schedule and put in the extra time my boss needs; I'm sure my parents will accept my decision to be a single parent if I buy the house they like;* and so on.

But can changes in another person's behavior really make everything better for you? If you believe this, then you probably look outward, rather than inward, for your needs to be met, for your fulfillment, and for your ultimate happiness. Like a boat caught at sea in a storm, you're at the mercy of the elements, buffeted and turned every which way.

But you can make your way to the safety and calmness of the harbor when you sail through life under your own power. You don't have to wait for your partner to finish school to get your needs met. You don't have to overwork to be rewarded. And you don't have to live up to your parents' expectations. Decide today what you need to be happy. Ask for a raise without sacrificing your personal time, make plans with friends when your husband is studying, and pursue parenthood with or without your parents' approval.

I won't wait for people to give me what I want or need. It's up to me to seize the day and make it mine.

. . . And if not now, when?

—*THE TALMUD*

I'll take care of that—sometime, I'll get to it as soon as I can, or *I'll handle it—when I'm ready,* are excuses often given to avoid tackling a project. Whether the project is as mundane as cleaning out a closet, as complicated as planning a new business venture, as dreaded as a family confrontation, or even as enjoyable as pursuing a favorite hobby, attending to a project can be difficult. It's often much easier to procrastinate.

But then projects begin to pile up like dirty laundry in a basket. Soon the basket is overflowing and there's never enough time or energy to tackle it. One uncompleted project can turn into two, two into three, three into four—and soon countless projects are hanging over you.

What are some of the projects you've been putting off? List them on a piece of paper. Now think about allotting time in the next few days to get at least one project done. Choose a top-priority project or one you think will be easy to complete.

Living life with a constant and unchanging list of Things To Do can add to the demands and pressures in a day. Why put yourself under more stress by avoiding those projects that, with a little time and attention on your part, can finally be scratched off the list?

Today, I'll eliminate the phrase "I'll get around to it" as I work on a project I've been putting off.

Shoot for the moon. If you miss it, you'll still land among the stars.

—LES BROWN

Winning is supposed to be the only goal in the National Football League, but not every team wins the Super Bowl. Only one team emerges the winner, which means there are a lot of teams, players, coaches, owners, families, and fans that have to cope with the fact that the other side of winning is losing. But is it right to be overly concerned with winning? Which should matter more: the amount of points on a scoreboard or the effort made to play the best game possible?

The drive to win isn't only evident in competitive sports; it's also part of the competitive world in which we live. You are already well aware of the intensity to get ahead on the job, to make the most money, to raise the best children, to have the perfect body, and to have more material goods than your neighbor.

But living each day concerned about who has the most or the best moves you away from what truly matters. How well you prepare a presentation at work should be more important to you than whether a colleague has a better office, and raising honest and considerate children should be your focus instead of whether your children test better than others.

Winning or losing should never matter as much as doing the best you can.

There's no scoreboard to record my performance today. No matter what I do, I'll focus on the effort and not the outcome.

. . . [Life is like] riding a wave: jump on your surfboard at six in the morning, wash up on the beach at ten that night.

—DIANE ROBB

Do you see time as an enemy—a heartless bandit that steals your valuable jewels of seconds, minutes, and hours and hides them so well that you can never retrieve them? *Where did the time go?* we often ask ourselves. *I can't believe the day's nearly over.*

Time Bandits have existed since the beginning of life. But their thefts have only recently become more evident as the pace of living has increased, thereby making time that much more precious. But trying to hold onto time, wishing there were more hours in a day, pushing yourself to do everything just a bit faster, or purchasing gadgets designed to save time can never get you more time. Time can't be controlled or hoarded.

You can, however, outwit the Time Bandits. Start by not wearing a watch, and stop glancing at the clock every five minutes. Focus on what it is that you need to do and then tell yourself, *I'll get it done when I can—and not one minute sooner!* Time is going to move on—there's nothing you can do about that—but remember that no amount of fretting or panicking will slow it down or bring it back.

I'll stop focusing on the clock and turn my attention to the tasks that lie before me. How well I get them done matters more than when I get them done.

The shortest recorded period of time lies between the minute you put some money away for a rainy day and the unexpected arrival of rain.

—JANE BRYANT QUINN

The feeling of never having enough money set aside for the things you'd like is all too common. It's frustrating when your hard-earned dollars barely cover the essentials like housing, gas, dry-cleaning expenses, and food, and rarely the luxuries you desire. Whether you crave a weekend away, a new dress, dining out, or an occasional massage, not having the money to do so can make you feel that money controls your life.

However, it's important to remember that *you* are in control of your money. You're the one who accounts for what your money pays for as well as how much is set aside for nonessentials. From large expenditures like insurance payments to smaller expenses like the morning paper and coffee, you have the power to examine where every penny of your money goes and to determine where small amounts can be redirected into a savings account.

That means you can save for the things you desire, no matter how much or how little you make. Even if you only set aside two dollars a day from now until the beginning of the summer, you'll have around three hundred dollars saved before the end of June. And that's more than enough to pay for a weekend in the country, a couple of dinners in an elegant restaurant, a new outfit, and several massages!

I can become a money manager instead of a money moaner. How much can I set aside today—and every day—for rainy days as well as sunny ones?

Tension is a habit. Relaxing is a habit. Bad habits can be broken, good habits formed.

—WILLIAM JAMES

Nail biting, smoking, daily alcohol consumption, overeating, snapping at others, and finger drumming are some habits used to relieve tension. Yet each does little to alleviate the actual tension. For example, reaching for a cigarette won't make a deadline easier to meet, just as snapping at your children won't ease a family conflict.

Daily tension can make bad habits almost a way of life. But if you can begin to recognize the early signs of tension—a headache, upset stomach, or muscle aches in your shoulders or back—you can use them as warning signals that you need to change your pace or take a moment to relax before you resume any activity.

What's your body saying to you right now? Are you relaxed and alert? Are you tired and sluggish? Are there muscles that feel tight or uncomfortable? Such body awareness can help you break bad habits you've acquired. By staying in touch with your body's reaction to stress throughout the day, you can be more aware of when you need to take a break. Then, instead of reaching for alcohol or biting your nails, you can go for a walk, prepare a cup of herbal tea, or close your eyes and do some deep breathing. Even a three-minute break can give your body a chance to relieve tension and renew its energy.

I'll replace my bad habits with good habits by listening to my body and taking relaxing breaks when I need them.

*There is no royal road to anything. One thing at a time,
all things in succession. That which grows fast withers
as rapidly; that which grows slowly endures.*
                              —JOSIAH GILBERT HOLLAND

During winter you can walk through a grocery store
and see an array of fresh vegetables and fruits on dis-
play as if it were summer. To perk up a salad, you may
select a tomato that took only a few weeks to grow in
a climate-controlled, enriched environment while a
snowstorm howled outside.

But a winter tomato grown in haste will rarely compare to the one that grew to fruition over months in
the natural sun and soil. And so it is with the things
you desire. Instant anything is like instant breakfast—
it fills you up for the moment, but doesn't satisfy you
over time.

It may seem that many things you want move at a
snail's pace—a project, a promotion, a relationship,
saving for a home, or making changes in yourself. But
to have meaning and permanence, such things can't be
forced; they need to happen at their own pace.

All you can do today about the things you want tomorrow is simply to let them happen in their own time.
Keep in mind the effort you put into them, trust that
it was the best that you could do, and then let these
things stand the test of time.

*Today I'll slow down my desires and try not to push
things to move more quickly. I will accept the pace and
know that everything will happen in its own time.*

Imagine how little good music there would be if, for example, a conductor refused to play Beethoven's Fifth Symphony on the ground that his audience may have heard it before.

—A. P. HERBERT

Are there routines you perform day after day that have become so tedious they make you tense even to think about them? *I'm so tired of this!* you might think as you pick up your kid's toys again, sit in traffic during your morning commute, answer the same questions from customers, or rehash the same issues in your relationship.

While some things will always stay the same—gridlock, for example, or questions about a store's return policy—what you can change is the way you *react* to them. Mundane tasks can take on new meaning when you let go of the desire to change them or revise your attitude toward them. Just as it can be fun to sing along with an old, familiar song, so, too, can you make some of the routine tasks in your life more pleasurable.

Instead of feeling frustrated with scattered toys, for instance, you can make a game out of returning them to the toy box—green toys first, blue toys next, and so on. You can listen to a book on tape when stuck in traffic. You can notice a customer's hairstyle. Or you can spread a blanket on the living room floor and have an indoor family picnic dinner. Sometimes just a simple change in attitude can make your whole world a little less routine.

I'll "tune in" to the same old songs in my life by listening to them as if it were the first time I were hearing them.

True love is not what you get—but what you sacrifice to give.

—Louis D. Izzo

The last thing anyone wants to do after coming home from an exhausting day at work is to start dinner, do the laundry, return telephone calls, pay bills, or go shopping. Yet when two people in a relationship work outside the home, these are the things that confront them the minute they walk through the door.

Harmonious two-career relationships are like riding a bicycle built for two. The most enjoyable ride is experienced when both riders exert the effort needed to scale each rise on the road so they can both earn the refreshing breeze and relaxation of every descent.

It's possible for you and your partner to function like the two riders if you can give to one another. Begin today by sharing equally in the responsibility of the household chores. Fold laundry together, make a salad to accompany dinner, or shovel the driveway together. Such simple, thoughtful, giving actions can help bring peace and harmony to a loving, two-career couple.

I'll ask for help or offer my help in order to share equally in things that need to get done around the house.

A journey of 1000 miles begins with a single delay of two hours before takeoff.

—BOB LEVEY

Wouldn't it be great if everything happened when it was supposed to? Meetings would begin and end as scheduled, rehearsals wouldn't run long, deliveries would be made at the specified hour, appointments would require no waiting, and airplanes would depart and land on time.

Living in the Not-On-Time World isn't easy. It's a world in which glazed eyes, tapping feet, and long sighs reflect the impact of delays. And it's a world in which excuses such as, *I got held up in traffic; I'm sorry, but the doctor was called out on an emergency;* and *The airport was fogged in,* are replete.

Living in the Not-On-Time World requires the flexibility to change or revise plans at a moment's notice, the ability to let go of frustration over situations out of your control, and the capability to make the best use of your time during unforeseen delays. Make arrangements with a friend to pick you up if your cab isn't at the airport. Catch up with your correspondence or read a good book at the doctor's office so your waiting time isn't wasted time. And take advantage of airport delays by conducting business over the telephone.

Things may not happen when I want them to today, and I need to make a Plan B just in case Plan A doesn't work out.

In a tight situation, remember that deep breathing clears the mind and relaxes the muscles.
—JEFF LOWE

Ice climber Jeff Lowe knows firsthand about tight situations, which he often encounters as he scales dangerous ice-covered slopes. He has learned that he must patiently and carefully maneuver his body and equipment through the narrow ice crevices in order to reach his destination.

Perhaps there are tight situations in your life in which you must maneuver patiently or carefully. For example, it's lunch hour, and you're waiting in line in a busy take-out restaurant. The line snails along. The cashier appears slower than normal. You tap your foot, glance at your watch, and visualize the pile of work on your desk. All you can think about is your time being wasted as your pulse speeds up and your breathing becomes rapid and shallow.

The best way to get through any tight situation is to stay loose and relaxed. Frequent deep breathing throughout the day, accompanied by full-body stretching, can keep your body from feeling as tight as the situations you must deal with.

I'll stay loose so I won't get "uptight" in any of today's tight situations. Each time I breathe deeply and stretch, I'll imagine I'm on the top of a mountain touching the sky.

Great trouble comes
From not knowing what is enough.
Great conflict arises from wanting too much.
When we know when enough is enough,
There will always be enough.

—TAO TE CHING 46

Our society seems to encourage accumulating "possessions." Every day manufacturers announce new and improved products, must-have gadgets, and "in" fashions. As a result, your dresser drawers may be overflowing and your closets jam-packed, while your car sits in a driveway outside your stuffed garage.

Yet by learning to purchase only what you need, use it completely or frequently, or give it away to those who are less fortunate, you'll discover a simpler, less chaotic lifestyle. By not buying into the belief that you need to own everything, you can reduce the compulsive work ethic of having to work to support an affluent lifestyle.

How do you do this? Try shifting your focus from accumulating more to enjoying the things you already possess. Instead of buying new music, listen to your favorite old tunes. Instead of purchasing the latest novel, exchange books with a friend. Instead of buying new art prints for your walls, move the ones you already have to different rooms. Freedom from wanting everything can help you enjoy what you already possess.

Today, I'll clean out one area in my house, discard anything I don't need, and recycle or donate to a worthy cause.

*If a man had as many ideas during the day as he does
when he has insomnia, he'd make a fortune.*
                                        —GRIFF NIBLACK

Insomnia usually begins with a few bad nights, then
blossoms into full-blown worry about your inability to
sleep. The more you worry, the more tense you get
and the less able you are to get a good night's sleep.
Sleep then becomes a dreaded activity rather than a
safe and soothing reward after a hectic day.

Because life proceeds at a pace that doesn't account
for lack of sleep, it may be tempting to use pills or
alcohol to make you drowsy. But while a pill or night-
cap may help you get to sleep, it won't deal with the
reason why you can't sleep and may lead to a dependency on it.

The best "cure" for insomnia is to make changes in
how you wind down before you get into bed. Don't go
to bed until you're tired. Read, listen to music, meditate, or watch TV until you feel drowsy. Set aside a
half-hour Worry Time in the evening to write down in
a journal the things that make you feel worried or anxious. Create a relaxing atmosphere in your bedroom.
And keep your mind focused on relaxation. Instead of
thinking *I've got to get to sleep; I've got a big meeting
tomorrow,* think *I'm filled with peace and able to let go
of all thoughts about today and tomorrow.*

*I'll stay away from stimulants like caffeine and instead
take a long walk after dinner. This will help me unwind
so I can sleep tonight.*

We want to be somewhere else, and don't know where—want to be someone else and don't know who.
—JEAN HERSEY

Self-acceptance means accepting who you are, what you look like, how you act, and where you are in your life at any given moment. But that's not always easy. Just as life has its ups and downs, so does your self-esteem. You're influenced not only by how you feel about yourself, but also by the opinions of others.

Yet, ultimately, it's how *you* feel about you that determines your level of self-esteem. Do you wake up each morning and, no matter how you look, or what others say, like your appearance? Do you appreciate your strong qualities? Do you feel happy with the things you do and the way you do them? Do you accept who you are without reservation, even if you want to change one or two things?

Even though you may want to change things about yourself—a scar or a blemish, wider love handles than you'd like to have, or your behaviors with others—these things make up who you are. A healthy sense of self-esteem accepts the negative, as well as the positive.

To develop self-acceptance, think about something you don't like about yourself. Then say aloud, *Even though I don't like_____ , I still like myself.*

No matter what my defects or imperfections, no matter what my wishes for changes in my life, and no matter what others say today, I'll accept myself.

You cannot be anything if you want to be everything.
—SOLOMON SCHECHTER

An actor is often a great master of disguise. In one movie he might be a World War II soldier, in another a missionary in Africa, and in another a dashing romantic hero. Even though you know who the actor is in "real life," in the fantasy world created by the movies, you learn to accept the different roles played by that one actor.

Are there times when you feel like an actor as you try to assume many roles in a day? You may jump back and forth from striving to be the best employee to the perfect parent to the greatest lover to the wisest friend to the smartest shopper to the most sparkling conversationalist.

But isn't it hard to try to be all things to all people? Taking on too many roles can leave you feeling scattered rather than focused, directionless instead of driven, and confused instead of certain. Rather than be effective in any one area, you usually end up ineffective in *all* areas.

Today, imagine you're an actor who has won the part for just one role in *Your Life*. Then channel your energy into giving your greatest performance in that role. Let the other roles wait in the wings until tomorrow.

Rather than waste my energy forever changing costumes and practicing new styles of behavior, I'll take center stage today in the role that best suits me.

I trust Lisa to drive the car . . . I can relax and enjoy the scenery . . . while she rages at all the drivers in her path, and even not in her path, who can all be counted on to do the wrong thing, and who must be taught by Lisa at the top of her lungs even though they cannot hear her.
—EDITH KONECKY

Is driving in your car making you crazy? Whether you commute to work, drive your family members to their commitments, or drive for a living, you know how frustrating it can be to get from one place to another. The roads are always crowded, no matter what time of day. Construction delays and accidents can result in long periods of sitting in traffic. And everyone behind the wheel has their own agenda and style of driving, no matter what the rules of the road are.

The only thing on the road you can control is *you.* That means tailgating a slower vehicle doesn't make the driver go faster, honking your horn at those who make sudden turns doesn't teach them to use signals next time, and screaming at others doesn't change their style.

Rather than spend your drive time continually frustrated, make it a more pleasurable experience. Listen to a book on tape or soothing classical music. If traffic is at a standstill, you might look at the sights around you. Finding something to enjoy can make your ride much more relaxing.

I'll make the most of my drive time today by learning or experiencing something new rather than by venting my frustrations at people and circumstances out of my control.

*Why hoard your troubles? They have no market value,
so just throw them away.*

—ANN SCHADE

Do you always feel there's some trouble—big or
small—that needs your attention? If so, you may be
the perfect guest to appear on *The Solution Series.*

The Solution Series is a family television show in
which, every few minutes, a new trouble arises that
needs to be solved. And you're the one who has to
solve it.

Each show in *The Solution Series* takes you through
a typical day, from the moment you awake to the time
you fall asleep. Right from the start, minor activities
turn into problem-solving dilemmas: *What route should
I take to get to work on time? When can I drop off the
dry cleaning? Where will I find the information for my
report?* Even enjoyable activities become troubling dilemmas: *What should I make for the picnic lunch? Will
I need to take a sweater? How long will it take to drive
to the park?*

But today you can turn off *The Solution Series* and
begin to enjoy life. How? Whenever a problem comes
up, ask: *Will the world come to an end if I don't solve
this right now?* Then make a cup of coffee, talk to a
friend, read a chapter in a novel—simply enjoy your
time away from problem solving.

*Today, I'll conserve my problem-solving energy for the
truly important dilemmas. I'll make just one decision—
to let things happen so I can enjoy myself in everything
I do.*

It happens every morning now.... You look at your watch. It's 9 o'clock. You go for coffee, and it's 10:30. Ten minutes later it's 11:15. Another morning lost in HyperTime.   —BRUCE WATSON

Does it seem that some days you're shortchanged on the amount of time you have? Does it feel like your day is only twenty hours long, while everyone else has a twenty-four-hour day?

There's a powerful scene in the movie *Hoosiers* in which the coach of a small-town basketball team takes his players into the arena where they'll be playing the championship game. As they walk onto the big-city court and look around them at the enormous stadium, they're visibly shaken. The coach then hands them a tape measure and asks them to measure the court. The point the coach makes is that the court is the same length and width as any other they've played on, so all the team has to do is play to the best of its ability.

Like the lesson taught to the basketball team, you need to stop focusing on how little time you have to do the things you need to do or how efficiently it seems those around you handle their time. Everyone has the same twenty-four hours in their day. Decide now what *one thing* you want to do in the next hour, then do it. When the hour's up, decide what one thing you want to do in the next hour, and so on. You can make the most of *your* time today by using it to do the things you decide to do.

Time truly does fly when I'm always on the run. Perhaps if I slow down my pace today, I can feel like I have more time.

Expecting the world to treat you fairly because you are a good person is a little like expecting the bull not to attack you because you're a vegetarian.
—DENNIS WHOLEY

One of life's hard lessons is that not everyone lives by the Golden Rule. So just because you're honest at work doesn't mean your boss will be honest with you. Just because you're devoted to your lover doesn't mean your lover won't fall out of love with you. Just because you do everything for your kids doesn't mean they'll appreciate you. And just because you're a success doesn't mean your parents will stop criticizing you.

The standards by which you treat others will not necessarily come back to you in kind. So how can you maintain inner peace when the positive energy, self-lessness, openness, and honesty you may try to bring into your home, work environment, and relationships is met with deception, tension, conflict, or confrontation?

First, keep in mind that everyone will behave as they want, no matter what you do. Then, rather than spend time trying to change their way of thinking or behaving, let go of the expectation that they will always treat you as you deserve. Instead, go for a walk, rent a favorite video, or make plans with a friend. Act, rather than react.

If I feel good about the way I've treated another, then that should be all that matters. So my primary focus should be on my actions, not on their reactions.

Surely this must be an ancient proverb: If the situation is killing you, get the hell out.

—HUGH PRATHER

At some time in your life you may experience an emotionally or physically painful situation. Perhaps you dislike your job so much that you feel tired and run-down all the time. Maybe your relationship makes you so unhappy that you can't seem to concentrate on anything else. Maybe your son or daughter has an alcohol or drug problem and you're worried sick about it. Or perhaps you're continuing to work out with an injury that needs more time to heal.

Imagine that whatever situation you're in is like wearing a pair of tight, uncomfortable shoes. Obviously you want to take the shoes off. But how? Start by being honest with yourself. Are there situations in your life that cause you physical and emotional distress? Identify these "shoes," then explore resources that can help you "remove" the shoes. Make an appointment with a career counselor to discuss a career that's right for you. Ask your partner to talk about issues in the relationship. Attend Al-Anon meetings to learn more about living with addictions. Consult a sports physician about a rehab program for your injury. Starting today, you can take steps toward easing your pain.

Staying in an impossible situation is impossible. Today, I'll think of things I can do or say to alleviate the pain caused by a circumstance or a person in my life.

*Temperance and industry are man's true remedies;
work sharpens his appetite and temperance teaches him
to control it.*

—JEAN-JACQUES ROUSSEAU

Years ago, working people labored on the farm, at
home, or in a shop or factory. For the most part, their
work required the physical stamina necessary to meet
the demands of routine tasks such as harvesting or
assembly-line operations.

Today, however, the work environment has changed
so drastically that working people need strong mental
and interpersonal skills rather than physical strengths.
In order to keep up with a rapidly changing world and
a fast-track pace, today's workers are expected to be
multifunctional. They must be able to work well in
groups, deal with clients from diverse cultures, digest
and disseminate new information and trends, manage
their time and tasks effectively, and identify and
achieve their professional goals.

Is it any wonder that you leave your job each day
feeling beleaguered, bothered, and burned out?

That's why it's important to have a quiet place to go
to after work. There—in your garden, at the beach, in
the bathtub, or in your favorite easy chair—you can
close your eyes and experience the peace and contentment you so deserve.

*Today, I'll create a peaceful sanctuary for my after-
work experience. Whenever I'm in my sanctuary, I'll
turn off the work demands and turn on serenity.*

*What is originality? It is being one's self and reporting
accurately what we see and are.*
                                        —RALPH WALDO EMERSON

As president, Abraham Lincoln faced divisions
between North and South, black and white, and slave
owners and emancipators. In his brief but powerful
Gettysburg Address, he voiced views that weren't popular or readily accepted, but in which he strongly believed.

How much do you enjoy sharing your beliefs? Perhaps you're vocal only when your opinions echo those
of others. Maybe you're quick to state your feelings,
but just as quick to revise or soften them when others
disagree. Maybe you pride yourself on being an agree-
able sort who enjoys hearing what others have to say.
Or perhaps you're too afraid to say anything for fear of
what others might think.

To say how you really feel can be intimidating and
scary. You may make yourself vulnerable to attack, criticism, and judgment. But sharing what you believe and
how you feel can earn the respect and caring of others,
which can provide you with a source of satisfaction.

Today, rather than be weak, meek, or silent, take a
stand. State just *one* of your beliefs freely, firmly, and
without fear. Do so to please yourself, not others.

*Saying how I feel is a way of opening, rather than clos-
ing; revealing, rather than hiding; and trusting, rather
than fearing. I'll gladly share my thoughts and opinions
today.*

*The pessimist sees the difficulty in every opportunity;
the optimist, the opportunity in every difficulty.*
                                        —L. P. JACKS

Do you think that a crisis is an opportunity to experience something new and exciting or a chance to
practice a new skill? Or do you see a crisis only in
terms of how poor the timing of it is, how much it's
going to cost you, or how much time it'll take to fix?

In China, bamboo can be seen as a powerful symbol
for how to deal with crises. Because bamboo is hollow,
it bends with the wind; but because it's straight and
strong, it doesn't break. Bamboo thus teaches that to
be "in crisis" means learning how to be flexible and
yet strong, to adjust to life's changes, and to remain
open to new possibilities.

How can you be more like bamboo in any crisis you
face today? Ask yourself: *What's the good in this? How
can I grow from this?* You can choose to see only the
difficulties created by a crisis. Or you can be more
flexible in your outlook and learn to look at the crisis
as a chance to experience change, plan new goals, or
experiment with something new in your life.

*Like the bamboo, I can bend and grow as I adjust to
the winds of change. Today, I'll treat any crisis as an
opportunity.*

When you love someone, you do not love them all the time, in exactly the same way. . . . And yet this is exactly what most of us demand. We leap at the flow of the tide and resist in terror its ebb. . . .
—ANNE MORROW LINDBERGH

Hollywood often presents a view of fairy-tale-come-true love that stops at the happily-ever-after ending. As the music swells and the happy lovers ride off into the sunset, unanswered questions hover in the air: *But what happened* after *the handsome knight on the white horse won the hand of his fair lady and brought her to his kingdom?*

Most often what happens is that the lady and the knight discover how cold the castle is in the winter. They argue over whose turn it is to throw more logs on the fire, who gets to put their cold feet on the other's warm body, or who hogs the blankets at night. What they discover, after the honeymoon period is over, is that love isn't always wonderful, warm, and witty.

Wanting a love relationship to be strong, safe, and secure all the time is normal; expecting that it'll always be that way, however, isn't realistic. The love that lasts is the love that stays in your heart even when it doesn't feel strong or wonderful. Today, create a Valentine for the one you love that conveys that your love is always there, through the good times as well as the bad.

Today is the day of love. I'll express my love through my actions, the things I say, and what I can give of myself to another.

*A man sentenced to death obtained a reprieve by as-
suring the king he would teach his majesty's horse to
fly within the year.... "Within a year," the man ex-
plained, "the king may die, or I may die, or the horse
may die. Furthermore, in a year, who knows? Maybe
the horse will learn to fly."*

—LEONARD LYONS

Never giving up is not only a test of belief in yourself
and what you can do. It's also a symbol of how you
approach life. When confronted by failure, disappointment, or rejection, it may be far easier simply to give
up. But this attitude can spell the difference between
long-term success and a series of defeats.

When Thomas Edison's manufacturing facilities
were heavily damaged by fire in 1914, Edison lost
nearly one million dollars' worth of equipment and all
the records he had kept. But the next morning, as the
inventor surveyed the charred embers, he said: *There
is value in disaster. All our mistakes are burned up.
Now we can start anew.*

Imagine what our world would be like today if Edison hadn't continued his work after the fire. His positive approach to personal disaster reflected a "can-do,"
rather than a "can't-do," philosophy. Today, in every
situation, strive to foster the same philosophy by eliminating *I can't* from your vocabulary and saying instead,
I'll try.

*A positive, tough-minded approach can turn certain fail-
ure into assured success. The difference between failure
and success rests on my attitude.*

Those things people work for ... material goods ...
weigh life down. That mark of success, a large house,
doesn't bring pleasure. The bigger the house, the more
pipes there are to burst, the more plaster to crack, the
more wallpaper for children to peel off.
                                    —SAMUEL F. PICKERING, JR.

How do you feel about money? Do you believe you
would be happier if you had more of it?

The subject is an emotional one. Money issues break
up marriages, cause resentment, and foster competitiveness. People are often quite willing to put themselves into financially shaky situations—mortgaging,
borrowing, or charging more than they can actually afford—in order to feel more successful, more powerful,
or more valuable as a human being.

It's important to keep money in perspective. You'll
never be able to be financially secure as long as you
woo money as you would a lover, worship it as you
would a god, or pay more attention to it than you would
yourself or those you love.

Today, rather than focus on your salary, what's in
your wallet, or what's in your checking account, think
of at least five valuable things in your life that are
priceless to you—but that money didn't buy.

I'll keep in mind that money is just metal and paper and
something nice to have around for a rainy day. Money
isn't the indicator of my success.

*The next time you're off to work, dreading the day
ahead, stop yourself. Decide, just for one day, to think
in a whole new way.*

— BENJAMIN J. STEIN

There's a cartoon that shows the different facial expressions of a man at work, depending on the day of
the week. On Monday, he looks grumpy. On Tuesday,
he looks tired. On Wednesday he looks tired and
grumpy. On Thursday he looks tired, but hopeful. And
on Friday, he looks happy.

You may note these same expressions on the faces
of commuters you see on buses and trains, sitting in
gridlocked vehicles, hurrying on the crowded city side-
walks, or dropping their children off at school. These
same expressions may even be reflected in the mirror
as you prepare for the new day.

Beginning each workday with a preset emotional
outlook can determine the events of the day and how
you handle them. So you can begin each day by thinking uplifting thoughts such as *It's going to be another
great day for me,* by setting a goal of smiling five times
on your way to work, or by getting up early and beginning the day with a relaxing bath. Any day that
starts with a positive, relaxing outlook will be less
stressful and much more enjoyable.

*It doesn't matter what day of the week today is—I'll
look forward to experiencing it.*

*The true spirit of conversation consists in building on
another man's observation, not overturning it.*
                                        —EDWARD G. BULWER-LYTTON

Have you ever looked back at times and wished you
hadn't said something to someone? Did your harsh or
insulting words cause another sadness or pain? Was a
snide or impatient comment delivered sharply to an
unsuspecting friend? Did angry words push aside a lover's desire to be close?

By the same token, you may recall times when you
delivered a friendly greeting filled with warmth or
whispered loving words in someone's ear. You may
have made someone laugh or smile despite tears, or
you may have been able to point out a different view-
point to someone blinded by rage or impatience.

Words can be powerful weapons that hurt. Or they
can be gentle healers that sweeten life's bitterness.
Freedom of speech doesn't mean you can say anything
you want whenever you want, just because you feel like
it. Communication with others is an action that requires responsible use.

Today, no matter how you feel or how your day goes,
strive to use words that let others know how they make
life easier for you to bear. Phrases like *Thank you; I
really appreciate your help;* and *How thoughtful of you,*
can lead to healthy and more relaxed interactions with
others.

*The things I say today can sweeten my relationships
with others or make them go sour. Today, I'll think before I speak.*

*It is a mistake to look too far ahead. Only one link in
the chain of destiny can be handled at a time.*
                                    —WINSTON CHURCHILL

Are you more aware of your future plans—those
made for days, weeks, months, or even years from
now—than today's plans? Like many people, your body
may be physically in the present, but your mind may
be racing ahead to the future.

Planning for the future is good. It can help you organize your life, coordinate your schedule with others,
and help you set effective goals. But *living* in the future
isn't a good idea, especially if you tend to be worried
or anxious about upcoming events.

The often-stated slogan *I'll cross that bridge when I
come to it* is an appropriate phrase to keep in mind to
help modify your future-thinking tendencies. Whenever you find yourself trying to predict or imagine what
will happen in the future, cut your thoughts short. Say
aloud, *I can't deal with that right now. It hasn't happened yet. I'll cross that bridge when I come to it. In
the meantime, I'll enjoy the present.*

*I know there are many bridges ahead to cross. But I
want to take my time before I reach them. Today, I'll
keep my feet firmly planted in the present.*

Any concern too small to be turned into a prayer is too small to be made into a burden.

—CORRIE TEN BOOM

Each day you meet your physical needs by eating, sleeping, and exercising. You meet your intellectual needs by solving problems and expanding your wealth of knowledge. And you meet your emotional needs by sharing your feelings with others.

But how can you meet your spiritual needs? These needs may include quiet time for meditation, connecting with the wonder and splendor of nature, developing inner peace through relaxation, and asking for spiritual guidance and support through prayer.

Perhaps the only times you meditate are when you're stressed out. Perhaps the only times you take a walk in the woods are when you have no pressing commitments. And perhaps the only time you pray for help is in the middle of a crisis.

It's certainly easy to ignore spiritual needs. They don't cry out for attention like your other needs do; you won't starve if you don't meditate, and you won't pull a muscle by not praying. But you also may not be able to handle stress in your life as effectively as you could.

Meditation, quiet time, appreciating nature, and prayer can help you cope with even the most minor of hassles so they don't become major burdens. Try finding twenty minutes today to pay attention to a spiritual need.

I'll make time for prayer and peaceful contemplation today, to help me become quiet and calm.

Men travel faster now, but I do not know if they go to better things.

—WILLA CATHER

How do you accelerate through each day? From the moment your alarm rings, you may taxi down the runway of your life and then become airborne at Mach 2 speeds like the Concorde jet.

You jump into your car, screech into traffic, hug tightly to the bumpers of cars ahead of you, and frantically cut in and out of travel lanes trying to better yesterday's drive-time record. You roar into the parking lot, jump out of the car, greet others with a rushed *Goodmorninghowareyouhaveaniceday,* and leap into your desk chair as the telephone rings and piles of work multiply before your eyes.

After going through day after day at this speed, isn't it time to ask, *What am I really accomplishing by functioning at such a superhuman pace?* The reality is that for all the speed and prestige of the Concorde, it guzzles too much fuel, carries too small a passenger load, and makes so much noise that thirty countries have restricted its use.

So today, whenever you feel the urge to zoom through each minute like a jet, stop and take a deep breath. Cease all physical movement and concentrate on filling your lungs. After three deep breaths, resume your activities—but at a much slower pace.

Moving faster doesn't necessarily bring goals closer. Today, no matter where I want to go, I'll move at a pace that's right for me.

*I'm too busy. I can barely see the numbers on my cal-
endar for all the meetings, talks, appointments, programs, deadlines and classes penciled into . . . [the] little
squares.*

—LINDA WELTNER

Self-inflicted stress is the voluntary creation of too
much to do in too little time. It usually begins simply
and innocently enough, with an offer on your part to
"help out." What happens next is like a snowball rolling downhill. "Help out" turns into support, which
turns into share, which turns into organize and, finally,
into single-handedly manage.

Yet rather than cease to offer help when you're already overwhelmed, you may actually jump at the next
opportunity to lend a hand. Why? Perhaps it makes
you feel good. Maybe you enjoy keeping busy. Or perhaps you just can't say "no." But what you may not
realize is that the real reasons for your giving nature
could be unhealthy: You may help others because you
want them to like you; you may like being busy because you're afraid of unstructured time; or you may
feel good only when satisfying the needs of others.

The next time you take on an additional responsibility, ask yourself, *What is it that I really want to get
out of this?* Then be sure to set aside as much time for
yourself so you can do the things you want to do.

*I'll stop structuring my life as an endless series of tasks
and responsibilities. Today, I'll allow myself some unstructured time.*

You can't have everything. Where would you put it?
—STEVEN WRIGHT

Greed isn't just about money; it's also about having the biggest house, the fanciest car, the cushiest job, the most famous friends, the best stereo equipment—even the biggest slice of pie.

But think of what your life would be like if you had everything you wanted—all the money, clothing, cars, furniture, jewelry, and other material things you want. How would you feel?

Most people would say, *I'd feel great! I'd have all the things I ever wanted.* But think of those who have achieved great success and found themselves with millions of dollars. You read and hear about such people often—through their divorces, their run-ins with the law, and their assorted other difficulties. Money may have gotten them what they wanted, but it certainly didn't give them what they needed—self-esteem, acceptance, and love.

Today, list your nonmaterial needs on a piece of paper. Then circle the one that's most important to you. Perhaps it's growing closer to your children, dealing with difficult childhood issues, or taking better care of yourself. Then take steps to meet this need by spending time with your kids, beginning counseling, or joining a health club. It's the fulfillment of this need that will bring you the happiness that money can't buy.

Simplicity, as well as greed, is a choice of living I make. Today, I'll make a choice and be happy with it.

I try to be as philosophical as the old lady from Vermont who said that the best thing about the future is that it comes only one day at a time.

—DEAN ACHESON

Those who belong to self-help groups such as Alcoholics Anonymous, Smokenders, and Weight Watchers know the value of the saying "one day at a time." The slogan makes it much easier to say, *I won't smoke for the next hour, I won't have dessert with lunch,* or *I won't stop for a drink after work,* so the focus is on the moment rather than tomorrow, next week, or next month.

"Live for today" is another slogan you can use to help you focus on the present. This focus can prevent your mind from wandering to worry, anxiety, and fears about tomorrow and keep you in the place in time where you can do the most good—the present.

Life cannot be predicted or even imagined. It can only be experienced each minute. So don't try to write the events of tomorrow until after they've happened. Instead, see today's sunrise and sunset. Be free to experience all that's in store for you—fresh and new and exciting—right now.

Whenever I feel like I'm getting way ahead of myself, I'll use the slogans "one day at a time" and "live for today" to keep my mind focused on the present.

The other day a friend said, "In five years I'll be in the tropics, sipping pina coladas with my fiancé who has just made a million dollars . . ."

—BECKY ROIPHE

When you were growing up, you probably had lots of plans and dreams. But as you got older, your childhood dreams may have faded as you faced the pressure of getting good grades and learning as much as you could so you could go to a good college, join the work force, or raise a family. Now, as an adult, you may look at your life and think, *I have no idea what I want anymore. I don't know where I'm going, and I don't know what will make me happy.*

What happened to your childhood plans and dreams?

The difference between the carefree optimism of your childhood dreams and your inability to find happiness in adulthood lies in how you view life. Children view the world without limitations or restrictions; adults often see a very limited, restricted world. But you can realize your childhood dreams when you teach yourself to become familiar with seeing the potential and possibility in life. To do so, rather than think, *I can't do this because* _____, think instead, *I can do this because* _____ *and here's how I'll start.*

I can see my life as an open road with no end and no limits. It's up to me to remove the self-imposed restrictions that prevent me from letting my imagination run as free as a child's.

If you are lonely when you are alone, you are in bad company.

—JEAN-PAUL SARTRE

Imagine for a moment that you have no plans today. There's no job to get up for, no class to attend, no errand to run, and no one who needs your time and attention. Initially, you might think this would be great. But how comfortable are you being totally alone, with no place to go and no one to be with? Think back to the last occasion you had to spend by yourself. Were you content to sit comfortably with yourself, enjoying the pleasure of your company? Or was your first instinct to turn on the television or pick up the telephone so you could escape being with you?

While you live in a world with others and need to feel connected with them, you also need to feel connected with yourself. When you like who you are, it doesn't matter whether you're with others or alone. Both are enjoyable.

Today, you can take steps to become more comfortable being with yourself. Set aside time to be alone, then eliminate any diversions created by television or projects. Record in a journal how you feel about your time alone and how you feel about yourself. By doing this on a regular basis, you'll not only discover who you really are, but also find that you're not a bad person to spend time with.

Today, I'll take fifteen minutes to sit quietly alone and listen to my inner thoughts and feelings.

Success is to be measured not so much by the position that one has reached in life as by the obstacles which [were] overcome while trying to succeed.
—BOOKER T. WASHINGTON

When hurdlers race, they face a track lined with obstacles. They must maintain top speed as well as successfully clear each hurdle in order to win a race. Yet not all of life's obstacles are as easy to see and overcome. Some are invisible obstacles that you carry with you as a result of growing up in a dysfunctional home.

In adulthood, obstacles from the past can complicate even the simplest tasks. You may fear asking your boss if you can leave work early because whenever you asked for anything as a child you were punished. Or cleaning your house may exhaust you because you feel you have to maintain your mother's standards of neurotic cleanliness. Or becoming intimate with another may cause you to withdraw or run away because of childhood incest.

Obstacles from the past can stunt your growth in the present, create problems and difficulties, and affect your overall happiness. But seeking help from support groups, consulting reading materials, asking for help from professionals, and giving yourself credit for surviving your childhood can help you overcome the hurdles the past presents in your life as an adult.

Today, I'll talk to a trusted friend about the problems in my childhood home and ask for support as I seek further help.

If we let things terrify us, life will not be worth living.
—SENECA

When electricity was first installed in the White House, President and Mrs. Benjamin Harrison were so intimidated by it that they didn't dare touch the switches. Because of their fear, if the servants didn't turn off the lights when they went to bed, the Harrisons slept with the lights on!

When you're faced with a new or unknown situation, are you similarly terrified? Perhaps you have to give a presentation at work, discipline your child, discuss problems in your relationship, or confront a parent. The last thing you may want to do is face what you need to do.

Fear and anxiety are normal reactions to difficult or new situations. So sometimes it's helpful to keep in mind that you aren't the first person to feel scared or anxious in the situation, and you certainly won't be the last. But if you allow fear and anxiety to dominate your thoughts and actions, you may end up as immobilized and intimidated as the Harrisons.

Being a confident speaker or being able to meet confrontation assertively and conflict head-on doesn't happen overnight. In such situations, it may be helpful to think, *I'll give this a try. It's okay to be afraid, as long as I don't let this fear rule—and ruin—my life.*

No matter what I need to do today, I won't be paralyzed by fear or anxiety. I can trust that as long as I try, I'll do fine.

*Time is like a river made up of events that happen . . .
as soon as a thing has appeared it is carried away, and
another comes in its place . . .*
                                        —MARCUS AURELIUS

Is your life an endless list of chores, meetings, errands, piles of papers, phone calls, and meal preparations?

You may notice that every time you cross one completed task off your endless list, there are other tasks
that magically appear at the bottom. Like a video battle
game, there may always seem to be more enemy creatures that need to be annihilated—no matter how
many bombs or laser bursts you use to eliminate the
ones already there.

It's fruitless to try to keep pace with the never-
ending list of tasks and responsibilities that face you
every day. So instead of feeling as if you can't slow
down until you accomplish everything, take a moment
to ask, *How long has it been since I've devoted a few
hours to my personal enjoyment?*

You can take time today to do things you'd like to
do. Read a book. Take a long walk. Play with your pet.
Go out for a cup of coffee. Relax in a soothing bubble
bath. Prepare a special meal. Today you can add to
your list—*Make time for me.*

*What can I do that's special for me? Today, I'll be sure
to set aside time in my schedule to pamper myself.*

Is there any miracle on earth to compare with that of discovering a new friend, or having that friend discover you? So much is at stake, but I will gladly risk everything to give a promising relationship a chance.
—ALEX NOBLE

Fear of intimacy in any relationship—be it with friends, family members, or a lover—can put you on the defensive and make your relationships stress-filled. Rather than be open to exploring new relationships or willing to grow closer in those you already have, you may be so busy building barricades between yourself and others that interactions become feared rather than favored.

While you may think that shutting others out closes the door to such stressful feelings as hurt, anger, pressure to meet the needs of others, or rejection, in reality what it shuts out are the possibilities for wonderful, calming feelings like love, sharing, and connection.

Defensiveness builds walls, but openness builds bridges that can lead to trust, wholeness, and peace. While getting through the fear of intimacy isn't easy, one way to do so is to start simply. Today, reach out to another with a kind gesture—call just to say hi, write a letter, or offer to run an errand. By letting another know you're willing to reach out, the door to caring can be opened.

Today, I'll show that I'm willing to be a friend and to have a friend. I'll start small so I can break down my barricade bit by bit.

The idea of calm exists in a sitting cat.

— JULES RENARD

How much time do you set aside as "free time"? Studies have shown that people spend fewer than three hours a week reading a book, newspaper, or magazine, and less than an hour a week relaxing and thinking!

Your free time may be packed with activities centered around household responsibilities, family obligations, errand running, or self-improvement. Whatever time left over after all those things have been accomplished may be relegated to activities that often require as much discipline and sustained effort as work—a rigorous rehearsal schedule for a community theater production, or taking a tennis or piano lesson. Any free time you have may make you feel uncomfortable or pressured to fill it with meaningful activities.

But if you can use your free time as the time in which you are neither too busy nor too idle—perhaps by reading a book, meditating, painting, or going for a run—maybe you can enjoy an hour of free time every day or every other day. One open, unscheduled hour can do wonders for your frayed nerves and end-of-the-day weariness.

There's no activity in free time. Today, I'll take advantages of the freedom of my free time by simply putting my feet up and enjoying every minute.

No man can tell another his faults . . .
                                    —HENRY WARD BEECHER

Everyone handles pressure differently. Deadlines may make one person frantic while another remains calm. Emotional tension may make one person feel the need to resolve the conflict immediately while another may feel it's "no big deal." Long hours may drain one person's ability to think clearly while another is as clear-thinking as at the beginning of the day.

Whether you're a man or woman, you may find how you respond to the same pressure differently than do members of the opposite sex. For example, men tend to react more strongly to the feeling of being over-worked, while women have greater difficulty with conflicts. Such differences can sometimes make it hard for men and women to support, validate, or understand one another in situations where they need to work to-gether. In lieu of trying to understand the actions of each other, fault-finding statements such as *You know what your problem is? You don't know how to handle such-and-such* may be delivered, which only add stress to the situation.

It's important to make an effort to learn how a mem-ber of the opposite sex feels in stressful work situations. "Check in" with that person by asking, *Is this okay with you?* or *Are there things I can do to ease the pres-sure you feel?* Such empathy and understanding will not only add to your productivity, but make the project more enjoyable as well.

I'll keep an open mind with both the men and women I interact with today so I can better understand the pressures they feel.

To be upset over what you don't have is to waste what you do have.

—KEN S. KEYES, JR.

WARNING: The following statements may be detrimental to your mental health: *I'm not good with numbers; I can't carry a tune to save my soul; I've never been good with kids.* If you think such statements about yourself or if you describe yourself to others in similar ways, then you may be guilty of nullifying who you are.

Such statements are nullifiers because they focus on the gifts or talents you feel you don't have. They convey your limitations, drawbacks, and weak areas rather than your many talents, capabilities, and gifts. As a result, your self-image and the image you present to others becomes based on your weaknesses rather than your strengths.

The solution is simply to drop such statements from your vocabulary. Try to follow a nullifying statement with a qualifying statement—one that identifies a positive quality, capability, or talent. For example, when you say, *I'm not good with numbers,* follow it with, *I'm much better with words.* Or *I can't carry a tune to save my soul* can be followed by *But I appreciate a good piece of music.* Then follow your words with supportive actions. Share something you've written or talk about the lovely Vivaldi concert you recently attended.

Today, I'll make a list of the things I do well. If I can't come up with any on my own, I'll ask a friend for help. Then I'll communicate these qualifiers to others.

I can feel guilty about the past, apprehensive about the future, but only in the present can I act.
—ABRAHAM MASLOW

Worry is an energy drainer. It can prevent you from living in the present as your mind wanders to what has already passed—an argument with a loved one—or what has yet to come—whether you'll be laid off from work.

How can you live each moment in the present and not somewhere in the past or future? The most important cure for worry is to distinguish between the facts and the fantasies of your worries. You may be worried that your partner will leave you because of your last argument, but ask yourself, *Is that a fact?* Whether you'll be laid off from work isn't a fact until you are.

Once you determine which is fact and which is fantasy, you'll be able to develop a plan of action. Instead of wondering what your partner will do, ask. Instead of worrying about the stability of your job, line up other possibilities.

When you focus on the facts, you can act. Then you can stop looking back or peering ahead and stay in the present moment—and enjoy it.

Worry depletes my physical and mental energy. Today, I'll conserve my energy by taking care of the present rather than worrying uselessly about the past or the future.

More . . . are killed by overwork than the importance of the world justifies. —RUDYARD KIPLING

Are you in love with your work? Perhaps you tote your work with you wherever you go. Or maybe you pride yourself on the fact that you're capable of doing several things at once—reading business mail during a lull in a meeting, or making business calls while working on your personal computer.

While the positive side of such work habits may mean you've found a job you enjoy, the downside is that in loving your work so much, you may lose sight of the rest of your life. You may find it impossible to fit everything and everybody into your life—business as well as pleasure, employees as well as family members, and company matters as well as personal matters.

While loving your work can be healthy, the effects of such an all-consuming focus can lead to problems. You may lose quality time with those you love. You may become alienated from your own personal needs. And you may have difficulty turning off work activities so you can relax and unwind.

Today, bring the rest of the world back into focus in your life. Make judgments about the things you schedule into your planning book. Before you pencil in another meeting or business-related activity, ask, *How important is this?* or *Would I be better off going out with a friend or being home for dinner?* Become more conscious of your time and how you use it.

Working rather than devoting time to others prevents me from enjoying important relationships. Today, I'll be more flexible with my time away from work.

. . . There's no other flight out tonight—so what? *I'll be an hour late for my meeting if I take a morning flight*—so what? *I may blow the deal*—so what?

—ROBERT J. RINGER

Life often presents itself as a seemingly endless stream of problems that can affect the flow of previously scheduled activities. As one situation after another crops up and messes up your plans, you may think to yourself, *Now what?*

But when an event occurs that affects your schedule or an anticipated outcome, you can take control of the situation by expanding your normal response of *Now what?* to *Now what can I do?* as you take action. For example, a canceled meeting may put the outcome of a major project on hold and send you into a frustrated rage. But instead you could look upon the extra time as a bonus—a chance to review the work you've already done and to refine it where necessary to make it even better. Or you may think that a delayed flight to an important meeting may result in the loss of your client. But you can prevent the possibility of such an outcome and solidify the business relationship by calling your client from the airport and exchanging ideas over the phone.

A positive outlook and creative alternatives can be much more effective than hand-wringing anxiety, mental paralysis, and noneffective *Now whats?*

No matter what roadblocks I run into today, I'll take care of things as best I can. Nothing will stand in my way unless I let it.

Whether we're battling personal demons or global ills, we need both the toughness to see problems for what they are and the faith to imagine that we can have an impact on them.

—MARIAN SANDMAIER

Although problems constitute a normal part of life, it's possible to solve most problems rather than let them upset you. The key to doing so lies in the way you approach any difficult or perplexing situation. If you believe a problem will get the better of you, it will. But if you believe there's a solution to every problem, then you'll be able to find it.

To become an effective problem solver, don't respond to your problem right away. Ineffective problem solvers tend to be impulsive, impatient, and quick to give up if a solution isn't immediately apparent. Then they become angry when their problem isn't solved after their first ineffectual try.

First, take a time-out or sleep on the problem. Then, follow the Number One rule for effective problem solving: A good problem solver is first able to identify what the *real* problem is. Perhaps it's not even related to a present situation but is an unresolved conflict from the past.

Once you identify the real problem, think of as many ideas as you can to solve it. The greater the number of solutions, the greater the likelihood of your being able to find the *best* solution.

Every problem has a solution. Today, I'll be persistent, confident that I can find the right solution.

Act nothing in a furious passion. It's putting to sea in a storm.

—THOMAS FULLER

Imagine filling a balloon with air, then continuing to blow into it as the balloon gets bigger and bigger. Eventually you'll fill the balloon with so much air that it'll burst with a loud explosion.

Angry outbursts are like the exploded balloon. They're the result of feelings that have been held in. Outbursts of pent-up feelings are usually not directed at the source of the stress, but at innocent victims. For example, you might snap at subordinates when your real concern is your own job performance, or you may yell at your children when you're really upset with your spouse.

While expressing how you feel is important, it's vital to use the principle of "seeing before screaming." Before you let out your anger, pay attention to who will receive your venting to determine whether this person is the actual source of your strong feelings. Blaming others for your shortcomings or shifting anger on someone else does little to alleviate anger or help identify the origin of your feelings.

Anger is only effective when it's communicated clearly and constructively to the right people.

Do I feel like I'm about to explode? I'll identify the source of my anger, then express how I feel without the intent to hurt another physically or emotionally.

One of the first rules of playing the power game is that all bad news must be accepted calmly, as if one already knew and didn't much care.

—MICHAEL KORDA

Reacting to bad news with feelings of anxiety, anger, or defensiveness can put you in the role of a helpless victim. This can take away your ability to face difficulties and effectively do something about them.

Remember when you were in grade school and your teacher taught you how to handle yourself during a fire drill? Your first instinct, when you heard the frightening alarm, was probably to shoot up from your desk and dash in the wrong direction. But your teacher's calm, firm voice told you, *Line up single file. Walk— don't run.*

By the same token, you can train yourself to react with calmness during any calamity. Rather than run, face your difficulty. Ask, *What's the worst possible thing that can happen?* While you may think it's the end of the world and you're going to die because your relationship just ended, this question helps you focus on what really could happen—you could be unhappy, you could feel lonely, or it might take you a while before you can relax and enjoy yourself with others. By facing the worst thing you can expect from a situation, you'll be better prepared to deal with it when it occurs. Then you'll be the victor and not the victim.

I can stay calm and focused even in the midst of terrible loss or disaster. Today, I'll remember that my actions can help me through any hard times.

God has given each one of us approximately 25,000 to 26,000 days on this earth. I truly believe He (or She) has something very specific in mind; 8,300 days to sleep, 8,300 to work, and 8,300 to give, live, play, pray and love one another. —QUINCY JONES

Musician Quincy Jones survived a brain aneurysm and two brain operations in 1974. Since that time, the highly successful and driven record producer, composer, and musician has renewed his belief in the importance of having a balance in his life. No matter how busy his schedule, he sets aside time for enjoying life to the fullest and for listening to the voice that comes from "divine guidance."

Many people believe that peace of mind comes from material success or financial security. So they devote the majority of their days on earth to working hard to achieve such things. But true peace of mind comes not from what you can get from your efforts, but from what you can give to others, from how well you can live each day—from how often you allow yourself to play, from your ability to reach out to a Higher Power, and from your desire to love others.

To find this true peace of mind, today resolve to give, live, play, pray, and love another. Pack a lunch for a friend. Enjoy the weather—no matter what it is. Play a game with your kids. Pray for riches in your life that money can't buy. And express your love to a family member.

Peace of mind, like the restless need to be always doing and achieving, is a habit. I can either nurture it or destroy it today through my actions.

Children are like wet cement. Whatever falls on them makes an impression.

—HAIM GINOTT

Are your methods of managing stress healthy or unhealthy? Healthy stress management includes exercising, relaxing, sharing your feelings with others, pursuing a hobby, and socializing. Unhealthy stress management includes "stuffing" your feelings, smoking, drinking, isolating yourself from others, and overworking.

How you handle your stress is most often learned in childhood. Although growing up in a nurturing and loving childhood home doesn't guarantee you can handle today's stress in healthy ways, it's a good start. But if you grew up in a dysfunctional childhood home, chances are you may have difficulty knowing how to handle stress effectively.

How did your working parent or parents handle stress while you were growing up? Look at how they juggled busy schedules, handled child care, managed finances, and dealt with problems in their relationship. You may uncover insights into why you manage your stress today the way you do. And you may also discover that the way you handle stress is actually a learned behavior and not a true indication of who you are.

Today, I'll welcome learning more about my behaviors. I'll look back at the past so I can discover the root of my stress response.

*. . . you must have faith in yourself—faith that you can
determine what must be done to solve the problem . . .
and faith that you will be able to take the appropriate
action.*

—MARSHA SINETAR

How would your life be different if, from this moment on, you made up your mind to do things instead
of just trying to do them? How would your actions be
different if you eliminated the word "try" from your
vocabulary and inserted "can"? Instead of saying, *I'll
try to stick to an exercise program,* say, *I can stick to
an exercise program.* Rather than saying, *I'll try to meet
that deadline,* say, *I can meet that deadline.*

Wouldn't your life be filled with potentials rather
than possibilities, intentions rather than insecurities,
and results rather than repeated attempts? The difference between believing you can try and believing you
can is the difference between having doubt in your
abilities and faith in yourself.

How do you foster faith in yourself? Start by tackling
simple things. Bake a cake, not a soufflé. Jog three
blocks, not three miles. Enroll in one class, not in a
long-term program. Then, once you achieve these
smaller goals, you'll be ready to face even greater challenges.

*Today, in everything I approach, I won't try. I'll make
up my mind that I can do them.*

*To embark on a new quarrel is to wander hand in hand
through the barbed wire and minefields of memory.*
                                        —KEN KOLB

Fighting with an intimate partner is like stepping
into the boxing ring with a familiar sparring partner.
You may be so used to how the other behaves that what
you each say and do may seem choreographed. So
while the actual cause of the hostility stays shrouded
in mystery, your "dance of disagreement" begins: walking away when one person is talking, rebuffing physical
intimacy, maintaining feigned politeness, blaming, or
name calling. But such a dance maintains disconnec-
tion and may only serve to escalate a fight from a minor
skirmish to a major battle.

Conflict and confrontation can be healthy when dealt
with in positive, specific ways. First call for a time-out
if anger or resentment clouds communication. Then,
when you can talk, focus on one issue at a time. If other
issues come up say, *I'd like to talk about A first and be
clear about it before we talk about B.* Take turns
listening to one another without interrupting. Then
together devise solutions or compromises to make positive changes in the area at issue.

*In any disagreement today, I won't complain just to
complain. I'll make a genuine effort to focus and communicate clearly on one area of conflict so it can be
resolved.*

*I went back to being an amateur, in the sense of some-
body who loves what she is doing. If a professional loses
the love of work, routine sets in, and that's the death of
work and of life.*

—ADE BETHUNE

Did you ever meet people who love their work? To
them, work is an expression of their energy and creativity—an experience that gives them satisfaction, challenge, and fulfillment. At the end of each workday they
aren't tired, and at the end of every work week they
aren't exhausted.

How you feel about your work creates an attitude
that influences the energy you bring to it. Your attitudes can be invigorating—*I love what I do,* or *I'm
excited about working on a new project*—or tension-
producing—*I deserve that promotion,* or *Why can't my
boss ever show any appreciation for what I do?* If you
only see your work in terms of your gain—what you
can get from it or how much others can give you—
rather than how much you can learn from it, grow from
it, or even what it can help you give others, then you
most likely view your work as draining.

The secret to fulfillment and happiness at work is to
do what you like not only because you can get something from it, but also because it can give something
to others.

*What does work mean to me? Today, I'll think of the
ways my work encourages me to be creative and the
positive ways my work makes me feel.*

You must have long-range goals to keep you from being frustrated by short-range failures.
—MAJOR GENERAL CHARLES C. NOBLE

The technological products we take for granted today—the sewing machine, the telephone, fax machines, or airplanes—weren't created overnight or even on the first try. The first models didn't always work as intended; sometimes even the thousandth prototype broke down. But inventors continued the process of reworking and revising until they found what did work. What motivated them was keeping their long-range goal in mind.

Without having long-range goals to work toward, the daily struggles can become overwhelming. Rather than see the light at the end of the tunnel, you may see no tunnel at all—no path to follow from one day to the next. Living each day without a distant dream or a new horizon to reach offers little hope of change, growth, or faith in the future.

Today, you can set long-range goals. Think about your lifestyle: Do you want to be married or single? Have children? Live in the city or the country? Rent an apartment or own a house? Consider your dreams: Do you want to go back to school? Write a book? Travel? Today, set one long-range goal and then keep that goal in mind whenever a day-to-day failure gets you down.

Long-range goals can help determine my direction in life so I'll know where I'm going and how I plan to get there.

I'm very competitive. However, I'm not so obsessed with winning that I cannot one day walk away from this occupation.

—ROBERT PARISH

The desire to win can be addictive. It's fun to win. Winners receive recognition. Winners earn rewards. Winners get ahead.

Competition, like excitement, thrills, challenges, and risks, can be seen as a positive stress. It's what most people expect to find in the job world and what motivates many to try their best.

But there's a fine line that, when crossed, can change the stress of competition from positive to negative. This can happen when the obsession to win becomes too consuming, when the pressure to win changes from a challenge to a burden, or when the thought of losing induces paralysis or fear. Then competition can turn into compulsion, where winning is the only acceptable outcome.

The key to working with the competition in your life is to stay focused on yourself, not the outcome. Always strive to maintain the attitude: *It's not important whether I win or lose; it's how I play the game.*

Today, I'll remember that any effort I make can make me a winner. I'll let competition motivate me, not overwhelm me.

Let our advance worrying become advance thinking and planning.

—WINSTON CHURCHILL

Do you ever find yourself beginning your thoughts with the famous pair of Worry Words—*what if ? What if my car isn't repaired on time? What if I don't get a raise? What if I can't get to the store before it closes?*

Worrying over events that haven't happened puts you in a state of mental disharmony, where you waste incredible amounts of energy agonizing over things you can't control.

Rather than build stress through worry, you can avoid stress entirely by thinking about more rational responses to the "what ifs" you pose and ponder. For example, rather than worry about whether your car will be ready on time, you can decide what you'll do if it isn't. Create a What If? Solution List that can help you plan your options in advance: *I can call the service station to see if they anticipate any delays; I can call a cab so I can get to my appointment on time;* or *I can rent a car for a few hours so I can run my errands.*

By turning your worrying into planning, you can find a solution that avoids a stressful problem.

Worrying can't change anything, but planning can. Today, I'll plan ahead rather than worry about what may come.

Americans generally spend so much time on things that are urgent *that we have none left to spend on those that are* important.

—HENRY WARD BEECHER

Do you marvel at those people who seem capable of juggling many things in their lives at one time—a full-time job, parenting, taking care of a home, pursuing a hobby, and so on? Do you ever think, *I wish I could be as productive?*

Just because some people can get many things done in a short amount of time doesn't mean they're working effectively. Vilfredo Pareto once created the following time-management principle: *Twenty percent of what you do nets eighty percent of your results.* So when you're faced with a number of projects that need to be done, it's important to make the right choice so you complete the one that will garner the greatest results. Targeting the most important project—not necessarily the most urgent—can help you receive the proper recognition, promote your position or salary, or give you the greatest satisfaction.

To become a more effective worker, focus on results rather than the process of getting a number of things done. That may mean putting off the urgent, but easy-to-accomplish, low-reward tasks in favor of the important, harder-to-achieve, yet high-reward projects.

Today, I'll use my time and energy effectively and begin work on projects that will net the greatest results.

There are always two voices sounding in our ears—the voice of fear and the voice of confidence. One is the clamor of the senses, the other is the whispering of the higher self.

—CHARLES B. NEWCOMB

There's a parable about a group of congregants who were asked by their pastor to share what they often prayed for. One who had just lost her job said secure work. Another who had medical problems said health. And another who had been raised in poverty said financial security.

But one congregant shook his head at the responses. When it came his turn he said, *I don't pray to escape the things that frighten me. Instead, I pray for the ability to trust that no matter what happens to me each day, it is the right thing.*

The voice of fear is high-pitched and stressed out; it whines and warns and whispers messages designed to scare you into action. But your voice of confidence is soft and soothing; it tells you not to worry, assures you all is well, and sometimes grows silent so you can listen to your Higher Power.

You can still your voice of fear and let your voice of confidence grow louder. Every day, pray for the wisdom to be able to live each moment to the fullest. A reassuring prayer is: *No matter what happens in the time between sunrise and sunset, I will never be surrounded by darkness.*

I'm connected with both the ebb and the flow of life. Despite fear and confusion, I can still feel secure.

The higher the flame has leaped, the colder and deader the ashes.

—OLIVE SCHREINER

The camp counselor was showing the campers how to cook a marshmallow over a campfire. *First you find a green stick and slide your marshmallow onto it. Then you hold it a few inches above the fire like so.*

But how do you know when it's done? asked a camper.

Well, uh, you just know, the counselor replied. *You see, it's not ready now because it's only a light brown.* A few seconds passed. *And it's not ready now because it's not quite golden brown.* A few more seconds passed. *And it's not ready now because it hasn't started to puff up yet.* A few more seconds passed, then suddenly the marshmallow burst into flame.

Is it done now? asked the camper.

The counselor held up the blackened treat. *No. Now it's ruined.*

Trying to do "just a little bit more" work, errands, or other obligations can leave you shortchanged on time you've set aside for yourself. And assuming that you'll always have some time left over at the end of the day for fun and enjoyment is a bit like leaving the marshmallow on the fire. So set aside time for yourself *now* and make it a rule that it can't be changed or shortened, no matter what happens today.

Today, before I'm as "done-in" as a burnt marshmallow, I'll stop whatever I'm doing and take time for myself.

See how nature—trees, flowers, grass—grows in silence; see the stars, the moon and the sun, how they move in silence. . . . We need silence to be able to touch souls.

—MOTHER TERESA

Meditation is the process of emptying your mind from stressful thoughts so you can experience physical relaxation and inner peace. It's a way to open yourself up to communication not only with your inner self, but also with a spiritual guide, such as a Higher Power. In making this contact, you gain knowledge, inspiration, and guidance about the people and situations in your life so you can handle them calmly and effectively.

How do you meditate? There are no hard-and-fast rules. Some people sit in a quiet, candlelit room, with their eyes closed; some listen to soothing music, recorded nature sounds, or a guided-meditation tape; some chant one word; others use running, bike riding, or walking as a chance to meditate.

To begin meditating, select a place where you won't be interrupted and an appointed time each day; in that way, you can become conditioned to calm and still your mind. When stressful thoughts occur, simply let them float through your consciousness. Rather than react to them, picture them slowly dissolving away like crystals of sugar in water.

Meditation can help me remain calm in the midst of stressful and conflicting situations. Today, I'll set aside a half hour for meditating.

I like trees because they seem more resigned to the way they have to live than other things do.
—WILLA CATHER

If a tree's soil becomes dry or low in valuable minerals, it can't pull up its roots and move to a better place. Instead, the tree spreads its roots deeper and wider, seeking more fertile ground. And it makes the surrounding soil richer by dropping its dead leaves and branches to decompose into mulch.

When you can effectively handle the stresses in your life, you're like a tree firmly planted. You can take care of yourself, whether or not others are there to take care of you. You aren't dependent on the people or things in your life to remain healthy. And when you're faced with difficulties or pressures, you are able to face them.

Whether you choose to live and grow in a "forest"—with a strong support system around you—or on your own, you can be flexible while maintaining your ability to handle the daily changes of life. Remember, in adapting to the conditions around it, the tree is always in control of its own destiny. So, too, are you.

In order to live well, I'll offer the correct responses to my environment, no matter how unpredictable and irregular this environment is.

Holding on to anger is like grasping a hot coal with the intent of throwing it at someone else—you are the one who gets burned.

—BUDDHA

Do you remember a time in the past when you felt anger toward a lover, child, sibling, parent, coworker, or friend, but didn't get it out at the time? Instead of working out the anger, you may have ignored it or tried to cover it up. But covering up the anger didn't "cure" it, and today you may still be experiencing past unresolved anger. And the longer you continue to go without expressing this anger, the angrier you will end up feeling.

Unresolved anger is like a bright red neon light that constantly flashes in your mind. Try as you might to ignore it, you can't. Attempt to shut it off, and you won't succeed. Soon the anger may overtake your life, casting its fiery red glow over everything and everybody you come in contact with.

Although unresolved anger is based in a past you can't change, you can still do something about it in the present. Talking to someone who's not involved with your past anger or writing how you feel in a journal can help you express it. These simple acts of letting your rage out are positive steps to take toward letting your anger go.

Today, I'll reflect on an incident that still makes me angry. Acknowledging this bad feeling and then expressing it can help me let it go.

The easiest kind of relationship for me is with ten thousand people. The hardest is with one.

—JOAN BAEZ

Inside you is a "light" side and a "shadow" side. The light side contains things you're comfortable sharing with others—your skills, strengths, and personality characteristics that make you feel happy and proud. Your shadow side, however, contains things you wish to hide from others—your unexpressed fears and weaknesses, and things that make you feel embarrassed, insecure, or ashamed.

Most people are willing to show their light side to others. But showing only one part of you prevents others from getting to know all of you, keeping intimacy and love at a distance.

Coming to terms with your shadow side means learning that each side works in harmony to provide you with a balance: Sometimes you need to be weak so you can be strong, fearful so you can be courageous, vulnerable so you can be secure, and uncertain so you can be confident. Today, embrace your shadow side with the same acceptance as your light side by acknowledging that each is part of the whole. Then you can show the *real* you to others.

I'll label both sides of me as good. Then I'll be less judgmental of myself and more willing to open up to at least one person in my life.

Habits are first cobwebs, then cables.
                                        —SPANISH PROVERB

You are a creature of habit. Some of your habits have become automatic, unconscious behaviors that result from feelings of fear, doubt, insecurity, tension, or worry. Nail biting, fidgeting, obsessing about one thing, or smoking are just a few. But until you become aware of your habits, you won't be able to change or stop them.

To become more conscious of the things you do, focus on your behaviors while performing a specific action. Think, for instance, about how you drive your car. Perhaps you're in the habit of tailgating slower drivers, honking at cars that don't signal, or speeding. The next time you drive, consider the repercussions that could result from your particular driving habit. Then ask yourself, *What do I gain from driving this way? Is it worth it?*

Positive replacements can also help you begin to change or stop a habit. For example, if you notice that you bite your nails when you're nervous, keep carrots, celery, or gum on hand during trying times. If a morning cup of coffee is tempting you to smoke, switch your drink to tea, cocoa, or plain hot water. Or set a goal of reading a book a week to divert your mind from focusing on an ended relationship. By becoming more aware of your bad habits, you can replace them with more constructive actions.

By consciously getting in touch with my habits, I can become more relaxed and accepting of new ways to handle routine tasks.

A customer in a crowded department store was writing a check. The cashier said that checks of such large amounts required a manager's okay. "I need approval!" she called to a nearby co-worker. Instantly he responded, "I love your sweater!"

—ADAM J. FECHTER

Are you an approval-seeker, someone who structures life around pleasing others and opts for what you "should do" instead of what you "want to do"?

You may feel that you're protecting yourself from the criticism and disapproval of others by acting, thinking, or verbalizing in ways you feel will earn their acceptance. But years of pleasing others can put you so out of touch with who you really are and what you really want that even the simplest choice can become a major conflict. Instead of knowing what you want, you're often more aware of what others want for you.

If trying to please others has made you unsure of your wants and needs, change the word "should" to "want" when you have to make a choice. So instead of thinking, *I should buy the dress my mother wants me to,* think *I want to buy the dress I saw in the window.* Over time, you can add a reason to help you understand your decision. For example, *I should attend my friend's exhibit* becomes *I don't want to attend the exhibit because I'm exhausted and need to get to bed early.* Identifying what you *want* can help you learn to please yourself—not others—first.

I won't be out of touch with what I want. Today, I'll focus on whether the choices I make are based on personal desire or feelings of guilt and obligation.

Blessed is the person who is too busy to worry in the daytime and too sleepy to worry at night.

—LEO AIKMAN

Your reward tonight for today's activities will be sleep. Although your body and mind may crave this slumber, it may take some time to "turn off" stressful thoughts so you can relax.

To release energy from your body and fill your mind with pleasant thoughts, set aside some time before going to bed for sleep-inducing meditation. Sit or lie down in a comfortable position, close your eyes, then picture walking down a gently winding, nature-filled path. Look around you as you walk. Perhaps you see a lake, its surface shimmering as it reflects a full moon. Maybe there are distant mountains that cast brilliant hues from a breathtaking sunset. Or maybe there's a nearby stream that soothes you with its flowing sounds.

Now shift your attention to your breathing. As you inhale, imagine clear, fresh air going into your lungs. Bring the air slowly and deeply into your abdomen. Then release the air in a slow, steady exhalation, feeling your abdomen sink and imagining your breath as a gentle breeze that barely stirs the leaves on a tree.

Regular presleep mind and body relaxation can train your body to enter into a peaceful state with only minimal concentration. Over time, this relaxation routine will also become a great stress reliever.

Tonight, I'll practice quieting my thoughts and then letting them go.

Emotions should be servants, not masters—or at least not tyrants.

—ROBERT H. BENSON

Nothing can rattle the nerves more than bottling up your feelings. Trying to keep your emotions under control or hidden from others can be like trying to keep the lid on a pot of boiling water. Try as you might, the feelings just keep bubbling to the surface and threaten to blow the lid off at any moment.

While internalizing feelings can be useful in some situations—for example, appearing calm under fire to show your boss a promotable employee or not having a heated argument with a spouse in front of others—in the long run it can create undue tension and unreleased stress.

The opposite of keeping feelings in is to let them out. The safest place to do so is not always with those who have been the cause of your emotions. Often, it's best to write down your feelings in a daily journal or share them with someone removed from the situation. In that way, you lessen the impact of your emotions rather than add to them.

Nothing can calm my nerves more than letting my feelings out. Today, I'll share how I feel with others by clearly expressing my emotions.

I was tired of feeling frazzled, stretched and over-worked, tired of the ache in my shoulders that signaled the beginning of another tension headache. Obviously, it was time for a change.

—ANNE CASSIDY

The next time you feel as if you're at the end of your rope, too stressed to hold on any longer, and ready to drop from exhaustion, practice the STOP message. STOP stands for Slow Down, Take a Time-out, Open Your Mind, and Practice Patience.

To Slow Down, first count backward from ten to zero as you picture in your mind a colorful hot-air balloon slowly descending to earth. Next, Take a Time-out—five minutes or more—from the situation causing your stress. Physically get up and leave or visually leave it. (Imagine, for example, lying on a tropical beach while sitting in traffic.)

Then, Open Your Mind to ways you can work through the stress. Can you change your attitude from negative to positive, find a solution to a nagging problem, or promise yourself that the next time you'll plan in advance how you'll handle that difficult client?

Finally, Practice Patience. Count to five before you respond, make a decision, or act. You may have to practice STOP a few times before you finally ease the racing feeling in your mind and body. But, over time, the STOP process *can* stop the stress.

I can control my reaction to stressful situations by stopping and listening to myself. Today, I'll practice helping myself rather than feeling helpless.

I've done the research, and I hate to tell you, but every-body dies—lovers, joggers, vegetarians and nonsmok-ers. I'm telling you this so that some of you who jog at 5 A.M. and eat vegetables will occasionally sleep late and have an ice-cream cone.

—DR. BERNIE S. SIEGEL

How do you approach life? Do you constantly push yourself to the limit? Do you take on every project that comes your way? Do you feel everything has to be done right this minute?

"Type A" behavior involves feeling as if you have to take on every job, do everything yourself, and con-stantly be in control, because if you aren't nothing will get done.

The best method for changing Type A behavior is to learn how to let go of the grip you have on at least one facet of your life: your desire to work a certain amount of hours each week, your wish to have things in your home a certain way, or your rigid diet.

But changing from a Type A to a Type A-minus doesn't happen overnight. You must ease yourself grad-ually into this new behavior. Just become willing to let go from time to time—to sleep in once in a while, to let magazines pile up on the coffee table, or to throw calories to the wind with a double-scoop cone.

I don't have to do everything. Today, I'll prepare myself for change by taking simple, easy, and gradual steps.

No bird soars too high if he soars with his own wings.
—WILLIAM BLAKE

Your life may be filled with perverse sacrifices made for something or someone else—a demanding boss, a hobby that's grown into an obsession, a lonely parent, or an unmotivated spouse. But is any person or thing more important than taking care of yourself?

Consider how you allocate your time and energy among the different areas of your life: work, relationships, family, and you. What you may discover is that one or two areas take up most of your time and leave you with little for yourself.

Now think about how much time and energy you'd *like* to devote to yourself—to all the things you've wanted to do, but for which you've rarely had the time or motivation. Like the gerbil that runs on its exercise wheel, you have a choice. You can continue to spin around and around, day after day, spending the majority of your time doing the same thing. Or you can jump off the wheel from time to time and experience a more well-rounded and balanced life.

What will you do for *you* today?

I need a balance of work and play, solitude and socializing, and activity and rest in my life. Today, I'll set priorities that include time for myself in each area.

We [men] define ourselves by our earning power, not by our human connections. Traditionally, our society has trained men to be comfortable with competition and uncomfortable with intimacy.
—HAROLD S. KUSHNER

Women are usually good at developing networks that provide them with the emotional support they need, particularly during difficult times. Men, on the other hand, are better at business networking and shared activities such as sports. This can make it hard for men to develop intimate relationships where they can talk about feelings and personal experiences.

Whether you're a man or a woman, your mental health is often determined by the nature of your involvement with others and the supportive network you've created. If you lack a nurturing web of family, coworkers, friends, and acquaintances, you may find the burdens in your life more overwhelming than you would if you could share them with others.

How can you develop your own social support system? It's up to *you* to seek out other people. For instance, instead of eating lunch alone at your desk, ask someone to join you. Or take a class in a subject you've always wanted to learn about—or volunteer at your neighborhood soup kitchen. Remember, it's not *what* you know but *who* you know that's most important.

Today, I'll begin to widen my social support network. I'll strike up conversations with at least two people I've never spoken to before.

Nature is always kind enough to give even her clouds a humorous lining.

—JAMES RUSSELL LOWELL

Are you too nervous, too serious, or too busy to laugh? When was the last time you experienced a real belly-jiggling laugh—one that brought tears to your eyes, left you gasping for air, and made your sides hurt?

Laughter provides an enjoyable break from the tense moments caused by the not-so-funny things in your life. Humor can take you away from your problems and troubles, and give you a fresh perspective on them.

Yet humor is rarely recognized as a tool for coping with stress. After all, how can you laugh when you're feeling angry, anxious, or tense? Laughter, however, can provide a well-needed positive balance to such negative feelings. Norman Cousins was able to use laughter effectively to help turn the tide of his serious disease. He surrounded himself with *Candid Camera* videos, Marx Brothers films, and *Three Stooges* comedies, then had to check out of the hospital and into a motel because he was making too much noise healing himself!

Humor can be as beneficial to the body as aerobic exercise: a good hearty laugh can give every system in your body—your heart, your lungs, your circulation, your muscles—a rousing inner workout.

What makes me laugh? Today, I'll discover what I think is funny and gravitate toward those situations, people, or resources that make me laugh.

Take your work seriously but yourself lightly.
                                        —C. W. METCALF

Do you expect things to run smoothly twenty-four hours a day, 365 days a year, every year?

In every job, relationship, or life situation, there's inevitably going to be some turbulence. But rather than try to fix everything and change everybody, you could use your time more effectively by "lightening up" and simply letting things go the way they were planned.

One way to do so is to stop obsessing about the trivial, day-to-day matters and start focusing on the truly important things in life—like good relationships with the people you love. By devoting less energy to the little things and more to the meaningful matters, you can begin to recognize the good in your life.

Another way is to foster a healthier perspective on your problems by asking yourself, *Will this matter ten years from now?* The snafus that happen in a day are often minuscule when seen against the "bigger picture." By recognizing that ten years from now being stuck in traffic today isn't going to impact on your life, you'll see that life is too short to waste by taking everything so seriously.

There's no way I can have everything happen exactly the way I want. Today, I'll focus on the things that are truly important and "lighten up" my attitude about everything else.

Human beings are like tea bags. You don't know your own strength until you get into hot water.
                                        —BRUCE LAINGEN

Bruce Laingen was one of the hostages held in Iran. During his 444 days of internment, he stayed level-headed and optimistic by striving to think and be positive about the inner strengths he had developed that could help him face—and survive—his difficult circumstances.

You may often think how wonderful life would be if things were easier. But think back to a particularly rough time you went through in the past. Maybe it was a difficult childhood, a hurtful relationship, an injury or illness, or the loss of a job. Would you be as strong today if it hadn't been for that experience? Hasn't that experience influenced you in some way—left a piece of itself to influence your way of thinking, feeling, acting, and believing?

Today, when faced with a difficulty, don't try to find an easy way out or escape from it. Instead ask yourself, *What will getting* through *this experience teach me?* How will this make me a stronger person now—and in the future?

Today, I'll explore the ways that I can foster a positive and optimistic attitude to support me through the tough times.

It is against the will of God to eat delicate food hastily, to pass gorgeous views hurriedly, to express deep sentiments superficially . . .

—CHANG CH'AO

Do you prepare and eat fresh, wholesome foods each day? Do you chew your food slowly and thoroughly, enjoying every bite?

A proper diet and healthy eating habits keep your body in a constant state of optimal health. Yet, during a busy day, you may tend to please your watch rather than your digestive needs—by eating on the run or when you can fit it into your schedule—or your palate rather than your nutritional needs—by eating fatty, salty, and sweet-tasting meals or snacks rather than a variety of enriching foods.

To eat for optimal health and vitality, you should satisfy what your body needs rather than what your habits or emotions demand. The two cups of caffeinated coffee you have every morning may give you a burst of energy, but they may also make you restless and irritable. And the cheesecake that puts a smile on your face because it tastes just like your mother's can later make you feel heavy and lethargic.

Because each cell in your body is replaced every seven years from the nourishment you give it, that means you really are what you eat! So it's best to begin today to replace the unhealthy foods you crave with more healthful nutritional choices.

I need to relearn what foods my body really needs. Today, I'll start by eating at least one healthy balanced meal consisting of fresh, healthy foods.

There is more to life than increasing its speed.
                                    —MAHATMA GANDHI

Does it seem like the speed of living is accelerating? The telephone gives instant access to the entire world. News networks air late-breaking stories as they occur. Computers enable one person to do the work of many in considerably less time.

We're living in an age of one-minute managers, fax machines, instant replays, and microwave meals. Yet instead of making life easier or allowing greater leisure time, such time-saving devices actually cause more stress. Modern technology encourages you to think you can do more in a day. So you spend each day locked into "express stress," juggling many activities at the same time—watching television, talking on the phone, and microwaving dinner as you ride your exercise bike.

But it's the quality, not the quantity, of living that's important. While instant coffee is a great convenience, grinding your own beans is more enjoyable and tastes and smells better. Driving in the fast lane may get you to a destination faster, but you won't be able to enjoy much of the scenery along the way.

Living life to the fullest doesn't mean living it the fastest. Life isn't a race, so slow down your pace.

I'll keep in mind that life isn't a race won by the fastest. Today, I'll slow down so I can take time to notice and appreciate the people, places, and things around me.

True contentment depends not upon what we have; a tub was large enough for Diogenes, but a world was too little for Alexander.

—CHARLES CALEB COLTON

When actor Michael J. Fox left the successful television series *Family Ties* after seven years, his first movie was a $200 million box-office hit. People asked him, *Doesn't that put pressure on you to have to continue to be equally successful in your future roles?* But Fox said, *The most important thing in my life is my family. It's not the business. I just try to keep my life small. . . . I don't have any big agenda.*

What makes you feel true contentment? To some people, it's being a business success, with a corner office and gold-embossed business cards. To others, it's raising healthy, active children. Still others believe contentment is measured by popularity, recognition, or financial wealth. And there are those who believe that true contentment results from helping others.

How you identify what brings you contentment will help you determine what your "life agenda" is. By first identifying and then working toward your idea of what's most important to you, you have a better chance of experiencing true contentment—and, ultimately, success—in your life.

What's the most important thing in my life? Today, I'll experience the ways this brings me true contentment.

I am not an optimist, because I am not sure that every-thing ends well. Nor am I a pessimist, because I am not sure that everything ends badly. I just carry hope in my heart.

—VÁCLAV HAVEL

Do you doubt that after every downswing in your life there will always be an upswing? Because the up-swings are not always immediate, you may lose hope that the bad times will ever turn around. You may even say, *I don't think I'll ever see the light at the end of the tunnel.*

But rather than bemoan the downswings, today you can begin to trust that there's a natural up-and-down motion to life. Have faith that the bad times will even-tually come to an end and the good times will get even better.

How? By thinking positively. When you have a bright, hopeful outlook, then "the swings" don't matter as much—you trust that nothing, no matter how bad, will stay the same. And you can tell yourself, *Things won't get any worse. In fact, I know they'll get better.*

Today, I can believe that the tide always turns. I won't give up my hopeful, optimistic outlook.

We believe that according to our desire we are able to change the things round about us . . . we do not succeed in changing things according to our desire, but gradually our desire changes.

—MARCEL PROUST

Do you view your car as a mode of transportation on and off a battleground five mornings and evenings a week? Do you hold a "me against them" attitude that makes you drive as if you're on a speedway rather than a highway? And do you believe that your way of driving—tailgating, making quick lane changes, or running yellow and red traffic lights—is the only way to deal with drivers who can't understand that you're the most important person on the road?

No amount of reckless behavior on your part will change rush-hour traffic. To try only subjects you to a senseless, stressful struggle you can't win—and puts your safety (and that of others) at risk. So instead try focusing on changing what you can. Make your commuting a more relaxing experience by joining a car pool or taking public transportation so you can read, sleep, or converse. Or, if you prefer to drive alone, think of your car as a sanctuary where you can do what you want: sing, listen to a book on tape, learn a foreign language from an audiocassette, notice the sights around you, or simply unwind from the day.

When I'm driving, I'm in charge of my own behavior. Today, I won't fight the traffic or take my frustrations out on others at the risk of my personal safety.

We have not been sufficiently schooled in the moment.
—STREPHON KAPLAN-WILLIAMS

Imagine how you might live life differently if you were told today that you only had a week to live. How would you use your time? Would you obsess about all the things you're never going to be able to do, or would you simply start doing the things you've always wanted to do? Would you think about all the loose ends in your life you have to tie up, or would you let them go and do something you've never done before?

It has often been said that there is no tomorrow; there's only today, and time spent daydreaming, worrying, or bouncing back and forth between past and future will only prevent you from experiencing the moment in which you are living.

How you live each day can set the stage for how you're going to live the rest of your life. Can you treat this day as a twenty-four-hour period untouched by the past or present? Notice everything about today—the sights, the sounds, the smells, and the way things feel. And notice everyone in your day—friends, family, co-workers, and strangers. Living fully in the present can allow you to see how full the present really is.

I won't sleepwalk through today. I'll experience the joy of being fully aware of each passing moment.

*Action may not always bring happiness, but there is no
happiness without action.*

—BENJAMIN DISRAELI

Wishing problems away doesn't solve them. Neither
does avoiding, walking away, or denying them. While
it's human nature to delay doing anything painful or
difficult, procrastination only keeps problems tempo-
rarily at bay. Facing problems is the most effective way
of dealing with them. Talking through a disagreement,
making a difficult decision, asking for help when you're
stuck, or letting your feelings out can help you get
through trying situations.

But knowing you must face a situation and actually
facing it are two very different things. One way to ease
into the process of confronting a problem gently is to
write about it in a journal. Use your journal to explore
why you're having such a hard time facing a particular
situation. Then, when you're finished writing, imagine
the conversation you might have to resolve the situation. Listen to how you express yourself. Are you stat-
ing your needs clearly? Is your tone too harsh,
argumentative, or defensive?

By first writing out how you feel and then going
through a mental "rehearsal," you may be able to face
the problems in your life with a little less anxiety and
a lot more confidence and clarity.

*I know it's scary to work through some of the difficult
situations in my life. But today, I'll focus on one of these
situations and think about how I'd like to handle it.*

Do we all have nothing but time on our hands—to shop smart, decorate divinely, cook healthy, exercise madly, perform the most innovative sexual acrobatics, yet still advance in careers . . .?

—SUZANNE GORDON

The pressures on women today to do it all are phenomenal. They've been promoted from their past position of chief cook and bottle washer to career woman-housekeeper-nurse-caretaker-gofer-chauffeur—and more. No wonder the common refrain of women today is, *I'm always so tired.*

While husbands are beginning to contribute more time and energy to housework and child care, wives are often still the ones responsible for completing most of the duties. But today's woman doesn't have to do anything—or everything—unless she chooses to. Nor does she have to buy into the belief that because she's a woman, she's responsible for all the "female" duties like cooking, cleaning, and caring for the children.

Today's woman deserves the best of both worlds—a great job *and* a wonderful family—without having to shoulder all the responsibility. To support this, create a flowchart that details all the household chores, then negotiate with your spouse and children so each can help share in some way in those responsibilities. Then you'll all be able to have the best of both worlds—and time to enjoy it.

I can't be everything to everyone anymore. Today, I'll let go of at least one of my responsibilities and feel good about it.

*The noise level goes up year after year. . . . Few places
are quiet, even where we might expect it.*
—PETER ANDERSON

No matter where you go today for some peace and
quiet, it seems that loud music and voices follow.
Browse in a bookstore, and melodies waft around you.
Walk down the street, and passing cars thunder by. Sit
in a movie theater, and people converse loudly. And
what would a summer day on the beach be without the
ear-splitting, head-pounding battle between competing
radios and screaming kids!

Searching for silence in a world replete with boom
boxes, trucks, jackhammers, and jets, in a culture
where music is piped into every store, waiting room,
and elevator is as impossible as finding a "no screaming
kids" section in a family restaurant. But, whether you
know it or not, noise pollution is stressful and unhealthy: it makes your blood pressure soar, your heart
palpitate, your jaws clench, and your head pound.

It takes effort to locate silence or soothing sounds
like waves lapping on the shore. While you may have
to go out of your way to discover places where silence
reigns or nature's sounds can comfort you, the rewards
will be worth it.

*Are there places where I can go to escape noise pollu-
tion? Today, I'll take a new path on my daily travels to
explore quieter locations.*

I don't think God puts you on this earth just to make millions of dollars and ignore everything else.
                                                          —CHRIS AMUNDSEN

The hours that lead up to today's midnight deadline for mailing your federal and state income taxes are like the countdown for a rocket about to be blasted into space—a rocket that symbolizes your rising blood pressure and increasing edginess, anxiety, and tension. The stress over what you owe, how financially good or bad you did last year, and the changes you need to make in your spending habits for the rest of this year are enough to make you scream, *I wish I had a billion dollars. Then I wouldn't have to worry about anything.*

But while it may seem that bushels and bushels of money would solve all your problems, in reality it merely provides you with an illusion of security in an insecure world.

The desire to have "all the money in the world" can make you forget about the truly important things in life—close moments spent with family and friends, enjoyable holidays and vacations, times of fun and relaxation, and quiet times for nurturing your spirituality. Today, to ease your tax-time stress, embrace just one simple pleasure that money can't buy that brings great value to your life.

Today, I'll let go of my obsession about money and rediscover the joys of home life, basic values, and things that last.

*These are the soul's changes. I don't believe in ageing.
I believe in forever altering one's aspect to the sun.
Hence my optimism.*

—VIRGINIA WOOLF

In American society, aging is often thought of as an
entirely negative experience. Most people are so
hooked on youth that they haven't recognized that in-
experience and great reserves of physical stamina
aren't always virtues; rather, knowing what you're doing, where you're going, and the steps you want to take
to get there are the *real* strengths.

Maturity can give you the chance to do many new
things, to develop yourself in new ways, and to set your
sights on more distant goals. Just because aging can
physically erode your body and slow up your pace
doesn't mean that your mind is similarly eroded or that
your faith and determination is fading.

Today, find security in the knowledge that you've
still got many more goals to attain. Think of at least
one vital, challenging interest that you can either take
up now or when you retire. If you begin now to take
steps toward this venture—in advance of retirement—
then you'll be better able to make the transition from
all-consuming work time to all-consuming retirement
time.

*Wisdom can be gained, but I have to take steps to ac-
quire it. Today, I'll venture into the world and create
new challenges and goals for myself—no matter what
my age.*

Every morning at 8 o'clock, I pull a jumpsuit over my nightgown and, no matter what the weather, I walk Pierre, my dog. I buy the newspaper at the corner stand, and while I eat my ample breakfast . . . I read the front page. Later, when I have time, I read the rest of the paper, do the crossword puzzle and play out the bridge game.

—Beatrice L. Cole

Are there people you know who seem to get to every task they need to in a day, never appear under pressure, and have energy to spare at the end of the day?

Some people accomplish more than others, but not necessarily because they're more capable, organized, or intelligent. What they have is a clear understanding of what they want and how they can get it. So if today what they want to do is prepare their garden for planting, read a couple of magazines, watch their favorite television show, and eat a tasty dinner, they find ways to do it all. Perhaps they spend the morning doing some gardening, use the lunch hour for eating and reading, and order a take-out dinner from a gourmet restaurant to enjoy with their favorite TV show.

When you can see the things you want to do each day as links in a connected chain, then you can move easily from link to link, making a little time for each thing. Today, create your own chain of activities, and then structure your day to include time to linger on each link.

Spending time doing the same old things over and over is something I'd like to change. Today, I'll learn how to find the time to do a wide variety of things.

The other night it hit me. Thirty-one flavors, 57 channels, 285 types of vegetables just aren't that fun.
—MARK MURO

Have you ever stood in front of the racks in a video store and found yourself thinking, *I want to see everything, and I want to see nothing*? You may have then slipped slowly into a paralysis of indecision, brought about by the stress of having too many choices.

In 1976, the typical supermarket carried 9,000 products. Today, it bursts with 30,000. In 1975, the average household received six TV stations; now the stations number between thirty and seventy-seven. Massive bookstores brag of 150,000 choices. Even in a depressed economy, 21 percent more new products are introduced in supermarkets and drug stores than in the previous year.

While choice is what our consumer-oriented society is all about, selection can nag at contentment, so many options can create compulsions to want everything, and an infinite choice can be intimidating.

How can you cope with the stress of "choice glut"? Know what you want before you shop. Make lists before you leave the house to narrow the field of choices—three action-adventure videos, two brands of shampoos, or one make of automobile. And then shop from your list, not from the choices.

Today, I won't be overwhelmed by the choices I face. I'll be decisive as I focus on just one thing I'd like and do what I can to get it.

*So I close in saying that I might have had a bad break,
but I have an awful lot to live for.*

—LOU GEHRIG

Who has had a sadder break in life than Lou Gehrig,
the major-league baseball player who had to give up
his career because of amyotrophic lateral sclerosis?
Who knows what pressures and stresses he faced as he
lived through each day, knowing his body was weak-
ening while he was powerless to do anything about it?
Time couldn't heal his wounds. Nor could patience or
a positive attitude cease the spread of his illness. Yet
Gehrig coped with pride and dignity and drew on the
strength of those who supported and cared for him.
And in his farewell speech he proclaimed, *I consider
myself the luckiest man on the face of this earth.*

What inner strengths do you call on to help you
through troubling times? Do you use the support of
nurturing friends or the love of family members? Do
you rely upon the comfort of spiritual reading, meditation, or prayer? Does the ocean, a walk through the
park, or working in the garden restore your strength?

Now, not later, is the time to create and strengthen
your sources of support. Today, think of the ways you
consider yourself lucky—lucky because of the people,
places, or beliefs you have to lean on when you need
them.

*Who or what would I turn to if I needed help and sup-
port? Today, I'll think about the people or things that
would give me the most comfort, then open my life to
them now.*

One doesn't discover new lands without consenting to lose sight of the shore for a very long time.
—ANDRÉ GIDE

Imagine the stress Columbus and his crew felt as they set sail, knowing they might never see their homeland again. But that didn't stop them from beginning their risky voyage.

Risk taking means attempting something new, different, or unknown, without the comfort of knowing what the outcome will be. Sometimes you can take a risk and achieve positive results—for instance, you may ask your boss for a raise and get it. Or you can take a risk and feel you didn't succeed—being turned down when you ask someone out on a date.

But whatever the outcome, it's important to take the risk. Being ready to take a risk doesn't mean you won't feel afraid; fear is a natural reaction to the unknown. But fearing and *still taking the risk* is what risk taking is all about. That's why the best risk takers are the people who say, *What do I have to lose?* They have the attitude that even if they don't succeed, they're at least willing to try.

Today, think of a risk you'd like to take. On a piece of paper, write what you might lose in taking the risk. Then write what you might gain. Keeping the gains in mind, take the risk!

I'll work through my risk-taking fears by asking, "What's the worst possible thing that could happen if I take this risk?" Then I'll consider whether that's bad enough to stop me from doing it.

It takes two people to have a marriage, but only one is necessary to change it. We end up feeling helpless in our marriages because we can't control our partners. The truth is that we need only learn to control our-selves.
                          —MELVYN KINDER AND CONNELL COWAN

In any relationship, there's often mutual work that needs to be done by both partners to identify, confront, and come up with solutions to issues that are affecting the relationship.

But if you're unhappy with your relationship a good deal of the time or are threatened by the interests and achievements of your partner, then you may need to do some work on yourself. Making personal changes such as dieting to improve your self-image, going to therapy, spending time alone, developing a new inter-est, or dealing with an addiction can bring about healthy changes in yourself that positively affect your relationship.

The best relationships are those in which both peo-ple are happy with themselves first. So when you can abandon the desire to change your partner and focus instead on the changes you can make in yourself, you may be amazed at how your relationship improves. Feeling good about yourself *can* make you feel good with another.

Today, I can accept others for who they are, without trying to change them. I'll work on me *instead so my relationships can grow for the better.*

Everyone has an invisible sign hanging from his neck saying, Make Me Feel Important! *Never forget this message when working with people.*
                                                    —MARY KAY ASH

Today, few tasks are accomplished in isolation. Even if you work for yourself, there are many people on whom you depend to keep your business running—the postal service, the copying center, a part-time employee, or friends and family members who provide you with emotional or financial support.

Yet how do you convey your appreciation for the support you're given by others? Too often, you may find yourself so caught up in a tight deadline or heavy work load that you can't even set aside a few minutes to chat with a coworker or send a card to a friend. You may schedule more business meetings with clients than dinners out with a loved one. Or you may take off on more business trips than vacations with your family.

Today, take some time to show your appreciation for all the wonderful things others do for you that help you to feel important. Send a card to a friend, pick up the phone and say hello to a loved one, or take your children out for a treat. Show the people who make you feel important that they, too, are important to you.

Today, I'll take the time to pay attention to how I treat those with whom I interact. As much as possible, I'll let them know their importance to me.

Going to church doesn't make you a Christian any more than going to a garage makes you a car.
—Laurence J. Peter

Coming home at night to an unlit house or apartment can be frightening. Once the lights go on, you feel an instantaneous burst of relief. But you don't always need bright lights to find your way in the dark. Spirituality—a belief in a Higher Power who watches over you—can provide you with an inner light. By trusting this light, you can be secure, no matter where you are or how dark it is.

You don't need to go to church every Sunday to find this inner light. Many people seek a spiritual connection with nature because they feel a certain sense of faith and trust in it. There's a beauty and vastness to nature as well as a soothing rhythm—the change of seasons, the ebb and flow of the tide, the migration of the birds, the rising and setting of the sun.

Appreciating nature and then "connecting" with it in some way—by taking a walk in the woods, bird-watching, or planting spring flowers—can take you outside yourself, help you forget your difficulties and problems for a short time, open your mind and heart to new experiences, and show you the wonder of something greater than you.

Today, I'll lose myself in the natural beauty around me. With an appreciation of nature, I can trust that there isn't a problem that can't be solved or a weary body that can't be reenergized.

Don't Tell Me What Kind of Day to Have.
— Bumper sticker

Beginning each day with a chronically angry attitude can cause physical distress as well as have a negative impact on your interpersonal relations, work quality, and overall attitude.

Today, rather than walk around like a time bomb, try to identify what provoked your anger. For example, your frustration could have been caused by waiting several minutes in a store checkout line or by a stressful visit with your parents.

Then ask yourself, *How important is the cause of my anger? Will it be significant enough to remember weeks, months, or even years from now?* Often what you discover is that there are very few things that make you angry that need to be remembered for more than a few minutes.

Finally, think of ways to change, limit, or even eliminate the time spent in the provoking situation. Shopping at a different time to avoid long checkout lines or cutting short visits to your parents can help you deal effectively with your anger so it doesn't control you or the kind of day you have.

I can work through my anger by thinking creatively. Today, I'll alter my angry responses by developing effective strategies to deal with the provocations in my life.

The greatest success is not in never falling, but rising each time you fall.

—VINCE LOMBARDI

When Thomas Edison and his assistants had finished an improved prototype of the first electric light bulb, Edison handed the bulb to a young helper. As the boy nervously carried the fragile bulb up the stairs, he dropped it. Hours more work had to be put into producing another light bulb. When it was finished, Edison handed it to the boy who had dropped the first one. In that simple gesture, Edison may have changed the boy's self-image from one of failure and incompetence to one of success and confidence. Rather than let his young worker wallow in a mistake, by giving him another chance Edison taught the boy that he could rise above his failure.

Being unable to rise above failure can prevent you from getting up when you've been knocked down. But failure can be a learning experience. Look upon your mistakes or failures today as valuable teachers. Instead of saying, *I really blew it,* ask, *What can I learn from this?* And then, *How can I use what I've learned so I can try it again?* Your capacity to learn from your mistakes and move on will be key to your ultimate success and achievement.

I won't be burdened by the need for perfection, nor will I be inhibited by failure. Today, I'll strive to do the best I can in everything I do.

I raced through the springtime of my life. I wanted to grow, stay up late, to leave home, to get on with my life.

—DONALD M. MURRAY

You may live each day thinking that once you get what you want, you'll be happy and content—you'll finally be who you've always wanted to be, do what you've always wanted to do, or find what you've been searching for. But always looking ahead at what's to come or living in anticipation of a future time can deprive you of enjoying the present.

Imagine what American history would be like if every explorer had looked ahead to the destination and neglected experiencing and recording the steps and processes of the journey. The discovery of America would have been a mere voyage across a lot of water instead of a thrilling sea adventure, and the expedition to the Pacific Ocean would have been a long hike through a lot of woods instead of a fascinating discovery of the country's unspoiled beauty.

Trying to speed your journey through life to reach some distant destination can keep you from enjoying each day and learning from your experiences. Take a leisurely stroll today to a place you've never been before and imagine you're an explorer as you notice everything around you. Walking, not running through life, is the best way to see and experience it.

Today, I'll be aware of who I am, not who I'd like to be, and where I am, not where I'd like to be.

Most people ask for happiness on condition. Happiness can be felt only if you don't set any conditions.
                                                    —ARTHUR RUBINSTEIN

Everyone wants to be happy. Some people spend their lives searching for happiness. Others set guidelines to help determine when they've achieved it, such as when they attain a goal or purchase their dream house. Yet searching for happiness can be elusive, defining it impossible, and setting guidelines conditional. What you often believe will make you happy and what really makes you happy can be as different as night and day.

Think, for example, about people who seem to have everything: money, power, prestige, and popularity. You'd think such people would be happy, but most spend their lives feverishly collecting more and more things or chasing grand illusions in the hopes such things will bring them happiness.

When you place your happiness outside yourself, it only leads to endless struggle, competition, frustration, and disappointment. So rather than look outside, today, look within. Think about what makes you happy, no matter what you have or don't have. Maybe it's the warmth of a fresh-baked chocolate chip cookie, the smile of a stranger, or time spent with one you love. Happiness comes not from what's around you, but from what's within you.

Success, influence, money, or the approval of others won't make me happy. Today, I'll look for happiness in the joy I feel from myself and my life.

Not everything that is faced can be changed; but nothing can be changed until it is faced.

—JAMES BALDWIN

One of the most common causes of stress is change. Research has shown that people who go through several major changes in their lives within a year—either negative *or* positive—experience more stress than usual. As a result, they tend to run a greater risk of becoming ill, become more susceptible to injury, or have more difficulties coping than those who haven't experienced such changes.

Yet life without change is boring. And a person who hardly ever changes functions more as a robot or a machine than as a human being. Everyone needs a certain amount of newness, stimulation, and freshness in their lives.

But you don't need to make drastic, major changes in order to experience the rewards of change. You can start by looking at the familiar people, places, and things in your life in a different way. For instance, instead of seeing your job as the same old grind or your home as the same old place, you can see the contributions your occupation makes to the outside world or you can explore why you find one room in your home more comfortable to be in than others. Such small changes in perspective can help you see your world in a new and exciting way.

What is it I don't like about change? Today, I'll stop resisting change and look at it as something that can help me and improve my life.

There is no stress in the world.

—EARL HIPP

Where would you go if you wanted to find stress? A shopping mall? An operating room? An air-traffic controllers' tower? While such places can be stressful, they no more contain stress than anywhere else. Stress is something that happens inside you—it's the result of how you react to your environment.

There may be many situations in your life that trigger your "stress response" so you end up with tight muscles, a rapid heartbeat, sweaty palms, a headache, or an upset stomach. However, you can ease this response by first examining your perception of a situation. Ask, *Given the situation, am I reacting appropriately?* Next, get active so you can remove the stress-produced adrenaline from your system. Take a brisk walk, ride a bike, or go for a run. You can also focus your attention on something other than the stressful situation. Read a book, watch TV, or listen to music. Finally, you can practice the "relaxation response" by using quiet and deep breathing to oppose the stress state. With these methods, you can make sure there's no stress in *your* world!

I know that excessive stress has negative effects on every aspect of my life. Today, I'll get in the habit of practicing action, not reaction, to the events in my life.

*More important than learning how to recall things is
finding ways to forget things that are cluttering the
mind . . . empty your consciousness of unwanted things,
even as you empty your pockets.*
— ERIC BUTTERWORTH

You may begin each day by making lists of things
you need to do, run around frantically all day trying to
get those things done, then close each day by adding
more things to the list. But while such itemizing can
be effective when it helps you get things done, it does
have a downside. List making can so dominate your
thinking that you spend every free minute creating
more lists.

For many people, trying to stop list making is like
asking an alcoholic to turn down the next drink. List
making becomes an obsession, a driving force, a reason
for getting up each day. List making keeps you in a
"busy orgy," overloaded and overwhelmed.

How can you break the list-making habit? One way
is to transfer the workhorse energy you put into eliminating the items on your lists to pro-active leisure
activities. Racquet sports, high-impact aerobics, mountain climbing, and thrilling amusement-park rides can
all provide the necessary stimulation to help you ease
up on the list-making mentality and focus on more
physical stimulation.

*Today, I'll put away my lists, close my calendar book,
put away my course syllabus, and empty my mind of
obligations, tasks, and duties.*

Lost, yesterday, somewhere between Sunrise and Sunset, two golden hours, each set with sixty diamond minutes. No reward is offered, for they are gone forever.
—HORACE MANN

Do you often find yourself unable to complete tasks or projects? Indecision or procrastination may be the reasons. Stopping to weigh every little detail of a task before you make a decision on how to proceed can prevent you from completing it. And putting off a project because it seems too large or complex can result in your never being able to start it.

The key to effective time management is not to be intimidated by any task, but to look at how you approach and organize it so you can accomplish what you need to do. For example, when faced with a complex or sizable project, you can break it into small steps or enlist the aid of a partner or colleague who can provide help as well as much-needed encouragement and support. Or, if you find yourself unable to begin even a small, easy-to-do task, identify the payoff for its completion—recognition, monetary reward, or a feeling of accomplishment. This can provide an incentive to begin—and complete—what needs to be done, as well as give you something to look forward to when you've successfully completed your task.

Time is precious. Today, I won't spend time spinning my wheels. I'll decide what needs to be done, then I'll do it!

Life is like a ten-speed bike. Most of us have gears we never use.

—CHARLES M. SCHULZ

Often you react to a given situation with a familiar pattern of behavior. Rather than modify or adjust your response to each individual situation, you simply choose to operate in the same way every time. But in doing so, your responses may keep you locked in an ineffective way of doing things.

Whether you realize it or not, your responses are under your control and, beginning today, you can learn how to alter them. Each time you face a new situation, stop and ask yourself: *What would be the best response to this situation?*

After you respond, ask: *Did my response help the situation or hinder it? On a scale of one to ten, how would I rate my response?* Then think: *What would have been a more effective response?*

By becoming aware of the habitual ways you deal with situations you can learn, like a bicyclist, how to try out many gears in order to see what works best under what conditions. What you may find are new responses that bring about greater results.

Today, I'll challenge my responses so I can learn how to change them. Then I'll be able to find effective ways to handle every situation in my life.

Whatever men attempt, they seem driven to overdo.
                                        —BERNARD BARUCH

It can be very difficult to bring balance into all areas of your life. You may find it hard not to put in overtime at work. You may be compulsive about having the perfect yard or the perfect home. Or you may be so driven to live life differently from your parents that you may push yourself to live well—at any cost.

But becoming too absorbed in any area of your life can take time and attention away from other areas and make your entire life imbalanced. In your rise up the corporate ladder, you may be leaving your intimate relationship or children behind. Or in your mad pursuit to become physically fit, you may be forgetting to slow down and rest from time to time.

There's nothing wrong with focusing on one part of your life for a short time. But anything beyond that can negatively impact all other areas of your life. To restore balance, think about letting go of an activity that has received a lot of time and attention lately. Reassign its time, or at least a portion of it, to an area you've been ignoring—your family, socializing, or yourself. In doing so, you can gently and gradually begin to restore balance to *all* areas of your life.

I'll imagine placing each activity in my life on a scale and weighing it to measure the focus I give it. For those activities that weigh little, I'll readjust the "weight" by giving them more time and attention.

The pervasive cultural misconception is that it is possible for a person to have it all—*a happy family, a high-paying job, a nice home, good vacations, etc.*—all at the same time.

—DR. RAYMOND B. FLANNERY, JR.

A woman who recently graduated from college was buying furniture for her small studio apartment. She asked her father, a successful businessman, *How does it feel, Dad, to have everything you've ever wanted? You can buy anything. You have a beautiful house with lovely furniture, a new car, and you take lots of trips. It'll be years before I can have those things. You must feel great!*

The father was silent for a moment. Then he replied, *You know, some of the best memories I have are from the days when I lived in a small apartment like yours. I furnished it with orange crates scavenged from the trash. I was pretty happy back then. I have a lot today, but, well, the days of the orange crates were fun, too.*

Wanting it all means not finding contentment with what you do have, and only sets you up for failure. No one has ever "had it all." So, rather than engage in "all-or-nothing" thinking, it's more realistic to do what you can with what you have right now. And it's better to accept that while you may lack in some areas, you are rich in others.

Rather than look at what I want, I'll appreciate what I already have. Today, I'll recognize that I'm a lot richer than I think.

Rest is not a matter of doing absolutely nothing. Rest is repair.

—DANIEL W. JOSSELYN

When do you allow yourself time to rest? When you're sick? When your muscles are so sore it hurts to move? When several sleepless nights catch up to you?

If you're like most people, you probably don't set aside time for rest until your body cries out for it. But by getting into the habit of listening to your body, you can "tune in" to the messages your body gives you that signal a need for rest. Tight muscles, a backache, a slight headache, tired eyes, and poor concentration are just a few rest-related messages.

To take a rest doesn't mean doing nothing. It simply means slowing your pace, becoming less active, and easing some of your tension. Lying down for a few moments is resting, as well as going out to a movie, reading a good book, watching television, listening to music, or talking to a friend on the phone.

Rest allows the body time to release tension and return to a normal, balanced state. And when you're well rested, you're often more energized. As Winston Churchill, who was a vocal supporter of afternoon naps, once said, *I regretted having to send myself to bed like a child every afternoon, but I was rewarded by being able to work through the night until two or even later.*

When the batteries wear down in a flashlight, the light becomes dim until it finally goes out. Today, I'll recharge my batteries through rest so I can shine brightly throughout the day and evening.

Establishing goals is all right if you don't let them deprive you of interesting detours.
—DOUG LARSEN

What would happen if every once in a while you ignored the goals you've set for yourself and spent time enjoying non–goal-related activities? Rather than focus on the years of schooling for a degree or holding down two jobs to send your kids to college, you might focus on what video to choose or what you'll wear tomorrow.

While goal setting is good because it enables you to identify and meet your needs, a life that revolves around it can become so achievement-oriented that every task can turn into a goal. So rather than live life to the fullest and experience all the newness and freshness of each day, you end up living from goal to goal, focused solely on outcomes.

So, while it's okay to set goals, not everything in your life has to be one. Instead of missing out on the wonderful, fun, exciting, or challenging adventures in life, you can decide today to do one non–goal-oriented activity—read a romance novel instead of a business journal, discover a new running route, or feed the ducks in the park on your way to the library. Be spontaneous and be flexible. Keep in mind that while it's great to have the "destination" of a goal, it's even better to reach your destination after making some terrific side trips.

Today, I'll decide whether I want to stay on a steady course, focused solely on a goal, or take some interesting side trips.

We should investigate and accept ourselves as nature made us, but realize that She also gave us the power to improve ourselves.

—ANONYMOUS

Some people wear troubles around their necks like strings of bangles and beads. But troubles are nothing to be proud of or to show off. In fact, they're worthless and usually just weigh you down.

You can get rid of such useless bangles and beads through meditation. No matter what kinds of problems you have—communication difficulties, anger, frustrations, unresolved issues or emotions, or habitual ways of acting or thinking—meditation can help you let them go so you can feel better about yourself.

To do so, first identify a problem and write how you feel about it. Ask what your attachment to the problem is and think of reasons why you hang onto it. Then place the paper in front of you as you sit in a relaxed position with your eyes closed. Breathe deeply until you reach a calm state, then say this affirmation aloud: *I am dropping and dissolving this problem. I no longer believe in it or in its power over my life.*

After repeating the affirmation several times, open your eyes. Then slowly rip the paper into tiny pieces and throw it away.

I can get rid of at least one of the troubles I continue to drag around with me. I know I'll feel much better without it.

*Laughing at ourselves is possible when we are able to
see humanity as it is—a little lower than the angels and
at times only slightly higher than the apes.*
                                                —TOM MULLEN

If you could learn to laugh at your problems, to see
the humor in nearly every situation, or even to laugh
at yourself, you would be more relaxed and much
healthier.

How can you add laughter to your life? Let the child
within you come out to play. Adults don't usually play,
because if an activity doesn't have a goal or an end
result, such as receiving recognition or some sort of
award, then it's often not considered a valid way to
spend time.

Play is lighthearted activity that has no expressed
purpose and only one essential ingredient—having fun.
Play can be a tug-of-war game with your dog, building
a sand castle, skipping rocks on a lake, or flying a kite.
Or play can be spending time with children—at a playground, at a children's museum, or at a weekend car-
nival. By interacting with children or simply observing
them, you'll see that they're never so busy that they
can't have fun, never so ambitious that they have to set
aside an hour of play time every day, and never so
serious that they miss out on the laughter in life!

*I can look at the world through a child's eyes and see
how wonderful and fun it really is. Today, I'll do something playful in this new world I see.*

Every man paddles his own canoe.
                                    —FREDERICK MARRYAT

Do you often do what others want you to or put the needs of others first? Or do you sometimes put yourself first, say "no" when you need to, and do things that feel right to you?

Assertive behavior can be difficult. Being assertive doesn't often make others happy, give others what they want, take care of everyone else's needs, or fulfill their image of you as someone who bends over backward for others.

But assertive people have learned to stand up for themselves and express their true feelings. They don't let others take advantage of them and are able to let go of the feeling that they have to "cave in" to the pressures and demands of others.

While being assertive may be hard, especially when it means doing or saying things that may not be viewed favorably by others, it is your way of protecting yourself. To learn how to be assertive, simply learn to say "no"—to working overtime, to making dinner every night, or to volunteering to head up a project. Standing up for and protecting your rights—not the wants or needs of others—is what being assertive is all about.

Today, I'll be more assertive in expressing my needs. If I don't want to work late or do something for someone, I'll say so.

Every mother is a working woman.

—ANONYMOUS

When you were growing up, it may have been common for a mother to stay at home and take care of the house and children. But today, nearly 70 percent of mothers work outside the home. That means that mothers today are faced with a multitude of options, not only in deciding how to balance a career and a family, but also in how they choose to raise the family.

This Mother's Day, it may be easy to dismiss the role your mother took when she raised you because life today isn't as simple as it may have been during your mother's or your grandmother's time. Yet no matter what generation, every mother has worked very hard at being a good mother.

Whether your mother worked full-time in the home, had a part-time job, or juggled a full-time career with raising you, you can reflect on the things your hard-working mother taught you. Keep in mind Henry Ward Beecher's thought, *A mother's heart is the child's schoolroom.* Then think of all the things you learned from your mother. Perhaps what she taught you was as simple as tying your shoes or baking bread, or as complex as how to get along with others or how to believe in yourself.

As I think about my mother today, I know she did the best she could with what she had. Today, I'll thank her for the things I learned and pass this knowledge on to others.

Fear is the darkroom where negatives are developed.
                                                    —ANONYMOUS

Remember some of your childhood fears—the ones
that used to keep you up at night, reduce you to tears,
or make you run to your parents? Many were probably
natural childhood fears: an imagined monster under a
bed, the first day of school, snakes or spiders, even the
dark. Now, when you think back on those fears, you
can laugh.

But what happens when you are confronted with today's fears: meeting new people, paying your monthly
expenses, speaking in front of others, spending time
with your parents, or giving up an obsession? Instead
of understanding why you fear these things, you may
let fear overrun you.

Today, you can put the things you fear in perspective
by asking yourself, *What's the worst thing that can happen to me?* Perhaps the people you meet won't like
you, you won't be able to buy the new shoes you
wanted, or you'll be a bundle of nerves before your
speech. Or, on the other hand, what you fear may not
be negative—maybe you won't have an argument with
your parents, or you *will* be able to kick your habit.

Whatever your fears may be, you need to see them
as instructive lessons—not frightening monsters. Study
one of your fears today to see what you can learn from
it. Once you understand each new lesson, you'll have
a lot less to fear.

*I believe that there's nothing in my life to be afraid of.
Today, I'll strive to understand my fears.*

Don't waste your time striving for perfection; instead, strive for excellence—doing your best.
—SIR LAURENCE OLIVIER

There's a story about a very promising young writer whose first novel was a critical and financial success. Her publisher immediately requested she begin work on a second novel.

At first the writer was ecstatic with her initial success, but then she began to worry. What if the second novel wasn't as good as the first? What if she wrote book after book, only to find the first novel was her best? The writer was so concerned about attaining the same acclaim on her second novel that she struggled day after day with the beginning of the novel. *I have to find the perfect words to create the perfect sentence to start the book,* she thought.

But years later, there is still no second novel. The writer still sits in front of her word processor, agonizing over her search for the perfect words.

You don't have to be burdened by this need for perfectionism in the things you do. Instead of setting your sights on a perfect outcome, focus instead on simply doing your best. Then, no matter what you do, you won't be paralyzed like this writer; you'll be stirred into action. And you won't be dissatisfied with what you do, but satisfied that you at least made an attempt.

Letting go of my need for perfectionism doesn't mean I'm letting go of my desire for excellence or success. It simply means I can be pleased that I tried my best.

I find no force so devastating as the force of "can't."
Within its meaning lie the roots of powerlessness.
Within its vulgar four letters lies the destruction of lives;
lives not lived.

—ANONYMOUS

Some words can weaken your strengths, impose limitations, or create pressure: "can't," "but," "should," "always," and "never." For example, saying, *I can't do that* can hold you back from achieving something you really can do. Confessing, *I like you, but I'm afraid to love you* can prevent intimacy and connection with another. Declaring, *I should go on a diet* or *I shouldn't get so angry* doesn't provide the impetus to make such changes. And the words "always" or "never"—*I'm never on time* or I *always have a hard time talking to my boss*—perpetuate the truth rather than encourage change.

By eliminating such words from your vocabulary and substituting more affirmative words, you can become more positive. For example, substitute "can" for "can't" to indicate you're willing to try—and then try. Replace "always" and "never" with "sometimes" or "occasionally"—and then strive to make the change. Use "will" rather than "should" or "ought to"—and then set a time when you will. Finally, instead of "but" use "and"—*I like you and I'm afraid to love you*—so you can examine each statement as a separate thought.

Today, I'll change my vocabulary so I can be heard as a stronger, more decisive and secure person.

Every man is the builder of a temple, called his body.
                              —HENRY DAVID THOREAU

Many of today's diseases are due to the wearing down of your body parts. While aging has much to do with the wearing-down process, chronic stress also contributes to the breakdown of your body. So many of your physical, emotional, and mental ailments—for example, headaches, ulcers, anxiety, depression, and insomnia—are stress related. Even germ-based illnesses such as colds and the flu have been linked to an immune system weakened by stress.

One way to protect your body from the effects of stress is to respond when your body reacts. "Listen" to your body to become more aware of what's going on so you can determine what you need. For example, chronic eyestrain can alert you to the need to restrict the amount of time you spend in front of a computer screen, or frequent indigestion may suggest that you need to eat different foods at a slower pace.

You can also explore ways to ease the impact stress has on your body. With professional care, blood pressure can be lowered through deep breathing and meditation, and tired muscles can be soothed by soaking in a fragrant herbal bath.

Although stress is a given in today's society, responding to it through such stress-healing methods can make you a healthier person.

My health and well-being are in my hands. Today, I'll regulate my activities so I place the least amount of stress on my mind and body.

Later. I'm still young. I'll think of spiritual things when I'm older. On my deathbed.

—GARRISON KEILLOR

Do you think about a Higher Power only in times of intense struggle or stress? Does it take something like death or a serious illness to open your heart to prayer? You may think that prayer is for the aged, the sick, or the dying. When you're young, healthy, successful, and busy, it's easy to think you don't need to communicate with a Higher Power.

But the time to establish contact with a spiritual source is now. From the minute you come kicking and screaming into this world until you take your last breath, there's a Power greater than yourself watching over you. This Power is always there for you, but you need to take the time to reach out to it.

Make time today—not when you can't take it anymore, don't know where to turn, or feel at the end of your rope—to open up to a spiritual source. You can begin the day with a prayer in which you ask to experience joy, serenity, and good, warm feelings. Throughout the day, you can share your feelings with a Higher Power as though you're talking to a close friend. And, when you lie down to sleep tonight, you can say good night to your Higher Power and give thanks for the day.

I need to open my mind and heart to a Higher Power. Today, I'll begin to develop my spiritual beliefs by reestablishing contact with my Higher Power.

Happiness is not something you can find like a stone in the road that has a beautiful color.

—MAY SARTON

Peter Lynch, the investment superstar who successfully built the Fidelity Magellan mutual fund, stunned Wall Street when he decided to give up his prestigious position and hefty salary. Even though he had everything he had always wanted, he realized he wasn't happy. So he went from picking stocks to packing lunches for his daughters because, he said, *I don't know anyone who wished on his deathbed that he had spent more time at the office.*

Many people believe happiness is measured in material terms—a house, money, lots of clothes. Others believe it's found in enjoyable moments: a sunset, dinner with friends, a walk in the woods. Although happiness can be all these things, it's also the feeling you get when you achieve something you've longed or worked very hard for—a promotion, passing a test, buying a home. But these personal victories don't have to be big. They can be as small as losing a few pounds, going a few hours without a drink or drug, not arguing with a family member, or taking an hour for yourself.

Today, think of something that will bring you happiness and then outline the ways you can achieve it.

Big or small, my personal victories are the key to my happiness. Today, I'll be happy for all my victories.

*Think for yourselves and let others enjoy the right to
do the same.*

—VOLTAIRE

Codependency is the act of becoming so absorbed
in other people, places, and things that you don't have
any time left for yourself. Caring so deeply about others or focusing so obsessively on externals can lead you
so far away from yourself that you may forget how to
think for yourself.

Losing yourself in a love affair or relationship, in
work or school obligations, or in caring for an aged or
ailing loved one can make you go days, weeks, or even
months without conscious contact with yourself. When
this happens you may forget that you exist apart from
whomever or whatever it is you're focusing on.

Today you need to tell yourself, *I'm still here.* Bring
some focus back to yourself by first writing in a journal
how the someone or something is impacting your life.
Then consider what it would be like to detach. Ask, *If
I didn't have this person or thing in my life, what would
I be doing with myself and for myself that's different
from what I'm doing now?* Make a list, choose one
thing—and then do it!

*"Detach" is the opposite of "attach." Today, I'll make a
choice about remaining firmly attached to someone or
something or gently detaching myself.*

People who suffer a trauma . . . must reinvent their lives.
—DR. KATHRYN D. CRAMER

If you've lost your job, experienced a serious illness, been through a divorce, ended a relationship, or are in the midst of some other major life change such as a move or retirement, then you know how stressful such times can be.

Some people approach traumatic life events with the attitude of a passive, helpless victim—*Nothing ever works out for me.* Others become angry, resentful, or full of blame or threatening thoughts—*I'll show my boss he can't lay me off; I'll take him to court!* Still others become negative, depressed, or apathetic about life, adopting attitudes such as *I don't care anymore; nothing I do matters.*

But there's a much better way to deal with traumatic life events. Rather than dwell on how devastating or painful the event can be, you can look at ways the experience is helpful to your life. For instance, an illness can encourage you to take better care of yourself; a divorce can give you the opportunity to focus on your own needs; a layoff can help you get out of a rut and pursue another career. Traumatic life events can be beneficial when you can see them as opportunities to reinvent the way you live your life.

Sometimes the events in my life can be devastating. But I can look at each event as an opportunity to learn, grow, and change as I develop a more positive attitude.

Ill habits gather by unseen degrees— / as brooks make rivers, rivers / run to seas.

—JOHN DRYDEN

How do you relax? With an alcoholic drink? A cigarette and a cup of coffee? A candy bar or a bag of potato chips? A tranquilizer? Watching TV?

Such habits may seem like they help you through stressful times, but they may actually add to your stress over the long run. Cigarette smoking increases your heart rate and blood pressure. A candy bar or cup of coffee gives you a high that's soon followed by a low. Frequent use of alcohol or drugs can lead to addiction. And watching TV helps you escape, rather than deal with, your problems.

Just as such bad habits are made, good habits can be made too. One good, mind-calming habit is color visualization. Think of a color that symbolizes your stressful feelings. Red can reflect anger, or a brilliant yellow-orange hue can portray frustration. Close your eyes and fill your mind with this color. See yourself and everything around you in this color.

Then think of a soothing color—sky blue, forest green, or rose pink, for instance. Picture a cloud this color floating above you, gently raining its colored drops upon you. Visualize the soothing color slowly "washing" the stressful color away as you breathe deeply. Unlike chemicals and other escapes, color visualization can be a calming, healthy addiction!

Relaxation techniques can be physically as well as emotionally beneficial. Today, I'll soothe myself with my favorite colors.

Joy enters the room. It settles tentatively on the windowsill, waiting to see whether it will be welcome here.
—KIM CHERNIN

Is joy a welcome feeling for you, or do you find it hard to be so positive?

If you grew up in a dysfunctional home, you may have learned early on not to trust positive feelings because they usually didn't last long. If you now live with people who behave in unhealthy ways, then you may find it hard to see any joy in day-to-day living. If you've gone through numerous personal tragedies, the constancy of negative emotions may overrule positive feelings.

How do you build up your ability to feel joy, increase your strength of belief in positive feelings, and shape your days to be more pleasurable?

Just as increasing your physical power takes time, dedication, and work, so does increasing your "positive power." You can enlist the help of a professional, a close friend, or a self-help group to help put a difficult past to rest. You can detach from the unhealthy behaviors of others by saying, *I want to see life through my own eyes—not through the dark glasses of others.* And you can build a strong relationship, through prayer and meditation, with a Higher Power who can take you through the bad times to the good.

Today, I'll think of ways to lift the weight of negativity from my heart. In that way, I'll be able to exercise my positive energy.

Whether you realize it or not, there are no boundaries, but until you realize it, you cannot manifest it. The limitations that each one of us has are defined in the ways we use our minds.

—JOHN DAIDO LOORI

How do you handle stress—by controlling or letting go, by worrying or moving on to the next task, by procrastinating or setting priorities, by wasting time or managing it?

Your "stress personality" determines how you handle difficult situations and whether your style of coping adds to the stress or eases it. You add to the problem when you see limits to what you can do to manage the demands in your life; you ease the stress when you see no boundaries and can plan and respond directly to the pressures.

Learning to change your stress personality will help you respond more effectively to problems. To do so, make a list of the three most stressful situations in your life. For each situation, think about how you usually respond. Then imagine fresh, new alternatives for each situation.

Picture yourself enacting these different responses so that you become comfortable with your "new" role. Making the actual change will then come when you're ready.

Today, I'll imagine myself responding differently to a stressful event. Trying out new possibilities in my head first can help me become more comfortable with my responses in the future.

Walking is an excellent technique to drain off panic and dangerous impulses . . .

—AARON SUSSMAN

Physical exertion is the most natural outlet for your body when it's in a state of stressful arousal. After fifteen to twenty minutes of vigorous exercise, neurochemicals called catecholamines are secreted into your brain and endorphins are released into your bloodstream. Catecholamines help fight depression and encourage creativity, while endorphins are natural painkillers and mood elevators. So after exercise, when your body returns to its normal equilibrium, you feel relaxed, refreshed, and capable of seeing your problems in a whole new light.

Exercises such as walking, running, swimming, cross-country skiing, or stair climbing are effective catalysts for such creative problem solving—particularly if you practice putting your source of stress out of your mind while you exercise.

Prior to your workout, identify a problem that's been on your mind. As you begin your exercise, put the problem aside. Concentrate on your stride or pace, your surroundings, the sound of your breathing, how you feel—anything but the problem. What you may find is that another way of looking at the problem springs to mind during your workout or right after you finish.

Today, I'll take a vigorous, twenty-minute walk, letting my arms swing and my muscles stretch as I set a good pace and just let my mind relax.

A compromise is an arrangement whereby someone who can't get exactly what he wants makes sure nobody else gets exactly what they want.
—BARBARA FLORIO GRAHAM

Because life can seem like it's one struggle after another, you may feel as if you're constantly battling and losing. So you may unconsciously draw "battle lines" in conflicts with others to force your will upon them, resist listening to their viewpoints, and eliminate the possibility of cooperation.

But when you do so, you only escalate the problem. The only way to resolve problems and difficulties with others is not by battling with them, but by showing your willingness to seek a peaceful solution.

This can be accomplished through compromise. Ideally, both parties clearly outline their positions or state what they want in such a situation. Then each makes concessions and considers counteroffers until an agreement is reached somewhere in the middle.

The road to peaceful compromise begins when emotions are first brought under control. Start with yourself, then appeal to the other party to do the same. You might say, *I know you're upset. So am I. But if we're going to resolve this, we've got to start talking about some alternatives. I'm ready to do that whenever you are.* Reaching a satisfactory conclusion requires that everyone must first yield so everyone can gain.

When a compromise is required, I'll listen to the other person. I won't interrupt, I'll try to be respectful, and I'll strive to see the other's point of view.

Speaking without thinking is like shooting without taking aim.

—SPANISH PROVERB

When you're under pressure, do you find yourself attacking those around you? While venting feelings of anger or frustration may be your first inclination, doing so at the expense of others can make a bad situation worse. Comments such as: *You're no help, Talking to you is just a waste of time,* or *How many different ways do I have to say this so you'll get it?* can greatly damage your personal relationships.

But bad days don't necessarily have to translate into bad relations with others. Before you launch—without thinking—into an angry tirade, first recognize your anger, bitterness, or frustration. Identify its source. Or, if you don't know why you're feeling the way you are, say, *I'm really upset, but it has nothing to do with you.*

Then meditate, take a nap, read a book, or go for a walk. Use the time spent in quiet rest, exercise, or other activity to readjust your focus from a defensive stance and give you the objectivity to communicate how you feel effectively—without traces of harsh, negative feelings.

Today, I'll communicate with myself first rather than use another as a sounding board. I want others to listen to me because they want to, not just because I want to vent my feelings.

Desire to have things done quickly prevents their being done thoroughly.

—CONFUCIUS

Doris Grumbach, an author in her seventies, has several works either in progress or awaiting her decision as to whether they deserve further effort. Yet she doesn't push herself to complete her books. *I get a great deal of pleasure out of finishing a work,* explains Grumbach. *I'm willing to wait. What I care about is the time and thought it takes to produce a book.*

What projects, tasks, or hobbies do you take pride in because you devote the time necessary to bringing quality to their completion? Is the finished product a cause for celebration because you have done the best job possible?

Rather than set time limits or goals for one of your projects, think instead of the ways you can bring the best quality to the project. Examine what that will take, not in terms of time, but in terms of expenses, research, your energy, or organization of the project. Then structure your goal for achieving this project to include all those things—and not a timetable.

Today, I'll take as much time as I need to bring quality to the things I do. I'll keep in mind that it's quality, not quantity, that will make me most proud.

Work of sight is done. Now do heart work...
                                    —RAINER MARIA RILKE

I thought we were going to have dinner together tonight....What do you mean, you'll call me later?...Listen, if I make an appointment, will you have time for me?

Most working couples begin their day frantically, part for the workday, then return home to renew the hectic pace of running errands, taking care of household responsibilities, preparing dinner, and then collapsing in bed for a few hours' sleep before repeating the process again. Very rarely is there time left over for fun things or even romance, so eventually a couple feels that life together isn't that enjoyable anymore.

Do you find you have a stronger relationship with tension than with touching? With intensity rather than intimacy? With stress rather than sex?

To change a stress-based relationship back to one built upon mutual caring and sharing, schedule time when you can do fun things together. Start by setting aside one weekend a month for the two of you to do something out of the ordinary—to spend time at a romantic country inn, to search for unique antiques, or to sign up for an interesting workshop.

If I'm not having fun out of bed, chances are I won't have fun in bed. Today, I'll work with my partner to find ways we can physically reconnect and emotionally draw closer.

I received my self-worth from work and it became my life.

—BYRAN E. ROBINSON

When you're on the job, do comments like *What a go-getter!* or *Boy, are you dedicated!* make you feel good about yourself? Do you find that work is your sole topic of conversation at social gatherings? Are you restless and irritable when you're away from work for more than a few days? Do you find that your unhappiness or low self-esteem disappears the minute you walk through your office door?

For many people, the workplace is the central focus of their lives. Like planets around the sun, everything else—family, social life, and self—revolves around it. But what if you no longer had your job? How would you feel good about yourself?

While work may evoke positive feelings, family members, friendships, and a connection with yourself also bring rich rewards. Restructure your "universe" today by placing yourself in the center. Scatter your "planets"—important people and things that matter to you—around you, and then think of ways each planet makes you feel good.

Do I only socialize with coworkers? Today, I'll spend some of my time with family members or friends outside work.

Lost time is like a run in a stocking. It always gets worse.

—ANNE MORROW LINDBERGH

At the beginning of each day, you may feel as though you have so much time ahead of you. But as each hour slips by, you may realize how little time you really have to do things. Poor time management can make you feel as out of control as a speeding train that's lost its brakes. But you can put the "brakes" on time by learning how to make better use of each hour.

To do so, divide your day into three segments—from waking to lunch, from the end of lunch to dinner, and from the end of dinner to retiring. Today, when you reach the end of each segment, make a list of every activity from that time period and the amount of time spent on the activity. For example, entries in the first segment could include: *Sleeping in, 20 minutes; showering, 15 minutes; getting dressed, 30 minutes; breakfast, 20 minutes; commuting, 45 minutes; chatting with coworkers and getting coffee, 20 minutes; meeting with boss, 1 hour; returning phone calls and organizing work, 1 hour; productive work, 45 minutes; lunch, 30 minutes.*

After a week, review your entries. You may be amazed at how much time you spend preparing to work rather than actually doing it. You can then use this information to make adjustments so you have more control over your time.

Time is a precious commodity. Today, I'll use my time productively so I can get the most out of my work time as well as my leisure time.

Most people are more aware of the weather, the time of day or their bank balance than they are aware of the tension in their own bodies.

—ALEXANDER LOWEN

Your boss's lousy moods or your children's cranky days may make your neck muscles stiff. Or your frantic schedule or a pressing deadline may make your head ache. Such muscular tension is simply your body's way of letting you know you're under stress. So even when your mind isn't aware of any stress, your body is.

Think about the parts of your body where you store tension. Common areas include neck and shoulder muscles, the forehead, the jaw, the lower back, and the stomach. When these areas become tight, try using deep muscle relaxation: Lie down or sit comfortably in a chair. Focus on tensing small muscle groups in your body, one at a time, for five seconds. Clench only the muscles in a group, then relax completely before moving to the next group. Start with your toes (curl your toes), then move to your calves, your thighs, your stomach, your chest, your hands (make a fist), your arms, your shoulders (raise them close to your ears), your neck (roll your head slowly from side to side), and finally your face (overexaggerate a smile). You'll find that instead of feeling muscular tension, you'll feel total muscle relaxation!

I can let go of my body tension through recognition and relaxation. Today, I'll take time to recognize how my muscles feel and how I can relax them.

If you don't make waves, you're not under way.
—LEONARD P. GOLLOBIN

Do you want to make changes in your career, living situation, relationship, or personal habits? What efforts have you made? Or have you only paid lip service to making such changes by thinking, *I'm going to get around to that diet soon... send away for college catalogues when I've got time... eventually look for a new apartment... bring up an issue in the relationship when the time is right?*

There may be many things you want to alter in your life. But unless you stop talking and start doing, those changes won't happen.

You can start today to make at least one change by setting a small, easily attainable goal. For example, if you want to cut down on your daily spending habits, you can set this goal: *For the next 24 hours, I'll set aside money for the morning paper and coffee, my lunch, and subway tokens. Then I won't spend money on anything else.* When that goal is achieved, you can set another small one. Breaking down each change you want to make into small, easy steps makes change a gradual and more successful process.

Today, I'll set at least one easily attainable goal. In a journal, I'll keep track of my progress toward that goal—and all other goals I set.

*Most successful people are not working for the money.
They're working for the rewards . . . the satisfaction . . .
the challenge of it all . . .*
                                            —MICHAEL J. CUTINO

What would it take to make you feel totally happy
with your job? More money? Greater challenges? More
recognition? Better benefits? A promotion? Now think:
What are the chances of these changes happening?

One way to make work a more meaningful experience is to explore your work expectations: *What do I
want?* and *Can I realistically get it?* You may discover
that what you want may be very different from what
you really can get. For example, you may want your
supervisor to be your mentor, but can your supervisor
deliver that? Is it realistic to think you'll be promoted
in two years, when it takes most people in the same
job three to five years?

Whether or not you're happy in your line of work
has a lot to do with the expectations you bring to it.
Today, keep your work expectations realistic. Don't set
your sights so high that you set yourself up for disappointment. You'll be more able to achieve satisfaction
and fulfillment when your expectations are in line with
reality.

*I know that expecting my work to meet all my demands
is unrealistic. Today, I'll focus on what I can honestly
expect from my work and accept it.*

*If this were a fantasy world, there would be ten of me
and we would each be doing what we wanted to do.*
—GEORGE LUCAS

Do you ever wish you could be in two places at the
same time? You may fantasize, *I'd like to relax and take
it easy at home, but I'd also like to clean my parents'
garage;* or *I'd like to get together with friends, but it
would also be great to go camping with my partner so
we could spend some time together alone.*

No one can possibly be everywhere or do everything
at the same time. To attempt to do so is like trying to
fit more and more items inside the confines of a rubber
band. There's only so long you can keep stretching the
band until it finally snaps under the pressure.

Today, rather than think about *all* the things you'd
like to do or places you'd like to go, decide on just one.
It may be the most important thing on your list of priorities (such as making your vacation plans), the most
time-consuming or complex (finishing a report for your
boss), or the one you need most for your peace of mind
(relaxing at home). By narrowing your focus, you'll get
a lot more enjoyment and reward than when you scatter your time and attention.

*What's my choice for an activity today? First I'll make
a list, then circle just one. I'll keep my mind focused on
what I choose so I can get the most out of it.*

One of my lawyers told me to read the sports section first every morning. It talks about mankind's successes, while other parts talk about mankind's problems or failures.

—MICHAEL R. MILKEN

Do you begin your morning or wind down your day reading about car accidents, murders and mayhem, destruction, criminal actions, and financial losses? After focusing on the stress and strife in the world, it may be hard to have a positive outlook for the rest of the day or evening.

But what would happen if today all the stories you read or the news items you heard were focused on uplifting tales? Perhaps a beloved dog, lost for weeks, was found safe and healthy. Maybe a missing child was reunited with her distraught parents. Perhaps a good samaritan retrieved an elderly couple's money from a robber. Or maybe an airbag enabled someone to walk away from an accident. Wouldn't such stories add a more positive influence to your day?

While you can't depend on the media for happy and satisfying stories, you can bring such stories into your life by turning off the bad news and "turning on" the good. Skim through magazines that cover interesting features. Read biographies of people you admire. Listen to programs with entertaining or educational topics. Or read the sports pages in the newspaper.

Today, I'll foster a positive attitude by looking for the good in everything and everyone around me.

In the old days, if a person missed the stagecoach he was content to wait a day or two for the next one. Nowadays, we feel frustrated if we miss one section of a revolving door.

—MODERN MATURITY

A few decades ago, corporate deals were made at a moderate pace, the lunch hour was spent eating and socializing, and most people left work at a reasonable time. But today, new technologies accelerate the pace of work and cause people to work longer hours.

But faster work doesn't necessarily mean better quality work; it just means more work needs to be done in less time. This sense of work-time urgency can spill over into your non-work time as well. At home, you may try to do several things at once—shaving while reading the newspaper, while talking to your children. Rather than handwriting a note to a close friend or family member, you may leave messages on their answering machines. Or you may perform routine actions at a breakneck pace—eating without tasting or chewing, talking without breathing, or walking at a quick clip.

To cope with time urgency, you need to force yourself to take a break every once in a while. When you catch yourself trying to keep up a breakneck pace, take a fifteen- or twenty-minute break. Go for a walk, take a few deep breaths, or simply look out the window.

Today, I'll break out of the whirlwind of doing. Rather than operate in a frantic mode, I'll really take the time to notice what I'm doing.

I have never been able to conceive how any rational being could propose happiness . . . from the exercise of power over others.

—THOMAS JEFFERSON

Are there people with whom you must work or interact who are controlling, manipulative, untrustworthy, or selfish? If such behaviors are infrequent occurrences, the best way to deal with the person is to offer support and understanding. But if the behaviors are repetitive, then you may need to treat that person differently.

When you have no choice but to interact with a difficult person—your boss or a member of your committee—you need a great deal of patience. But that doesn't mean you have to accept their behaviors or let them treat you the way they do. You can communicate to them how their behaviors impact on you. For example, you could tell a critical boss, *I'm not encouraged to come up with new ideas when you're so quick to find ways that my ideas won't work. Why not look at the positive elements first before you point out the negative?* Making such a specific and clear suggestion gives you the opportunity to air how you feel and makes interacting with a difficult person a more positive experience.

Some difficult people don't realize they're being difficult. Today, I'll focus on the behavior, not the person, as I offer constructive advice for change.

The two words "peace" and "tranquility" are worth a thousand pieces of gold.

—CHINESE PROVERB

Are you in touch with your inner self? If you're like most people, you're probably more in touch with your outer self—the active part of you that's always moving, thinking, and striving to deal with problems and hassles, failures and successes.

Getting in touch with your inner self through meditation can help you balance activity with inactivity so you can rejuvenate and recharge the depleted energy of your outer self. Meditation needs only a quiet, peaceful place (a cozy room in your home or a favorite spot in the woods), a comfortable position (sitting cross-legged or lying down), an object to dwell on (a word such as "peace," a lit candle, or a specific thought or feeling), and a still mind. Having a still mind—one that's free of activity—puts you in touch with your inner self so you're aware of your thoughts, perceptions, and feelings, yet feel total tranquility because there's no pressure to act or react.

How would I be different if I were more in touch with my inner self? Today, I'll give meditation a try.

*Man is a pliant animal—a being who gets accustomed
to anything.*

—FYODOR DOSTOYEVSKY

The ease with which people can adapt to their surroundings is often a positive trait. Military families
adapt when they move from one country to the next.
New Englanders easily accept seasonal changes. Those
who live by airports or close to train tracks learn to
tune out the deafening sounds of jet engines or loco-
motives.

However, adaptability and flexibility is not positive
in *every* situation, particularly when a situation can
harm your health or well-being. Living with an alcoholic, working for a boss who treats you badly, or sacrificing your needs to do things for others are situations
where pliancy is not healthy.

Knowing when to adapt to particular situations and
when to rectify or move away from a situation requires
courage and patience. Putting your own needs ahead
of the needs or expectations of others may result in
anger or personal attack from them. But knowing when
to say, *Yes, this is right for me,* or *No, this isn't right
for me,* can spell the difference between adding to or
easing the stress in your life.

*Today, will I just go along with a situation, or will I be
able to question its significance in my life? I need to be
thoughtful first, rather than pliant, in my considerations.*

*Golf without bunkers and hazards would be tame and
monotonous. So would life.*

—B. C. FORBES

What would life be like if everything had a happy
ending, every relationship was perfect, and things went
according to plan?

Desire for a life filled with stress-free situations is
like playing on a golf course without sand traps, water
hazards, trees, or difficult holes. While you may enjoy
the practice the course gives you, in the long run it
will offer you little challenge or opportunity for developing the skills necessary to play well.

There's no such thing as a life—or even a day—
without stress. Every day is different. Some days may
be enjoyable experiences while others may be difficult
to get through. But each day, no matter how it turns
out, plays an important part in your development.

Instead of longing for today to be free from all stress,
you can see today as a teacher. Ask, *What can I learn
from today?* and then treat each difficult "hazard" and
"trap"—as well as each successful "hole in one"—as a
daily lesson you can apply to your life.

*Today will happen just the way it's supposed to, with
its stressful moments as well as its relaxing ones. Rather
than fight it or wish it away, I'll learn from it.*

Ancient religion and modern science agree: We are here to give praise. Or, to slightly tip the expression, to pay attention.

—JOHN UPDIKE

How aware are you of the world around you? How often do you take time to smell the outside air on a spring day, notice the colors of leaves on the trees, distinguish the sounds of morning songbirds from evening songbirds, taste a raindrop or fresh herb, or look up at the sky—no matter what the weather—to notice the shapes of the clouds?

Often people think their reason for being is to stay active until they can't be active anymore. They become so caught up in activity that they equate rushing around with being alive. Yet there's a difference between being alive and living. Being alive means you're breathing and functional. But living means you're connected to all that's breathing and functional.

Unless you take the time to pay attention to what's around you, you'll never have a sense of connection to the world and the people in it. You won't notice the vastness, beauty, and marvels of nature, or the fascinating differences between people. Living means seeing everything and ignoring nothing. So open your senses—sight, sound, taste, touch, and smell—to the world around you. Then share something wonderful you notice with someone else.

What haven't I noticed before? Today, I'll take a few minutes to pay attention to the world around me and experience it in a new way.

Every artist was first an amateur.
— RALPH WALDO EMERSON

Did you ever stop yourself from trying something new—painting, singing, or writing, for instance—because you felt that you'll never be a Rembrandt, Streisand, or Brontë?

Believing that some people are simply born with their talents is a fallacy. Every successful artist has had to work hard at his or her craft. Rarely have masterpieces been created on a first try. For example, while the preteen Barbra Streisand who sang on the *Ed Sullivan Show* displayed an incredible talent, she was nothing like the gifted actress and singer who, years later, wowed audiences in *Funny Girl*.

If you let the thought that you can never be as good as the best prevent you from exploring what talents you have, you deny yourself wonderful creative outlets that not only release daily tension, but also teach you something about yourself. As Billy Joel, gifted and successful songwriter himself, said about the work of Beethoven: *This guy knew something. He didn't have tape recorders on which he could instantly play back what he was writing. He had to laboriously write music dot by dot . . . [and] I want to know how he did it.*

Today, I'll keep in mind that the world needs more artists who can create more great music, more beauty, and more joy. I'll allow myself to be an amateur as I explore my abilities.

We're becoming more comfortable with processing information and less comfortable with genuine communication.

—CRAIG BROD

"Technostress" can lead people to interact with others in the same way they interact with machines. There are computer programmers who sit in the same room, yet communicate with each other through electronic mail messages rather than talk face to face. There are people who believe computers don't make mistakes, so they apply the same standard of perfection to others. And there are people who are so accustomed to the instant gratification provided by fax machines that they expect the same speed from others.

But technostress leads people away from one another rather than bringing them close. Technology handles information, but it can't help you handle an emotional crisis, take away your loneliness by having lunch with you, negotiate conflicts with your partner, or offer ways to help your family spend quality time together.

To foster more human interaction, avoid using machines as substitutes for talking face to face and spend your off-work time in nontechnical pursuits with others—going to movies, working in the garden, reading fiction, or conversing with no set goal in mind.

Instead of looking for rationality and logic in my relationships, I'll look for fun and frivolity. Today, I'll spend time enjoying people, not machines.

Mtoshi Yamada . . . has big plans for the next 10 years.
He wants to pass . . . exams in . . . health and real estate,
read 480 books and buy some land to build a home. . . .
he intends to bicycle around the world, go to art school
and volunteer his services to a government-sponsored
Peace Corps . . .
                                            —KUMIKO MAKIHARA

There's a story about a forty-three-year-old Japanese
workaholic who was forced by illness to slow down.
Where he used to give 100 percent to his job, he now
gives sixty. Like most Japanese, it wasn't easy for him
to let go of the long hours on the job; he wasn't interested in time away from work. So the National Rec-
reation Association of Japan was formed for people like
him; now he attends classes to learn how to become a
"leisure counselor"—someone who can set aside and
enjoy more free time in his life.

Do you need to become a leisure counselor so you
can work less and enjoy your free time more? Here's
how. First think about activities that interest you, then
determine how much time you can devote to one of
them in a day or week. Your leisure time can include
group activities such as an art class or individual activities like taking golf lessons.

You'll be an effective leisure counselor when you can
choose activities that you like and that suit your interests and schedule—and set aside a half hour each day
or two hours each week to enjoy them!

Starting today, I'll try my hand at painting, learn how
to play a musical instrument, garden, cook, write a
poem, or build a model airplane.

*His life was one of perpetual labor and jet lag. It was
not an unusual life at all.*

—ANONYMOUS

Are you a superbusy person? Do you have little or
no time to return phone calls, answer letters, or get
together with friends? On weekends and vacations, do
you find yourself cramming as many activities as you
can into the available days and nights? Is your schedule
chock-full of deadlines and crises, all of which require
your immediate attention?

Superbusy people are breathless people who rarely
have time to sit and chat. When they do, the conversation is usually focused on how very busy they are
and on all the things they need to do.

For many superbusy people, staying active is used
to avoid intimacy, to eliminate the discomfort of having
nothing to do, to build low self-esteem with the impression of importance, or to gain sympathy and/or recognition from others. So if you take a look at your need
to stay busy, what you may find is that you've made
busyness a full-time job.

The key to managing such superbusyness is to stop
for a moment and ask, *Is my busyness productive?* You
may discover that you're spending more time using up
your time than spending it doing the things you really
want to do.

*How would I feel if I took a half-hour break today and
simply did nothing? Today, I'll use those thirty minutes
to question my need to structure each day as a frenzied
race to nowhere.*

A man that studieth revenge keeps his own wounds green.

—FRANCIS BACON

Past incidents that still arouse your anger prevent you from living a healthy and happy life today. Hurt experienced in a former marriage or relationship can prevent you from having a warm and loving relationship today. Or anger at an alcoholic parent may prohibit making a connection with that parent today, even if the parent has stopped drinking.

How can you let go of deep-rooted anger from the past so you can get on with living in the present? First, recognize that your anger is often a response to feelings you didn't express at the time you experienced them in your childhood, in a former intimate relationship, or during an incident that happened years ago. Because you didn't express them, they remained "alive" and grew into the anger you feel today.

Then let go of your anger by completing the following sentence: *I felt angry when _____, and I'm still angry.* As you bring up the past memory and its feelings, you may feel hurt, anxious, fearful, or even sad. Such responses are normal and, like the past anger, should be acknowledged rather than suppressed. By recognizing past hurtful feelings, you can begin to put your anger behind you rather than carry it with you in the present.

Holding on to past anger doesn't help me. Today, I'll let go of something that hurt me in the past by remembering how I felt then.

Today's opportunities erase yesterday's failures.
                                    —GENE BROWN

Although you exist in the present, you're also determined by the experiences of your past as well as your visions of the future. Because it's so tempting to review the past and dream for the future, it can be hard to keep your primary focus in the present. And, after all, how can you set goals unless you're able to look ahead to your dreams and desires? Or how can you make changes in yourself unless you reflect on past actions or behaviors?

Yet spending time interpreting and labeling past experiences—*I should have handled last week's presentation better*—or looking ahead to the future—*If I get that promotion, I'm going to find a new place to live*—competes with your ability to process present thoughts and can prevent you from dealing with current situations.

Being able to live in the present is one of the best antidotes to handling the stress of judging the past or wishing for the future. How can you stay focused on the present as much as possible? Picture the three parts of your life—past, present, and future—on a theatrical stage. Imagine there's only one spotlight, which means only one part of your life can be illuminated at a time. You control the light. In which direction will you make it shine?

When I'm in the past or future, I'm there. But when I'm in the present, I'm here. Today, I'll concentrate on being here instead of being there.

*One of my worst fears, as a child, was having to sell
Girl Scout cookies. The terror of ringing someone's
bell. . . . I wanted to sell the cookies to my mother. She'd
have none of that.*   —DR. JOYCE BROTHERS

Speaking in front of strangers—for business, through
community or volunteer service, or as part of recovery
work in a twelve-step program—can take you to the
heights of terror and anxiety. The night—or even
weeks—before your scheduled speech may be filled
with nervous tension. Then, when you speak, you may
stammer through your delivery until you can bolt out
of the room and escape that petrifying fear. Only then
do you feel safe—until the next time.

How can you feel more relaxed as a speaker? Use
P.A.U.S.E.—Preparation, Attitude, Undressing the Audience, Speed, and Experience.

The better prepared you are, the more comfortable
you'll be. Outline your presentation, provide handout
materials, and rehearse your talk—this will result in a
confident attitude. Prior to speaking, undress your audience. Smile or laugh as you imagine them in under-
wear decorated with cartoon characters. Then keep the
speed of your delivery at a pace that's easy to follow.
Finally, remember each time you speak in front of others, you'll gain experience that can make future public-
speaking engagements less frightening.

*Today, when I speak before others, I'll think of it as a
time to be less intimidated, more secure about the things
I have to say, and more confident in my abilities to say
them.*

Nothing is more seductive, and at the same time more deceitful, than wealth. It is extremely troublesome to acquire, to keep, to spend and to lose.
                                                        —HINDU PROVERB

Money is the number-one cause of arguments between couples. Couples who don't fight about anything else may fight about money; couples who have lots of it still argue about it. Money is such a volatile issue because it symbolizes different things to people—love, power, security, dependency, freedom, control, and self-worth. Therefore, it's important that you and your partner communicate your individual views on spending and saving money. For example, are you a saver while your partner is a spender? Are you a sharer who wants to pool the money—or a divider who wants all of your money kept separate?

After determining your individual money styles, you can then share what you don't like and what you admire about the other's relationship with money. You might say, *I don't like how much money you spend, but I admire how you reward yourself. I wish I could learn how to spend money on myself.* By airing the negative as well as the positive, you can ease money conflicts and foster a more relaxed attitude with your partner about future finances.

Today, I'll let my partner know my views on money to facilitate understanding about why I save and spend the way I do.

Mistakes are a fact of life. It is the response to error that counts.

—NIKKI GIOVANNI

I'm not perfect. Say that statement aloud and assess how you feel. Are you tense or nervous? Angry or frustrated? Ashamed or guilty? Relieved?

Living life striving for perfection can be as difficult as making a movie without rehearsals or retakes. And when you fall short of the high expectations you set for yourself, you probably end up feeling all is lost rather than something's gained.

There are two important lessons to learn from making mistakes. The first is that doing your best is as close to perfection as you can really get. So while you may play an errorless game of tennis today, that doesn't mean you'll play perfectly tomorrow. Recognizing that can help you enjoy the game each time you play rather than becoming upset whenever you miss a shot or double fault.

The second lesson is that mistakes are the guideposts to destinations you're headed for. They point out your weaknesses and help you to refocus your concentration. So there's a value in mistakes; they're what you learn from, not the things you do perfectly.

What, if anything, is lost when I make a mistake? Today, I'll keep in mind that mistakes can help me learn and grow.

*Even though you have ten thousand fields, you can eat
no more than one measure of rice a day. Even though
your dwelling contains a hundred rooms, you can use
but eight feet of space a night.*

—CHINESE PROVERB

Chinese art has long affirmed the beauty of simplicity and the concept that less is more. The works of the masters are models of effortless grace: a branch of blossoms, a simple stalk of bamboo, a boat on a small pond. There are no extra strokes, no embellishments, no majestic backgrounds. Instead, the Chinese emphasize the importance of having empty space and feeling comfortable with that space.

How much empty space do you have in your life? Look at your calendar, your desk, the rooms in your living space, your closets and drawers, your car, and your glove compartment. Are they crammed full of things? Now focus on one cluttered area in your life— a closet, perhaps, or a kitchen cabinet. What things do you really need? What can you do without?

Henry David Thoreau once praised his stay at Walden Pond by saying, *I love a broad margin to my life.* You, too, can experience a broad margin in your life by simply cutting down on some of the chaos in your schedule or getting rid of some of the clutter in one area of your living space.

*Do I have more things than I really need? Today, I'll
think of ways I can eliminate some of the clutter in my
life.*

Instead of canoeing for three weeks, Americans want to buy a power boat and spend one week with it. Instead of skiing in New England for two weeks, they buy a plane ticket and ski for a week in the Rockies.

—LESTER THUROW

Competitive vacation planning means opting for the most impressive and elaborate vacations—ones that cost a lot of money or require a great deal of activity in a short period of time.

But there's a big drawback to competitive vacation planning. The true purpose of a vacation—to relax and unwind—is usually ignored. Because a competitive vacation often involves travel to an exotic locale or participation in a unique activity (such as a camel ride across the Sahara Desert), there's an intense amount of pressure to see, do, touch, taste, and feel as much as possible in a limited amount of time.

This summer, you might want to avoid a complicated, exhausting, or expensive vacation and opt for something more relaxed, inexpensive, and closer to home. What about renting a cabin by a lake in a nearby state, visiting friends or family members, or using the time for day trips and puttering around the garden? Your vacation is yours, so be sure you make it what you want.

This year, I don't want to end up exhausted after my vacation. Today, I'll think of vacation options that'll be fun and still give me time to unwind.

Whatever happened to those flying cars like in the Jet-sons we were supposed to have by now?
                                                    —BRIAN BASSETT

   Traffic is bumper to bumper this morning. Even the alternate routes are all tied up. . . . Do you ever wish you could press a button in your car so your vehicle could swoop up and over the stream of traffic that slows you down? Do you ever dream of owning a robot that would clean your house, do your laundry, and have dinner prepared by the time you arrived home? Do you ever fantasize about a simple shot that could cure the common cold?

   Even though space travel is possible and technology has made living easier, gridlock, household chores, and the common cold still exist. Until these things change or disappear, you need to approach them with a more relaxed attitude. So plan to leave the house twenty minutes earlier to avoid morning rush-hour bumper-to-bumper traffic. Hire a teenager or professional ser-vice to do your household and yard chores, or alternate weekly with your partner or roommate. Strive to keep yourself healthy and, when you're sick, allow time for proper rest and recovery to avoid relapse.

   Dealing with life, rather than dreaming about how life could be different, is the best way to handle daily hassles.

Today, rather than complain about how difficult life is, I'll focus on the things I can do to make my life easier.

My father taught me a good lesson: Don't get too low when things go wrong. And don't get too high when things are good.

—ROBERT PARISH

Robert Parish once let his legendary coolness heat up in Game 5 of the 1987 NBA Eastern Conference Finals. When Detroit Pistons center Bill Laimbeer elbowed him, he punched Laimbeer. Parish wound up paying a $7,500 fine and was suspended for a game. *I allowed him to break my concentration,* Parish explained to the press. *There's a lesson in everything. In this case I learned that I must be more protective of my concentration.*

There are many lessons in life, some learned from positive experiences and positive people, and some from negative experiences and negative people. This Father's Day, think about a lesson you learned from your father. It may have been a positive, uplifting lesson from a successful man; a simple, helpful lesson from a hardworking man; a kind, loving message from a warm man; or a difficult lesson from an unhealthy or unhappy man.

No matter what the lesson, reflect on its meaning for your life. Whether you've added the lesson to your life, struggled with it, or chosen to exclude it from your life, there's a reason why you needed to learn it. And that makes the lesson a valuable one.

Today, I'll reflect on positive memories of my father and accept that no matter how close or distant our relationship is or was, he's still a big part of my life.

*All our efforts to beautify and condition our bodies have
not made us, as a nation, any happier with the way we
look.* —BARRY GLASSNER

Has the quest for the perfect physical condition left
you worried and exhausted? You may diet continually,
but still agonize about gaining weight. You may exercise relentlessly, but live in dread of heart disease.
Even sunbathing brings worries of skin cancer.

The maniacal American pursuit of perfect health and
physique can often be taken to extremes, leaving you
ready to embrace the latest nostrums and potions—
from patent medicines to vitamin treatments—or eager
to part with hard-earned money for health-club mem-
berships, exercise equipment, or diet foods. Such ob-
sessiveness can leave no time or energy simply to enjoy
the benefits of good health.

That's why it's important to discover, as an individual, the value of simple, healthy living. Then you can
let go of the constant worry about staying fat-free and
the obsession to work out to the point of physical exhaustion, illness, or injury.

Today, set up a weekly exercise program that gives
you an occasional day off or allows for a "light" workout
day—a three-mile, untimed run instead of a five-mile
timed run. And, at the end of a week of healthy eating,
reward yourself with a small portion of a "forbidden"
food—and enjoy it!

*Today, I'll begin to think of my health as a sense of
well-being rather than a paramount aim in my life.*

Solitude is the mother of anxieties.

—PUBLILIUS SYRUS

It's a rare person indeed who never feels lonely. Even when you're surrounded by coworkers, friends, or family, you can still feel lonely. So you have to recognize that your happiness and well-being come from within you, not from others.

There are ways, however, to alleviate your loneliness and learn to enjoy your own company. For example, instead of reaching for the phone when you're lonely, you can listen to your favorite music. Or you can use your time alone to give yourself a manicure, massage your feet with an aromatic oil, or create different outfits from the clothes in your closet. Connecting with yourself, rather than relying on others, is the best way to combat loneliness.

Today, listen to yourself so you can "hear" the times when you're lonely. Then pay attention to those feelings. By being there for yourself, you can learn that loneliness doesn't have to be bitter, and solitude doesn't have to be frightening.

Today, I'll savor the pleasure of my own company. I'll think my own thoughts, rent a favorite movie, curl up with a good book, or take my time touring a museum or art exhibit.

*When you have power over yourself, circumstance has
no power over you. Your inner weather is at your command.*

—OLGA ROSMANITH

Do you ever find yourself thinking things like, *I
know I'm not going to do a good job; I'm too nervous
to handle this; I know he/she doesn't like me;* or *I can't
do this?* Such thoughts are stress thoughts, and they're
often based on a fearful or anxious interpretation of an
incident, as well as on your feelings of self-worth.

Stress-coping thoughts, on the other hand, act as
tranquilizers that calm you and push aside the feelings
of panic and fear. Stress-coping thoughts tell your mind
there's no need for arousal so your body can relax.

How do you encourage stress-coping thoughts rather
than stress thoughts? In the midst of any stressful situation, say or think a series of statements such as, *Stay
calm . . . everything's okay . . . you've handled worse before . . . relax and take a deep breath . . . take it step by
step and don't rush . . . I can get help if I need it . . .*

The more attention you pay to creating and keeping
such stress-coping thoughts in mind, the less impact
stress thoughts will have upon you.

*Today, I'll make a list of stress-coping thoughts and
memorize them. Then, at the first sign of stress, I'll begin thinking them or reciting them out loud.*

What are my chances when they load the bases with nobody out? I never doubt myself. I just step back, take a deep breath, and figure out what I have to do.
—Dwight Gooden

Proper breathing is an antidote to stress. Yet you may not be in the habit of full, deep breathing. Instead, you may only take shallow breaths, or even hold your breath during times of stress or exertion.

To become aware of how you breathe, lie down on the floor. As you breathe gently, move your hand over your chest and stomach until you locate the spot that seems to rise and fall the most as you inhale and exhale. If the spot is in your chest, you're not making good use of the lower part of your lungs.

To learn deep breathing, sit or stand up straight. Breathe in through your nose. As you inhale, fill the lower section of your lungs so your diaphragm pushes your abdomen out. Then fill the middle part of your lungs so your lower ribs and chest move forward. Finally, fill the upper part of your lungs by raising your chest slightly and drawing in your abdomen a little. Hold your breath for a few seconds, then exhale slowly.

By practicing this deep breathing several times a day, eventually you'll perform the three steps in one smooth, continuous, stress-reducing inhalation.

Today, I'll practice breathing deeply and fully during times of stress as well as times of relaxation.

. . . God give us a mind that can or can't believe, but not even God can make us believe . . . you have to believe first before you can pray.

—HARRIET ARNOW

Sometimes it may be difficult to focus on your Higher Power after a stressful day at work, after an argument with a loved one, after the frustrating experience of a flat tire, a long bank line, or any of the other nuisances that are part of your day. During such times, it may be easier to believe that a Higher Power is out to get you rather than being there to help you.

But a Higher Power doesn't choose sides in arguments or single you out for punishment. Your Higher Power is on your side, but only if you choose to open your heart and believe that. Your Higher Power is there to help you every minute of the day.

During times of stress, do you think to ask your Higher Power for help—for guidance, for understanding, for patience, or for support? Today, you have a choice. You can "go it alone" and complain about any and all difficulties that happen to you. Or you can believe that your Higher Power is there for you and ask for help.

Today, I'll remember that a difficulty shared becomes a lighter burden. I'll ask my Higher Power to share those times with me.

Results! Why, man, I have gotten lots of results. I know several thousand things that won't work.
— THOMAS A. EDISON

When you're under pressure, are you able to foster a positive, lighthearted, or even humorous outlook to help you through your time of stress?

While negative attitudes can take a toll on you, positive approaches can strengthen you. A perfect example of this is provided by field hands living in Louisiana's depressed sugarcane region. The workers once labored in the fields for only seventy cents a day and lived for years in homes that were merely tottering piles of rotting wood. But rather than feel sorry for themselves or hopeless about their plight, the workers described their long days in the fields with a smile. One said, *We used to work from can't to can't. You go to work, it is so dark you can't see your hand, and when you finish, you still can't see your hand.* Today, these workers are learning how to rebuild their homes with the help of a government grant—and their positive attitudes.

By switching your own attitude from can't to can and can't do to can do, imagine what you can achieve!

Today, I'll strive to change my negatives into positives and employ this attitude in my conversations with others.

*Do not be too timid and squeamish about your actions.
All life is an experiment.*

—RALPH WALDO EMERSON

Are you willing to take chances, or does the thought of taking a risk scare you?

The experimental pilots who were the inspiration for the book *The Right Stuff* were well known for their lack of fear and their desire to challenge both the limits of man and the boundaries of space. They were unafraid to fly higher, to travel faster, and to push themselves and their jets to the edge.

Within you is that same "edge," which defines the boundary of your "comfort zone." When you do things that are comfortable and familiar to you, you're operating within your comfort zone. But when you seek to transcend past performances, explore new capabilities, take chances, and risk failure, then you're operating close to the edge of your comfort zone.

How can you expand the edges of your comfort zone so you can take greater risks and try more new things? Begin by taking small risks and achieving them first before you try to tackle bigger adventures. Before you sign up for a skydiving course, watch a skydiving film or talk to other sky divers about their experiences. Preparing yourself to take a plunge, rather than actually taking the plunge right away, can help build your confidence and conquer your fears.

It's been said that "the only thing I have to fear is fear itself." Today, I'll rule my fears rather than let them rule me.

*A test of friendship: If you find you can't be with some-
one unless you're doing something together—skiing, going to a play, in other words, a third thing to which you
both direct your attention—then that person may not
be as good a friend as you think.*

—EUGENE KENNEDY

Today, it's often hard for people to maintain close,
long-lasting friendships. People relocate with fre-
quency, move around in their jobs or careers, change
marital status, and raise families. As a result, your more
intimate relationships may be disrupted, leaving you
with a large number of work- or group-related acquaintances with whom you do things for entertainment.

Fostering friendships, rather than maintaining ac-
quaintanceships, requires interacting with others in
ways that steer you away from work or planned activities so you have time to get to know one another.
While going to a movie can be enjoyable, it isn't a time
for conversing, and writing letters is nice, but it doesn't
truly enable you to communicate with the other person
as much as a visit does.

A friend is someone you need to pay attention to. By
showing a genuine interest in your friends, listening to
what they have to say, and taking time for long walks
or heart-to-heart talks over lunch, you're creating a
bond that can remain unbroken no matter what
changes or distance occurs in the future.

*Today, I'll renew an old friendship or build a new one
by inviting a friend simply to spend time with me.*

One cannot collect all the beautiful shells on the beach,
one can collect only a few.
                              —ANNE MORROW LINDBERGH

The lovely coastal town of Pacific Grove, California, was once known for the monarch butterflies that returned every year. The butterflies even became a town symbol as they highlighted tourist brochures, street maps, and town landmarks. But when development began, the butterfly population decreased. The desire of developers to clear and level as much land as possible to build homes and hotels resulted in the eradication of the shrubs and flowers that were once the natural habitat of the butterflies.

How often do you do the same thing in your life, but on a smaller scale: in your struggle to attain more, do you actually deprive yourself in the end? For example, giving up a small, quaint apartment in a city neighborhood for a large, modern penthouse apartment in an exclusive suburb may give you a more prestigious address, but may deprive you of the sense of community you had in your old neighborhood.

The lesson in wanting more is that you often end up with less. Rather than focus on getting, why not focus instead on giving? Volunteer one or two hours a week in a soup kitchen, offer your services to a summer camp program, or read aloud at the children's story hour at your local library. You may find that in wanting less, you actually get more.

Wanting everything is stressful. Today, I'll believe that
I have everything I want—and more.

For peace of mind, resign as general manager of the universe.

—LARRY EISENBERG

Do you sometimes see yourself as the director of a play called *Life* as you strive to supervise, manage, delegate, and dictate to those with whom you interact? Perhaps you attempt to control your boss, coworkers, bank teller, children, or partner.

But there's a difference between controlling and being in control. When you're controlling, you want people to do what you want them to do, when you want them to, and in the way you want them to. Being in control, however, is the feeling that you can get what you want without needing to dictate to others. When you're in control, you're more willing to accept that other people have their own direction and that it's not up to you to direct them.

Instead of managing everyone else, manage only yourself. First, catch yourself when you feel the urge to control others. Then strive to discover what's best for you, not someone else, and do it. Ask: *What do I want?* And then: *How can I get it?* By focusing on how *you* can get what you want, rather than on how others can give it to you, you assume a much more active role in determining what you can get from life.

Many people share the stage of life with me. Today, I'll realize that it's not up to me to direct them. They, like me, have their own direction.

There are people who don't like vacations . . . and sim-
ply shouldn't take them. Vacations are not an obligatory
part of life.   —DR. HY DAY

In one episode of the television show *Cheers*, manager Rebecca Howe discovers that bartender Woody
hasn't taken a vacation since he was hired. She informs
him that he has to take a vacation. *But I don't want to,*
Woody moans. *I like it here at Cheers.* The storyline
then focuses on how Woody is so happy with his work
that the thought of taking a vacation anywhere—even
to an exotic location—makes him unhappy.

Do you find that taking a vacation sometimes makes
you unhappy? People who develop vacation depression
often do so because they take vacations that aren't right
for them. If you're someone who craves excitement and
adventure, spending a vacation touring museums isn't
going to make you happy. If you're someone who
craves order, you're not going to enjoy an unchapero-
ned trip through the jungles of Africa.

To plan a vacation that can make you happy, first
determine what your vacation goal is. Do you want to
be active and playful, or quiet and peaceful? Do you
want set plans or the freedom to be spontaneous? Do
you want to be at a familiar location or somewhere
new? Do you want to go alone or with a group? And
finally, the most important question: Do you even want
to go on vacation at all?

Today, I'll think about whether I want to take a two-
week vacation, two one-week vacations, or simply
spread my vacation time out over several long week-
ends. I can design my vacation any way I want.

I could almost dislike the [person] who refuses to plant walnut trees because they do not bear fruit till the second generation...

—SIR WALTER SCOTT

A man wanted to give up his lucrative job to start a Christmas-tree farm. He told his friends about his dream. They asked how much money he would make. *A lot,* he replied, *after it gets going. Well, how long will that take?* they asked. *Years,* he answered. *First I have to purchase the land. Then I have to prepare the soil, plant the seedlings, and tend them until they mature. By the time I'm forty-five, I'll have my first trees to sell.* His friends just stared at him and shook their heads; they couldn't understand why he would want to take a risk on such a long-term venture.

In these times of instant gratification, you may be accustomed to setting goals that give you prompt results. When you choose to diet, you want to lose weight right away. When you want more money, you ask for a raise. When you crave human connection, you sleep with someone.

But not all your dreams and desires can come true right away. Sometimes the things that can make you the happiest for the longest period of time are distant dreams—those you feel can only happen in the future. But unless you start today to work toward a distant dream, it may never come true.

Do I have a distant dream? Today, I'll think about how to reach my dream and take the first step toward making it come true.

*Freedom. A whole new world opened to me. I had a lot
of possibilities after the Olympics, but I wasn't able to
do them. It was like being in a box, knocking on the
walls, screaming, "Let me out!"*

—KATARINA WITT

Gold medalist Katarina Witt, who took the women's
figure-skating title at the 1984 and 1988 Olympics, was
a revered athlete in East Germany. Yet she was also a
virtual prisoner in the Communist country until the
two Germanys became one. Then, everything in her
life changed. She discovered she could keep her own
passport, earn her own money, and go where she
pleased.

Do you take your freedom for granted? Just imagine
what it would be like to live in a country where you
had no choices, no sense of individuality, numerous
restrictions, and very little personal freedom. Before
East and West Germany united, Witt was told what to
do; now she's asked what she'd like to do.

Freedom allows you to live your life fully. It gives
you choices, lets you make mistakes, and enables you
to explore the possibilities of life. Yet do you take full
advantage of the freedoms available to you? Take an
hour today just for yourself and do whatever you'd like
to in that time. Nap, read a book, go for a drive, or
blast your favorite song. Truly experience your freedom!

*Today, I'll celebrate the independence of America and
my own independence by doing something just for me.*

Striving for success without hard work is like trying to harvest where you haven't planted. —DAVID BLY

When a garden is choked with weeds, a farmer doesn't stare at it and think, *Well, I guess I'll have a lousy crop this year.* Instead, the farmer starts pulling out the weeds to give the plants room to grow.

When you're faced with days choked with problems, worries, pressures, or uncompleted projects, what's the first thing you do? Tense up? Think that you'll never be able to handle it? Put off or avoid what you need to do?

Charles B. Newcomb once said: *Life is an experience of ripening. The green fruit has but small resemblance to that which is matured.* When you think back to some of your past successes—solutions to perplexing problems or completed tasks that resulted in great rewards—you may realize that they started out like the seeds of unformed ideas or desires and then reached fruition through the energy you put into achieving them.

To become more willing to face what you need to do, focus on the results rather than the process. Decide right now what your payoff will be when you complete a task. By looking ahead to a well-deserved rest, more money, the opportunity to have fun, or the chance to do something you'd really like to do, you'll be more motivated to put the time and energy into getting things done.

My garden's growth depends on the energy I put into it. Today, I'll face the work I need to do in order to reap the rewards of achievement.

The cure for moving too fast is just to slow down.
                                        —WILLIAM E. COLES, JR.

The players on the field were running ragged, so their coach called a time-out. The players listened to the coach's motivating words and then, at the whistle, charged back onto the field. Their defense held tough as their offense scored. At the end of the game, the team came from behind to win.

While you may be familiar with time-outs in the heat of an athletic competition, you may not realize that you can take a time-out from any stressful activity. A time-out can be used on the job, during family conflicts, or even in the middle of an argument. A time-out is simply a brief suspension of activity that allows you to slow down, catch your breath, and refresh your outlook so you can handle an activity more effectively.

It's your responsibility to determine when you need a time-out and how long it should last. When a child's behavior gets out of hand, you might want to set a five-minute time-out where you suggest the child sit still with a favorite stuffed animal or book. Or, with a partner who has arrived home from work angry, you may suggest a half-hour time-out apart from one another so your partner can "decompress" from the day. Think of yourself as the "coach" so you can create time-outs that are right for you.

Today, I'll use time-outs wisely—to help provide distance from difficult people or situations, to collect my thoughts, and to renew my perspective.

Shooting here is just so much slower. The Italian crew works hard during the day, but come 5 or 6 o'clock, that's it. They don't even want the overtime to keep going. It's a whole different philosophy of working. In the States, we live to work. Here, they work to live.
—MICHAEL DRYHURST

The filming of the movie *Hudson Hawk* revealed to coproducer Michael Dryhurst the differences between American and Italian priorities. For most Americans, work is a top—if not sole—priority. Statistics show that today we're working the equivalent of one month's extra time per year than we were in 1970. Since 1973, our leisure time has fallen from twenty-six hours a week to fewer than seventeen.

This helps explain why conflicts occur when you try to find enough time and energy to do everything you want. Work may eat up so much of your time that there may be little left over for personal growth, relationships, relaxation, and enjoyment.

How can you change this? Keep in mind that while it's okay to work hard, you need to know when to stop and play. Make the decision now not to do any work over the upcoming weekend. Instead, make plans to attend a movie, dine out, or take a day trip with a friend or partner.

Unless I make time for personal enjoyment, I'll never have it. Today, I'll look forward to the pleasure of making nonwork weekend plans.

Happiness, in this world, if it comes at all, comes inci-
dentally. Make it the object of pursuit, and it leads us
on a wild-goose chase . . .
                                    —NATHANIEL HAWTHORNE

Do you believe happiness comes from attaining or
amassing material things? Yet electronics break down,
fancy clothes become worn, and expensive cars get
dented and scratched. Do you believe happiness comes
from a promotion or a new place to live? Yet new jobs
and new homes soon become old jobs and old homes.
Do you believe happiness comes from being with the
"right" person or having perfect children? Yet even the
most loving relationship and the most well-behaved
children can't provide you with lasting happiness.

That's because happiness comes from within. It's not
from the things you buy, you get, or are given. Happiness is the sense of contentment, peace, or joy that
comes from within, based on how you feel about yourself and your life.

Take time today to explore the simple things that
make you happy. Is it laughing and joking with friends?
Seeing a beautiful sight or a happy child? Feeling pride
when you look in the mirror?

Happiness isn't something you search for; it's something that can gradually grow within you. Sometimes
happiness can come from just being yourself and doing
what you want to do.

What makes me happy? Today, I'll be happy with my-
self and where I am right now.

When a baseball player makes an error, it goes into the record and is published. How many of us could stand this sort of daily scrutiny?

—SYDNEY J. HARRIS

Sometimes you may struggle so hard to do things perfectly or to never make mistakes that when a minor error does occur, you may view it as an earth-shattering mistake from which you'll never recover. Instead of seeing a mistake as evidence that you tried something, you may see it simply as an example of how you failed.

Similarly, you may treat others who make mistakes with the same kind of negative outlook. When the cashier overcharges you, the post office loses your package, or the mechanic doesn't fix your car's problem, you may react to such failures without an ounce of patience or understanding.

But everybody—including you—makes mistakes. Learning first how to view your own mistakes with a more positive outlook can help you change your attitude about the errors we all make.

How? See your errors as indications of future potential and reward. The next time you make an error think, *I'm glad it turned out this way. I've learned _____ from this. And, in the future, I can do _____ because of what I've learned.*

Today, I'll be more positive about my mistakes and use them to move forward. In doing so, I'll learn how to overlook the mistakes of others as I would want them to overlook mine.

Our true life lies at a great depth within us. Our rest-
lessness and weaknesses are in reality merely strivings
on the surface.

—EMANUEL SWEDENBORG

Have you ever seen the ocean in a storm? The water
is in constant, frightening motion, capable of sinking
boats, eroding shorelines, and sweeping away entire
homes. Yet below the churning surface is a stillness
that enables the tiniest fish to dart gently to and fro.

Within you is a similar "center"—a part of you that's
capable of being calm and still in the most nerve-
racking and restless moments. Being centered is like
being a tree in a storm: while wind, rain, and lightning
may affect you on the outside, your roots hold you fast
and firm in the ground.

How long has it been since you felt the sensation of
having your feet firmly planted on the ground? Aikido
masters who teach their students to maintain their centers claim it can generate incredible personal force that
enables one to withstand the power of many. To gain
your center, stand with your feet a foot apart. Keep
your spine straight. Bend your knees slightly. Hold
your hands in front of you with elbows bent, slightly
above waist level. Now inhale deeply. Imagine energy
rising up through your feet. Then exhale, feeling the
energy flow out through your hands. Repeat three
times, continuing to center and strengthen yourself.

Today, whenever I feel my stress or the stress of others
moving me away from my center, I'll do my centering
meditation.

The disease of men is this: that they neglect their own fields, and go to weed the fields of others.
—CONFUCIUS

Body awareness is the cornerstone of self-care. When you neglect physical symptoms of stress such as headaches, insomnia, digestive problems, or muscle tension, you are only setting yourself up for even bigger health problems.

It can be easy to dismiss your body's reactions to stress when you're accustomed to them. *So what's a little heartburn?* you might think. *I have it all the time.* Or, *I always get a headache in the late afternoon. That's just the way it is.* But such ongoing stress symptoms, if not attended to, can develop into more serious conditions over time as the body wears down under pressure.

To relieve body tension effectively, you need to stop neglecting yourself and find activities to help you relax. One group of activities involves relaxing diversions such as reading, watching a video, or spending time with a friend. Another group involves physical exercise—running, swimming, bike riding, and so on. And another group involves passive relaxing through meditation, talking things out with a therapist, massage, or sitting in a whirlpool.

Think about one activity from each group you'd like to do on a regular basis. Then, on your calendar, set aside time each day for the next week to do them.

My body is my friend. Today, I'll listen to the messages it gives me and be alert to any stress-related signals.

Patience! The windmill never strays in search of the wind.

—ANDY J. SKLIVIS

Being laid up with an illness or injury can be frustrating. Pacing the sidelines when your softball team is playing, staring at a tennis racket you won't be able to use for weeks, or having to cancel plans to go to the beach because you're feeling under the weather can sometimes make you feel even worse.

Although the healing process may seem slow, every day your broken leg, sprained ankle, or summer cold gets better. Each day you may feel a little stronger, a little more capable of functioning at full capacity.

Wanting to speed up the process of healing only leaves you feeling frustrated and helpless. That's when patience can truly become a virtue. Patience requires acceptance of a current condition and trust that it will change.

Developing patience is simply a matter of focusing your attention on something other than your injury or illness. Even though you can't help your teammates on the field, you can cheer them on or keep the scorebook. You can read all you can about tennis to sharpen your strategy for the time you're back on the court. Or you can catch up on reading while you nurse your cold.

Patience sometimes means waiting for things to happen that are not on my timetable. Today, I'll practice patience by trusting that time will heal my wounds.

It's one of the least understood laws of physics that time spent enjoying oneself always passes faster than time spent in drudgery. I'm certain that an hour spent in pleasure has about forty-five minutes, while an hour spent in toil—working one's taxes, or suffering in the dentist's chair, or cleaning house—has seventy-five.
—LAUREN WRIGHT DOUGLAS

You may feel that the phrase *Time flies when you're having fun* comes true whenever you're enjoying a weekend, on vacation, or taking a day off from the office. It may seem that you just begin to relax when it's time to go back to work or return home.

How can you make the most of your time away from work or home responsibilities? First, leave the office at the office. Don't bring work home or make any business calls while you're away. Just as your personal life doesn't belong in the office, so should your office life be excluded from your personal time. Weekends, holidays, or vacations should begin the minute you leave the office and not end until you return to work.

Second, if you're away from home, stop worrying about people and things back there. Remind yourself of everything you've taken care of, such as stopping newspaper or mail delivery, as well as the trustworthiness of those you left in charge.

Then enjoy yourself. The time you take off is probably minuscule compared to your "time on," so don't waste any of it on anything other than pleasure.

Whenever I'm physically away from my home or the office, I also have to be mentally away. Today, I'll make sure that work tasks stay at work.

Your trouble's easy borne when everybody gives it a lift for you.

—GEORGE ELIOT

Are you afraid to ask others for support? Are you hesitant to approach others for assistance because you believe your requests will be turned down?

Asking others for help can be stressful. Just the thought of someone saying *No* to a request can be intimidating. Even when someone does consent to help you, you may feel pressured to do something in return.

As a result, you may ignore your basic need for assistance in certain situations. When you cut yourself off from seeking such assistance, you may end up in a more stressful situation by having to take on everything alone. In so doing, you may place your company's schedule in jeopardy or take on an unhealthy burden.

Is there an area in your life where you need to ask for the help or support of others? Think about what others could bring to this area: valuable resource information, creative input, solutions to problems, emotional support, or accomplishing a lot in a little time. After you focus on what you can gain from asking for help, write out your request on a piece of paper. Then practice it before you make it. This can help you feel more relaxed and comfortable reaching out to others.

I can't manage everything in my life alone. Today, I'll ask someone to join with me to help ease part of my burden.

Doing things out of obligation, no matter how much effort you put into it, will always be like dragging a ball and chain.

—J. L. MARTIN DESCALZO

Are there things in your life that you love to do? Albert Schweitzer loved to work in his clinic in Lambarene, Africa. Audrey Hepburn loved her work with needy children overseas. Eleanora "Billie" Holiday loved to sing. Amelia Earhart and Charles Lindbergh loved to fly. John F. Kennedy loved to sail and read.

When you love what you do, you can be creative and passionate. You can be energetic and enthusiastic. You can be joyful and positive. You can enjoy every minute of your life. And you can be so focused on what you do that external "rewards"—money, recognition, respect—pale in comparison to the emotional and spiritual rewards you get.

Make it a point today to devote at least half an hour to something you love to do. Take your pet for a walk, gossip with a friend, work on a craft, or create a new recipe. In doing so, you'll be adding thirty minutes of enjoyment to your day.

Today, I'll do something I love to do—even for a short time period—to help make the things I don't like doing more tolerable.

Sleep is when all the unsorted stuff comes flying out as from a dustbin upset in a high wind.
—WILLIAM GOLDING

Lying in bed at night and thinking about what you need to do tomorrow or this week can result in endless tossing and turning. Cloaked by the darkness of night and surrounded by stillness, it's easy to get worked up over problems that are best solved in the morning or when they finally do arrive.

Being unable to tune out worry and dread about the next day when you need to sleep can prevent you from tuning in to messages of closure, peace, and relaxation. To change this, you can use the message of the Serenity Prayer—*Grant me the serenity to accept the things I cannot change, courage to change the things I can, and the wisdom to know the difference*—to replace restless thinking. Or you can talk yourself to sleep by telling yourself peaceful and relaxing messages. For example, you can say: *I can relax my mind and body ... I feel the tension leaving my muscles ... I am breathing deeply ... I visualize a quiet, peaceful place ... Sleep makes me feel good ... I am content and at peace with myself ...* and so on.

Then you can close your eyes and give yourself one final message: *I am going to sleep.*

When I'm unable to doze off, my mind is usually going a mile a minute. Tonight, I'll still my mind by filling it with peaceful bedtime messages.

"It no big ting man," they'd say, "saafly, saafly, tiger ketch monkey" (meaning I'd get what I wanted eventually).

—ALAN RABINOWITZ

In 1983 zoologist Alan Rabinowitz ventured into the rain forest of Belize, Central America, to study the jaguar in its natural habitat and to establish the world's first jaguar preserve. As he did his research, he discovered how the hours flew by with little work to show for the time. He learned that he had to become accustomed to the pace of the villagers who were helping him: *Whenever I wished to get something done that involved people other than myself, I would estimate the time it should take and multiply it by four.*

You create pressure when you expect others to work at your own pace or to have an unreasonable amount of work produced in too little time. Effective time management involves not only considering how you approach and organize tasks, but also how others approach and organize them, so you can work together in a supportive and considerate environment.

Taking the time to understand how others work can make working together more enjoyable. Ask others first what commitment they can give to a project and what their expectations are for completing the task. By listening to their responses, you can create a working atmosphere that's pleasurable rather than pressured.

The best use of time makes the best use of everyone's time. Today, I'll consider the needs of others in making schedules and setting deadlines.

You let your kids stay up late so you'll have some time together. You take your daughter to a restaurant you can't stand because you don't want to have a fight. . . .You agree to the third bedtime story, even though you're so exhausted you could scream.
—BARBARA F. MELTZ

Are you a guilty working parent? Do you allow your children to do things you wouldn't let them do if you were a full-time parent, such as staying up past their bedtime? Do you push yourself beyond your limits so you have something to give your children? Do you tell yourself, *I'm away all day, so I don't want to say "no"?*

While most working mothers and fathers feel guilt from time to time over the office–home balance, it's important to distinguish between healthy guilt and the guilt that can eat you up. Unhealthy guilt makes you feel like there will be terrible consequences as a result of your work: *I'm ruining my child's life!* But healthy guilt is a natural response to the circumstances: *I wish I wasn't away from home so much. I miss spending time with my children.*

You can develop healthy guilt by first examining what you're doing. Ask: *Am I away from home too much? Do I have too many night meetings?* Then make adjustments, not retribution, so both you and your children feel better.

Today, I'll remind myself of my work choices and the reasons I'm making them, then accept healthy guilt as a natural response to my circumstances.

For many years a person may have been saying, "I can't sing." There's been a certain security in that [notion]. . . . But slowly, as they begin to hear and identify pitches and melodies and develop some breathing techniques, they realize "I can sing!"
—PAMELA WITRI

Almost every magazine devotes its cover to movie stars, famous personalities, and other beautiful people. They send the message that you should aspire to look and act like these exceptionally attractive and glamorous people. We end up believing that if we wear what they wear, eat what they eat, and fix our hair like theirs, then we can be like these supermodels and superstars. The message we subconsciously receive is: *Don't be yourself. That's not good enough. Be like someone else—someone better than you.*

Do you define yourself not by who you are, but by who you aren't? You might think: *I'm not glamorous like* _____ . *I'm not as good a dancer as* _____ . *I can't sing like* _____ . But there will always be someone who looks better, has better rhythm, or can carry a more melodic tune. That doesn't mean you aren't attractive or a capable dancer or can't sing.

If you're always measuring yourself against others, you'll always come up short. So stop focusing on what others have and what you *think* you don't have. Today, experiment with your talents and abilities. Dance! Write! Draw! Sing!

Today, I'll be myself. I will keep in mind that life is made up of people who are good and bad, happy and sad, rich and poor, beautiful and ugly.

The earth is everlasting
Because it does not live for self alone
But exists as one with life . . .
Through loving service
. . . [you can] attain fulfillment.

—TAO TE CHING

Focusing on global problems such as the poisoning of the planet, world hunger, overpopulation, nuclear testing, and the shrinking wildlife population can be overwhelming. Even the realization that one print run of a major city's Sunday newspaper can use 75,000 trees or that each person discards up to 165 pounds of paper, glass, metal, plastic, and kitchen waste a month can make you feel that your life—and the lives of future generations—is in jeopardy.

Rather than throw up your hands in dismay at the seemingly insurmountable problems facing the world, you can begin to live your life today in a way that can have a positive effect on tomorrow. You can make use of your town's recycling centers for bottles, cans, and newspapers. You can purchase biodegradable or "safe" products that don't harm the environment. And, when grocery shopping, instead of asking for paper bags that destroy trees or plastic bags that pollute the planet, carry your own reusable canvas bags. Using your resources wisely and making responsible choices *can* have an effect on tomorrow.

Today, I'll keep in mind the guiding principle that "Nothing should be wasted" in my purchasing and discarding habits.

*Time and distance, it turns out, have no power in the
face of . . . yearning. I can conjure up [her] voice at will.
In my imagination, I can hold her close with a single
thought. I re-create her presence when I write, as I
suspect she re-creates mine . . .*
                                                    —LINDA WELTNER

Times of separation from parents, children, friends,
or partners can be difficult. When you live with someone or close to them, your lives can be linked by
frequent phone calls, shared meals, and social get-
togethers. But when long distances separate you, letters and phone calls are often the only ways to stay in
touch. Yet letters are rarely timely or able to convey
all the things you want to say, and long-distance phone
calls can be expensive.

How can you connect with someone you love when
distance disconnects you? If someone is gone for a
short period of time—a month or the summer—you
can make and send weekly cassette tapes that contain
details of things you've done, messages from children
and other loved ones, and favorite songs or stories.
When the period of separation is longer—several
months or a permanent move—you can compile a
scrapbook of photographs to send or make a videotape
of the things you're doing and the changes in your life.

Even though those dear to you aren't physically near
to you, you can still be close.

*Today, I'll know that separation from a loved one can
never distance me from the love we feel for each other.*

In every real man a child is hidden that wants to play.
—FRIEDRICH NIETZSCHE

How many times a day do you laugh? How playful are you in your personal relationships? Can you let down your guard and respond spontaneously to things?

People who know how to play and have fun are often more relaxed and capable of handling stressful situations. Play is one of the most effective ways to manage and release the buildup of daily tension. So the best antidote to a stressful day is after-work play.

To help you focus on adding play to your life, create a "play list" of activities that are amusing, pleasurable, and filled with laughter. These can involve people, places, or things. They can include things you do alone—buying a pack of bubblegum and blowing bubbles—or with others, like playing a game of charades.

As you make your play list, be sure your activities are simple (flying a kite rather than learning how to fly an airplane), easy to do (baking a cake rather than making a first-time soufflé), and inexpensive (buying Chinese checkers rather than a plane ticket to China).

When you finish your list, keep it in a prominent place in your home or office. Add to the activities from time to time, but be sure to *do* some of them!

I need a balance of work and play in my life. Today, I'll add five new activities to my play list and do at least two of them.

Unless each day can be looked back upon by an individual as one in which he has some fun, some joy, some real satisfaction, that day is a loss.
—Dwight D. Eisenhower

On weekends, do you race from commitment to commitment? Are Saturdays days of "catch up"—times to run all the errands you can't do during the week—and Sundays the days you set aside to tackle laundry, pay bills, or do yard work?

If the tempo of your weekends ranges from busy to frenetic, punctuated by only brief periods of relaxation and enjoyment, then it's time to make a change. For if you don't use your weekends as true respites from work and obligations, you'll find yourself dreading the start of the work week and regretting not taking better advantage of your time off.

To decrease your weekend roster of responsibilities, try to run at least one or two errands during the week. Maybe you can go food shopping Friday evening or handle post office and banking tasks during weekday lunch hours. Then, on Friday evening, list the things you have left to do, and set aside time Saturday morning *or* afternoon—not both—for them. Finally, create a three- or four-hour "fun time" on Saturday or Sunday—a time that excludes errands, chores, or any task that isn't fun, relaxing, or enjoyable.

I know there will be some weekends when I'll feel the pressure of having too much to do. But today, I'll attempt to balance such times in the upcoming weekend with fun activities.

When you worry, you go over the same ground endlessly and come out the same place you started.
　　　　　　　　　　　　　　—HAROLD B. WALKER

The sole inhabitant of a small island has very limited space in which to move. When you worry, you're like that island inhabitant. Worry keeps your mind confined to one set of thoughts—a child who's out past curfew, missing information from a project, an ailing parent, or a financial problem. Worry keeps your body in a constant state of tension and anxiety. Even though you may believe that your worrying is helping you work toward a solution, in actuality all you're really doing is dwelling on the futility of the problem.

It's only when you're released from worry that you can see solutions clearly or make changes. To free yourself from worry's constraints, ask: *What can I do to change this situation?* What you may discover is that there's nothing you can do. And if there's nothing you can do, then continuing to worry is a waste of time—and it's time to focus your mind on the things you can change. Such thoughts are the keys that can release you from your worries and take you off your remote island of worry and onto "the mainland" of other activities.

Today, I won't be a prisoner to worrisome thoughts. I'll do what I can, then let go of things I can't do anything about.

There are two things to aim at in life: first, to get what you want; and, after that, to enjoy it. Only the wisest . . . achieve the second.

—LOGAN PEARSALL SMITH

How often do you take time to enjoy the fruits of your labor? When you make a gain in your life, you need to stop for a moment and enjoy it. No gain should be too small to be recognized and appreciated. Perhaps the hard work you and your partner put into couples counseling has resulted in fewer arguments. Perhaps your parents are finally beginning to see you as an adult rather than a middle-aged child. Maybe your child is finally behaving after months of patient parental coaching. Or maybe a long-deserved promotion came through.

How do you celebrate the gains in your life? Celebrating what's good doesn't have to be a planned or catered affair. It can simply be hugging your partner or treating yourself to something you've wanted for a long time. Or it can even be telling yourself, *Congratulations! You've done well.*

Today, I'll enjoy the fruits of all my labors and celebrate the gains I've made.

Men trip not on mountains, they stumble on stones.
                                        —HINDU PROVERB

There's a woman who, when she was laid off from work, began her own company and built it into a success. Because of her financial security, she then became a single mother to two adopted Korean children. When her surviving parent died, she singlehandedly managed all the funeral arrangements and the estate. Yet when this woman gets stuck in traffic, all she does is curse and shout at the other cars—and then burst into tears!

Sometimes it's truly the "little things" that drive you crazy. To prove this, think about things that add stress to your life. Whether it's your partner leaving the cap off the toothpaste tube, the dry cleaner folding your shirts wrong, or the newspaper deliverer tossing your morning paper on the just-sprinkled lawn, such little things can send your blood pressure sky high.

Handling the little things is often best accomplished with humor. The ability to laugh at things that make you the most riled up can ease your reaction when they occur. Keeping a jar of bubbles in your car, for instance, rolling down the window, blowing bubbles, and singing "Tiny Bubbles" when you're stopped in traffic can do more to release your tension than any amount of cursing or shouting!

Elating my spirits—and not elevating my blood pressure—is the result of adding humor to my life.

Living is a form of not being sure, not knowing what next or how. The moment you know how, you begin to die a little.

—AGNES DE MILLE

What do you want from life? Where are you going? How do you want to get there? Questions such as these can make you feel uncomfortable, especially when you don't have all the answers or don't know where to go to find them.

Sometimes you may find it disconcerting to go from day to day without a set plan in mind or a strong idea of who you are—especially when those around you seem capable of clearly defining themselves and what they want from their lives.

Some people view not knowing who they are and where they're going as a sign of weakness, indecision, or immaturity. Yet being flexible, spontaneous, and open can be signs of strength that allow opportunities to learn and grow.

One way to uncover some answers about yourself and the direction of your life is to ask: *What makes me different from the other people I know? What are some of the special contributions I make?* By focusing on your qualities and strengths, you may be better able to uncover who you are and where you want to go in life.

Today, I'll recognize the personality traits and talents that make me unique.

I have plumbed the depths of despair and have found them not bottomless.

—THOMAS HARDY

Sometimes the greatest achievements can come from the greatest pain, sadness, or depression. An alcoholic who hits bottom and then reaches out to Alcoholics Anonymous can find a new way of life without the bottle. A grief-stricken spouse can discover wonderful friendships with those who are there in time of need. Numerous rejections from employers can lead someone to become a more assertive interviewee who eventually lands a job.

Sometimes it takes reaching your lowest point to become ready to make a change or to see the same situation through a different perspective. Just when you feel you can fall no lower or that your situation is hopeless, what you may find is that some transformation happens—either in yourself or in your circumstance—to help you see your way out of your predicament.

A Sufi aphorism states: *When the heart weeps for what it has lost, the spirit laughs for what it has found.* Today, rather than bemoan the difficult circumstances in your life, remain open to new possibilities. Tell yourself, *I won't let _____ get me down.* Then compile a list of helpful resources—supportive friends, self-help groups, career counselors, or a religious or spiritual adviser—and make contact.

Today, I'll remember that I can always see a way out of any predicament.

Remember that you may have and not have. You may receive a property and not enjoy it. You may inherit wealth and not use it.

—H.C.G. MOULE

When you were growing up, did you imagine living a way of life different from that of your parents? Are you struggling today to make this happen in your own life or in the lives of your children?

The more severe the influences are from your past, the more determined you may be today to strive to achieve a different life. Rising above poverty, limited education, dysfunctional behaviors, language barriers, prejudice, divorce, or death can make you hungry for a life that's free from all those things. Even if you were raised in a home of wealth, unlimited educational opportunities, and healthy parents, you may still feel the need to make your life different from theirs.

As you work today at proving to yourself that you can have something more, keep in mind that it's a good habit to give this "more" back to others. If you are blessed by wealth, think about starting a scholarship fund. If you have overcome language barriers, offer your services to teach adults English as a second language. If you have dealt with prejudice, raise your children to treat others without bias or bigotry. In doing so, you'll appreciate what you've gained even more.

Today, I won't take anything for granted. I'll give thanks for the changes I'm making in my life and share these changes with others.

Attitude is everything. Mae West lived into her eighties believing she was twenty, and it never occurred to her that her arithmetic was lousy.

—Soundings

How do you feel about growing old? Do you fear the physical and mental limitations that lie ahead? Are you anxious about lengthy illness or death? Or are you looking forward to retirement and being able to do the things you've always dreamed of doing?

Although you have no control over the advancement of time and your individual aging process, what you do have control over is the attitude you bring to growing old. If you believe, for example, that turning sixty-five means your life is over, then on your sixty-fifth birthday you'll probably locate the nearest rocking chair and wait passively for death to arrive. But if you think now, *I want to still be jogging when I'm seventy,* or *I'm going to travel and see as much of the world as I can,* then it'll be all you can do to keep up with yourself as you grow older.

Which way you choose to see your life in the future depends on your attitude today. To get in touch with your attitude, compose a letter to "Dear Older Self." Detail in your letter how you'd like to see yourself grow older. Then, on each birthday, open the letter, read it, add whatever you'd like to it, and seal it to be read again on your next birthday.

As I look ahead to my "golden years," how do I see myself? Am I fragile and slow or strong and spry?

You can't please everybody. Don't let criticism worry you. Don't let your neighbors set your standards.
—ROBERT LOUIS STEVENSON

A man sat in his therapist's office, telling the therapist about a recent dilemma. He wanted to take a vacation during the first two weeks in August. But his parents wanted him to paint their house then, his girlfriend wanted them to take a vacation together in the fall, and his boss asked him to move his plans to the last two weeks of August in order to work on a special project. *Well, what do you want to do?* asked his therapist. *I don't know,* he replied. *I don't know what I should do.*

Living a life that's structured around pleasing others—parents, friends, employers, or an intimate partner—can put you out of touch with what you really want. Instead, you may feel like you're at the hub of a wagon wheel, with each person you try to satisfy connected to you like a spoke. Rather than choose your own direction in life, you're forever welded to traveling around and around in the same circle with the same people.

If trying to please others has caught you in conflicting commitments, eliminate the words "should" and "ought to" from your vocabulary. Replace them with "want" and "need." Whenever you begin to say, *I should . . .,* say instead, *I want. . . .* Then you may find that what you really want becomes clear.

I won't know who I am unless I do things that are right for me. Today, I'll answer to myself, not to others.

I been so busy ... I never truly notice nothing God make. Not a blade of corn (how it do that?), not the color purple (where it come from?). Not the little wild-flowers. Nothing.

—ALICE WALKER

How often do you take time to notice the wonders of the natural world—the rainbow after a storm, the birds frolicking around your bird feeder, or the silvery brilliance of a full moon? How often do you go out of your way to discover a new path through the woods or a less-traveled route to work? How often do you allow time in your schedule to connect quietly with nature in some small way—whether by getting up early to sit in a city park and watch the sunrise slowly awaken the city or by planning weekend getaways to the country?

The mad rush of living and the mad crush of places to go and people to see can make you forget there's a world around you that's teeming with wonders. But these wonders won't come to you; you have to take the time to notice them.

No matter how busy you are, you can slow down your pace and notice the things around you. Pack a bag lunch for work and eat outside, feeling the sun on your face. Savor the food you're eating and marvel at its taste and texture. Take off your shoes and feel the coolness of grass. By taking time and opening your senses, you can notice a whole new world around you.

Today, I'll pay attention to the natural wonders of the world that are ever-present around me.

*Whether you realize it or not, there are no boundaries,
but until you realize it, you cannot manifest it. The limitations that each one of us has are defined in the ways
we use our minds.*

—JOHN DAIDO LOORI

In 1982, climber Hugh Herr and his partner Jeffrey
Batzer reached the top of Odell's Gully on Mount
Washington and decided to push for the summit. They
immediately stumbled into a blinding blizzard. Herr
and Batzer survived three nights in gale-force winds
and below-freezing temperatures. Batzer ended up losing one leg; Herr lost both.

Doctors warned Herr about the limits he would have
to accept. But Herr ignored them. Instead, he designed
artificial limbs that enabled him to continue climbing.
He invented a more comfortable socket for leg pros-
theses. And he became an advocate of technical solutions to physical disabilities and a role model in
overcoming limitations. *Limitations*, Herr says, *are illusions.*

In what ways do you limit yourself? Do you often
think you can't do something or that some risks are too
risky? Today, Herr's dream is to design legs for running marathons. Today, your dream can be conquering
one limiting attitude and treating it as an illusion.

*No matter what my health, fitness, intelligence, or skills,
I can do anything I set out to do. My limitations are all
in my head.*

I could have let eighteen firings prevent me from doing what I wanted. Instead, I let them spur me on.
                                        —SALLY JESSY RAPHAËL

In her thirty-year career, Sally Jessy Raphaël has been fired eighteen times. Every time, however, she focused on something she could do. When no mainland radio station would hire her—they thought women couldn't attract an audience—she moved to Puerto Rico, became fluent in Spanish, and proved them wrong. To sell her hit radio program, she pitched her idea time and time again to several network executives until it sold. Now she's the Emmy award–winning host of her own television show.

Are you such an achiever? Achievers may lose their jobs, get numerous rejections, watch their businesses fail, or see their ideas founder. But they take advantage of such difficulties and somehow find a way to make opportunities happen.

Real success in life is not measured by how much you can accomplish, but by how you accomplish it. Think about a situation in your life that makes you feel defeated. Maybe you've lost your job, can't sell your writing or paintings, or are just getting by in your business. Ask, *Is there something bigger and better I can move toward—a career change, a different market for my creative work, or a unique way to restructure my business?* By thinking beyond your immediate problem to a new idea or approach, you can use adversity to spur you on to greater achievements.

As long as I'm stuck in defeat, I'll stay defeated. Today, I'll think of ways to triumph so I can reexperience success.

*People can make time for what they want to do; usually
it is not really the time but the will that is lacking.*
—JOHN LUBBOCK

*How do you find the time to exercise, read the paper,
and eat a good breakfast every morning?* the woman
asked a coworker who came into work each day burst-
ing with energy. *Isn't it hard? I mean, don't you have
to get up early? Me, well, I just stay in bed.*

While some people may find it hard to do more than
get up for work, go to work, and go to bed, others have
no difficulty working full time and adding exercise, volunteering, family, travel, or a hobby to their lives.
Since both groups of people have the same amount of
time in their days, how does one group find more time
than the other?

People who find the time—no matter how crowded
their days and nights—aren't necessarily terrific time
managers. The secret of their success in balancing obligations with personal interests is their willingness to
make the time for what they want. You can make time
for a favorite activity by establishing a time slot for it—
for instance, 6:30 to 7:00 A.M. for exercise, 6:00 to
7:00 P.M. for time with your children, or 10:00 to
11:00 P.M. for reading. Treat the time slots as un-
changeable, and then take full advantage of them!

*All I need is desire and dedication to fit the things I
like to do into each day. Today, I'll be sure to make
time for me.*

Life is raw material. We are artisans. We can sculpt our existence into something beautiful, or debase it into ugliness.

—CATHY BETTER

Each day is a new beginning. No matter what happened yesterday or what will happen tomorrow, today is like a blank canvas on which you can paint whatever picture you want.

What will today be like? You can draw a picture that's peaceful and relaxing, gray and somber, or chaotic and busy. You can sketch a day that will be full of exciting opportunities and options, or you can draw a day that will be riddled with stress and strife. For the next twenty-four hours, the day is yours.

Although people, places, and things may impact on your vision of this day, they can never destroy your creation unless you let them. Although you may find yourself reacting to unexpected changes or pressures in ways that deviate from your original vision, that doesn't mean you can't calm your reactions and recapture the day you imagined.

Visualize your "painting" of today. What colors do you see? What objects are pictured? What feeling does it produce? Keeping this picture firmly in your mind, take a deep breath and plunge into today.

I'm on my way to painting a beautiful day. Today, I'll opt for soothing, rather than stressful, colors.

When you buy the land, you buy the stones; when you buy the meat, you buy the bones.

—VERMONT PROVERB

Perfection is something you may look for in your life. You may want the perfect marriage or relationship—guaranteed to make you live happily ever after. You may want the perfect house—right out of the pages of a magazine. You may want the perfect job—interesting, challenging, and glamorous. Or you may yearn to be the perfect employee who does everything right—from keeping the neatest files to making the perfect marketing plan.

Yet perfection requires that everything—including you—is perfect all the time. It means never making a mistake, never making a less-than-perfect decision, never misplacing anything, never looking less than perfectly put together—never even having a blemish. But who or what do you know is ever that perfect?

From time to time you may earn an "A," write a magnificent business proposal, play an error-free softball game, or complete a craft project without a dropped stitch. But not all the time. By telling yourself today, *I don't have to be perfect,* you can replace the pressure to be perfect with just the desire to be.

Only angels are perfect! Today, I'll keep in mind that the only perfection I can really expect is momentary. Perfection can never be a way of life.

Women feel that if they can run a big ad agency or write a column or present a show, by golly, they can make the best child that's ever been.

—PENELOPE LEACH

Sometimes, as a parent, you may unconsciously push your children into things you want them to do. Or you may focus too much on their winning at sports, earning awards, or receiving recognition. As a result, your children may pick up a subtle message: *If I win or excel or succeed, my parents will love and accept me.*

By simple observation, a child can recognize what actions and behaviors get the best rewards. So when a handpicked bunch of wildflowers elicits little or no response, while scoring a goal on the soccer field earns praise or even a material reward, the child learns that winning and succeeding are better than caring and sharing.

An upbringing that emphasizes competition and getting ahead rather than simple pleasures can push a child too soon into becoming a young adult. Right now, the most important thing you can give a child is love and attention—no matter what the child does.

Spend time with your child in unstructured activities like a bike ride, a picnic lunch, or playing catch. Focus on who the child is instead of what the child does. This will contribute to a strong self-confidence that the child will carry into adulthood.

Anyone—even a child—can learn to take life too seriously. Today, I'll let the children in my life enjoy acting their age.

Pressure should come from inside and then you transform that into a feeling of excitement and exhilaration.
—PAT RILEY

You don't have to be an NBA basketball coach, a Broadway actress, a brain surgeon, or a presidential candidate to know what it feels like to experience pressure.

Every day, you may feel pressure pushing you to conform; to please your parents, family, and friends; or to acquiesce passively to the policies of a group, committee, or company. Consider, for example, how influential you allow other people to be in determining your thoughts and behaviors. Do you fear people not liking you or disapproving of your actions or behaviors? Do you dress to fit in? Do you have a hard time holding or expressing divergent opinions? Submitting to pressures from others means bowing to their wishes rather than holding true to your own. When this happens, you become a jigsaw puzzle pieced together with little bits of everyone else rather than yourself.

The next time you find yourself torn between doing what others want or doing what you want, think, *I am a complete and whole person. I have a choice in this situation.* Then, no matter what you decide to do, it will be your choice.

Living with the courage of my convictions means thinking for myself and not allowing others to put pressure on me. Today, I'll be courageous.

*Like the body that is made up of different limbs and
organs, all mortal creatures exist depending upon one
another.*

—HINDU PROVERB

How often do you use the phrase, *I can handle this*?
You may believe that you—and only you—are the one
who should take care of your own problems and satisfy
your own needs.

Certainly there are some things that only you can
do. For example, only you can eat right, exercise, get
plenty of rest, and connect with a Higher Power. Yet
there are other things that you may not always be able
to take care of alone: solving business or personal problems, comforting yourself, developing intimacy with
others, or feeling loved and cared for. These are things
that need to come from others.

Imagine how dependent you would be if you lost
your eyesight, hearing, or mobility. But just because
you don't have a physical handicap doesn't mean you
can't ask for help.

Who are the people in your life you can turn to for
friendship, problem solving, fun and relaxation, or advice? Make a list of such people and identify the value
they bring to your life.

Whether one person provides you with many things
or many people perform several functions, the support
of others is an important factor in surviving everyday
stress and strain.

*Today, instead of saying, "I can handle this," I'll ask,
"Will you help me?"*

Men are not in such a privileged position in the family anymore, so it's no surprise that their distress levels are rising.

—NIALL BOLGER

Statistics show that a large number of men in relationships where both partners work feel threatened, resentful, and pressured because domestically the balance of power has shifted. The old male identity as the sole family breadwinner has changed, and many men find they're not comfortable in their new roles as nurturing parent and domestic helper. Because they grew up with fathers who were largely absent from the home front or were married to full-time mothers and homemakers, they have no positive role models to show them how to balance full-time work with additional familial responsibilities.

Men may have a harder time coping with independent wives who are contributing to the family income, as well as harbor resentment about household duties.

Yet it's important to recognize that there can be positive results from changing roles. Your children will become responsive to both parents—not just the mother—and learn from two positive role models. For men, there can be a sense of greater completeness in your having a career *and* being a parent. And for women, there's the opportunity to relinquish control at home and allow your husband to contribute in valuable ways.

Although being part of a working couple is hectic, I can feel like I have the best of both worlds. Today, I'll appreciate the contributions my partner makes.

People who fly into a rage always make a bad landing.
                                    —WILL ROGERS

Anger is an emotion that can easily escalate from resentment to rage. At its peak, anger can ignite explosively into verbal tirades or physical contact. At times like this, it can be almost impossible for you to act or think clearly or effectively.

De-escalating such intense feelings requires first that you take a break from the anger, and then that you patiently work through it. Taking a break involves a two-step process of saying out loud, *I'm beginning to feel angry and I want to take a time-out,* and then leaving the situation for the time you need to cool down.

Then, to work through the anger, try doing something physical. If you're at the office, go outside for a walk or sit in your chair and do several leg lifts. If you're at home, go for a run, vacuum your house, wash the car, or go work in the garden. This can help discharge some of the tension in your body and take your mind away from the situation or person that sparked the anger.

Then, when the time-out is over and you've cooled down, you can return to the person or situation and work things out with calmness and insight.

Taking a time-out provides me with a physical as well as mental cooling-off period. Today, I'll use time-outs to avoid volatile anger.

True affluence is not needing anything.
—GARY SNYDER

Do you feel like you can "afford" a certain amount of debt? Do you say you're too broke to go out to a movie or dinner, but then decide to apply for a loan for a new car or larger house?

Most people bounce back and forth between being terribly worried about money and not being worried enough. So one minute they're misers, trying to pinch every penny, and the next minute they're overspenders, acting as if they have money to burn.

How can you find a middle ground between the two? To become a better spender, accept that some of your major purchases—furniture, a car, or home improvements—may need to be made on credit. But, at the same time, you also need to consider the realistic amount of credit debt you can afford—and then not exceed this.

To become a better saver, first keep a log of where your money goes. Write down everything, not just your major expenses—you'll be surprised at how much taxis, snacks, and newspapers add up. Then set up a savings program in which money is automatically taken out of your paycheck and placed into a bank account. You won't miss the money you don't see, but you'll certainly benefit in the long run!

Today, I'll watch my spending and saving habits. To make purchasing less stressful, I'll try to set aside some money in a checking or savings account.

*Human beings are set apart from the animals. We have
a spiritual self, a physical self and a conscience. Therefore, we can make choices and are responsible for the
choices we make.*

—ROSA PARKS

No pain, no gain, is an often-employed rule by those
in exercise programs. It implies that if an exercise
doesn't hurt while you're doing it or your body doesn't
ache after you've done it, then you really haven't done
anything.

But now the growing body of sports medical data
has confirmed that there's really no connection between muscle strength and soreness. So you can get
stronger—and healthier—without the physical side
effects of pain. If your workouts begin and end with
pain, then you're creating a physically—and emotionally—stressful exercise program.

The one hard-and-fast rule of exercise that hasn't
changed over the years is to enjoy it. In fact, if you
don't look forward to your workouts or can't smile from
time to time while you're exercising, then it might be
a good idea to change your exercise program. While
it's okay to push your body, the idea is to remain below
the threshold of pain and to stay within the realm of
pleasure.

*Today, I'll enjoy a realistic and motivating exercise pro-
gram. I'll keep in mind that the point is not to punish
myself, but to make me feel good.*

Happiness is not having what you want, but wanting what you have.

—HYMAN JUDAH SCHACTEL

Complete this sentence: *I won't be happy until* _____ . Until what? Until you meet the right person? Until you make a certain salary? Until your kids get all A's? Until you lose all the weight you want?

Rather than say *I won't be happy until* _____, what would happen if you said, *I'll be happy when I* _____, and then you went out and did what you said? The first statement encourages you to wait for some external circumstance to happen before you are happy. The second statement, however, is motivating and requires action on your part.

Or what would happen if you said, *I'm happy right now with* _____, and you thought of at least three things in your life that currently bring you happiness?

Placing your happiness on conditions or on people, places, and things that need to change can keep happiness at a distance. But making your happiness your responsibility—something that happens as a result of something you do—can mean you're much more likely to get it.

Today, I'll remember that my happiness comes from what I have or what I can make happen. It doesn't simply come to me because I want it.

Men who try to do something and fail are infinitely bet-
ter off than those who try to do nothing and succeed.
                                    —LLOYD JAMES

One of the biggest roadblocks to taking a risk is the
tension such an action may create in you beforehand.
For example, wishing to confront your parents about
childhood issues such as incest or alcoholism can fill
you with such trepidation and anxiety that you find it
hard to take the risk.

To work through risk-taking tensions, create an ob-
stacle/solution chart. List all the obstacles that might
prevent you from taking the risk on one side of a piece
of paper. Then list the possible solutions next to these
obstacles. For example, if you want to talk to your parents about how you felt as a child, an obstacle could
be, *I might not be clear with what I say.* A suggested
solution could be, *I'll write down what I want to say
first.*

Then, after coming up with solutions to your obstacles, review your list, choose the best solution, and try
it!

*Anticipating the tension and coming up with solutions
can help alleviate it. Today, I'll "psych out" the tensions
before they psych me out of taking a risk.*

I enjoy early mornings on the porch; fresh corn; going barefoot; blueberries and strawberries and raspberries; sleeping without nightclothes or covers; the long evenings and the texture of the low western sun on fields that are still green.

—DONALD M. MURRAY

What makes you feel serene? Spending time with someone you love? Reading a book? Walking on the beach? Listening to a beautiful piece of music?

Finding serenity in a world that's often far from serene can be difficult. Trying to ignore city noises or finding a free evening to spend with a loved one can be almost impossible. As a result, it may seem as if you spend more time trying to find moments of serenity rather than actually experiencing them.

The teachings of the *Tao* say to *Be still and discover your center of peace.* One way to do this is through visualization. No matter where you are, you can take a minute to imagine yourself in a safe and beautiful retreat. It can be high on a mountain range, near the ocean, in the middle of a forest, or lying under a quilt with a good book—whatever image brings you the greatest sense of peace. Leave your tension and stress behind as you "travel" to your retreat and relax. Tell yourself: *This is my special place to relax, and I can come here anytime I want.* Then "return" to the present world and know that you can go back to your retreat whenever you need serenity.

Today, I'll use my imagination as I create a special place that fills me with a feeling of total peace.

If every morning Mom and Dad are rushing to get ev-
eryone out of the house, if things are so frenetic that
the homework gets forgotten one day and . . . lunch the
next . . . well, the message that begins to come through
is, "I must not be very important . . ."
                                        —ARNOLD L. STOLBERG

Do your kids ever say: *I don't want you to go to*
work! You never have any time for me! or *My friend's*
mother is always home and she bakes cookies? These
are the feelings of children who have working parents
and who need to know that they count and matter
enough to command your time, energy, and attention.

Responding to a child's anger, resentment, or hurt
over your choice to work outside the home with retorts
such as, *I'm working hard for you,* or *You're a selfish*
brat who doesn't appreciate the things I do for you, may
only end up making a bad situation worse.

Instead, you can validate your child's feelings by saying, *You know, sometimes I want to stay home with you,*
or ask, *What can we do to make both of us feel better*
about my work? Perhaps asking your children to draw
pictures for your office or planning a special dinner
menu together with their favorite foods can show them
that their feelings are important. Once your children
know that they have a voice in expressing needs, then
together you may be able to come up with positive
solutions to make a family of working parents work.

Today, I'll ask my children how they feel about me
working. I'll really listen to their responses and ask if
they'd like to have a family discussion every week.

The vultures live on what was. They live on the past.... But hummingbirds live on what is. They seek new life. They fill themselves with freshness and life.
— STEVE GOODIER

Experts in fine wines can often recall the sensory pleasures of a bottle of wine—its subtle flavors, its bouquet, and its color. They may say, when tasting a new wine, *Ah, but it will never compare to the* _____ *I had in 1968.*

Yet times from the past—like the vintage wine of the past—are gone. So living in the present by thriving on remembrances of the past is like trying to recapture the taste of a fine wine from its empty, dusty bottle.

To exist fully in the here and now, you need to enter into this moment without depending on what has come and gone. You need to leave your mind open to everything the new life of the present has to offer. This involves doing more than just thinking, *I'm in the present; I'm reading the meditation for August 18.* You need to feel yourself in the present. You need to experience this moment as fresh, clean, and exciting so you can savor each taste as if it were the first—and only—time.

Today, I'll open my senses—sight, sound, touch, taste, and smell—to each moment. In that way, I'll be able to feel each moment rather than let it pass by me unnoticed.

*There is only one problem with saving your dream for
someday. . . . Someday will always remain in the future.*
                                                    —ANONYMOUS

When you were a child and were asked, *What do
you want to be when you grow up?* your answers may
have included: *An astronaut. The president. A world
traveler. A movie star.* At the time, there was no reason
for you to think your dreams couldn't come true.

But as you grew older, you may have shed such
dreaming. Career realities may have forced you to be
practical—rather than become an astronaut, you may
have earned a degree in engineering—and family pressures may have pushed you into marriage, the family
business, or living in a geographical location not of
your own choosing. The excitement and limitless possibility once expressed by your childhood dreams may
have evaporated in adulthood. Even today, you may
dismiss most of your dreams as fantasies, silly notions,
and impractical castles in the sky that will never come
true.

Yet today's dreams don't have to be practical. After
all, it's the nature of a dream not to follow logic or even
rational thinking. So what's wrong with letting your
mind wander with the question, *What if . . . ?* It doesn't
matter whether you have all the answers to translate
What if . . . ? into *How?* Simply having a dream and
wanting to dream it is the key to creative living.

*Today, I'll wonder "Why not?" as I let my mind wander
with wild imaginings and fantastic fantasies.*

I think one must learn a different, less urgent sense of time here, one that depends more on small amounts than big ones.

—SISTER MARY PAUL

Do you ever wonder why back-to-school shopping has to be completed in August, why Halloween candy goes on sale in September, why the celebration of Thanksgiving begins in late October, and why the Christmas season commences as soon as fall officially begins?

The retail push to make holidays into month-long events can propel everyone into such a preholiday frenzy that people become stressed out long before the actual holidays arrive. Consumers rush to get the best bargains, buy the biggest bags of candy and the plumpest turkeys, and find the perfect Christmas tree.

Rather than give in to such frantic consumerism, you can make a resolution this year to make things happen in your life at the time they're supposed to happen. Stores rarely run out of school supplies, cartons of Halloween candy are always still available on October 31, there's often chicken or pheasant if turkeys sell out, and countless Christmas trees are chopped down that never see the inside of a living room.

By deciding now to let such events happen in their own time, you'll be better able to deal with events in the present rather than become frantic over events that have yet to happen.

Today, I'll mark on my calendar when I want to start thinking about the upcoming holidays. I won't let outside influences dictate my schedule.

It wasn't until late in life that I discovered how easy it is to say, "I don't know."

—W. SOMERSET MAUGHAM

In her book *The Tao of Inner Peace*, Diane Dreher tells the story of a Midwestern farm boy who was the only one in his family to go to college. He went to a state university, then earned a graduate fellowship to a fancy Eastern school. There, he often felt embarrassed when his classmates asked if he had read this or that learned book. He would remain quiet as his classmates discussed theories and authors he didn't know.

One day he decided to tell the truth. *No, I haven't read that book*, he responded. *Could you tell me more about it?*

The next time you face an area of ignorance in your life—on the job, with your family or friends, or with your children—can you admit you don't know and ask for more information? Honesty can provide you with the opportunity to learn, foster closeness with others who are happy to enlighten, help you gain the respect of those who may be afraid to admit limitations, and bring you peace of mind in removing the strain of defensiveness or egoism. As the *Tao* teaches, *Those who know they do not know gain wisdom.*

Today, I'll watch what happens when I admit I don't know something. Rather than lose respect from such a confession, chances are I'll gain respect through my courage and honesty.

*Use what talents you have; the woods would have little
music if no birds sang their song except those who sang
best.* —REV. OLIVER G. WILSON

When you lose your confidence, it may be easy to
doubt that you're good at anything. As a result, you may
have no desire to discover your hidden talents. Instead,
you may tell yourself, *If I can't do something better than
someone else, then I'm not going to try at all.*

As you look over pictures you've taken, you might
think, *I'm no Ansel Adams.* As you reread a poem
you've written, you may determine, *I'm no Emily Dick-
inson.* As you assess your current position in a business,
you may say, *I'm no Henry Ford.* Or you may tell the
parent in you, *You're no Dr. Spock.*

Such critical messages have an uncanny way of making you feel inferior before you even attempt something. They can also hurt or damage your attitude
about your creativity and talents so you give up even trying. *After all,* you might think, *I'll never be that good!*

But how do you know you won't be any good? It
doesn't matter whether you become famous or successful. What does matter is that with talent, determination, and effort, you give yourself a chance to
achieve splendid things.

To explore your talents, enroll in a community adult-
education course. You won't know what you can do
unless you try.

*To uncover my hidden talents, I won't be intimidated
by what others may think. Instead, I'll be curious about
what I can do.*

Time was my enemy, but now it has become my friend.
                                            —J.B.W.

In spite of its reputation for efficiency, rules encumber German society. In rural areas, grocery stores close between noon and three o'clock every day. Mowing lawns is restricted on Sunday, a statutory day of rest. There are laws telling you when to clip your hedges and regulations on when and how to sweep your stairs. Yet despite these rules, many Germans argue that such restrictions make them better time managers because they have to think before they can do.

How good are you at budgeting your time so you can be more efficient? What would your day be like if you had to abide by numerous rules that forced you to slow down your pace, reschedule activities, or regulated the events in your life?

Today, before you plunge into a day filled with numerous activities and endless things to do, *think*. On a piece of paper, list the hours from the time you get up to the time you go to sleep. Ask, *What things do I need to do at specific times?* Block out those times. For the remaining time, ask, *What things are priorities? When can I do them?* Block out time for your priorities. Finally, in the hours remaining, set aside time for the things you'd like to do.

Today, I won't be able to do all the things I'd like to do. But if I think before I do anything, I'll have better control over my time.

*The biggest lesson I've learned . . . was that if you have
all the fresh water you want to drink and all the food
you want to eat, you ought never to complain about
anything.*

—EDDIE RICKENBACKER

For almost twenty-one days, Eddie Rickenbacker
floated aimlessly in a life raft in the Pacific Ocean. That
experience helped him see life differently from most
people because he learned to focus on the very basics
of his happiness and survival rather than the extrava-
gances, desires, or cravings that many believe are the
source of their happiness.

How satisfied are you with what you have? Are you
content with your health, house, salary, and partner, or
are you looking for something more? Are you able to
appreciate the basics of life, or are you more apprecia-
tive of the finer things?

It has been said that money can buy a bed but not
a good night's sleep, books but not intelligence, a house
but not a home, and amusement but not happiness. Are
you able to give thanks for the simple things in life—
food to eat, a place to live, a way to make money, a
spiritual belief?

Using the phrase *Keep it simple* whenever you lose
sight of these simple blessings can remind you that
there's very little you really need to survive comfortably and happily.

*I'll create a list of only three things I need today to
make me happy. I'll be content with these three things
and not desire more.*

*I still find each day too short for all the thoughts I want
to think, all the walks I want to take, all the books I
want to read, and all the friends I want to see.*
                                        —JOHN BURROUGHS

The *yin* and *yang* life force is central to Eastern philosophy. This philosophy explains that yin is the phase
of repose while yang is the phase of activity, and all of
life emerges from the harmonious synthesis of these
two forces. You need both moments of reflection for
your actions to have purpose and meaning, as well as
moments of action so your thoughts can take form.

Western philosophy, on the other hand, proposes a
choice: action or repose. Americans prefer yang over
yin by accepting the Puritan work ethic, burning the
candle at both ends, and equating a successful day with
the number of tasks completed.

Yet without a balance between yin and yang, you
will bounce from one extreme to the other—going
from times of overwork to periods of exhaustion and
collapse. To restore balance in your life, ask: *Where in
my life do I try to do too much? As a result, what things
are lacking from my life?*

Imagine your yin and yang on opposite sides of a
scale. To bring them in balance, what can you add or
take away from each side? Then create a new, more
balanced pattern of yin and yang in your life.

*Today, I'll flow harmoniously from my vocal, outgoing,
and active yang to my quiet, peaceful, and reflective yin.*

Abel began talking to himself. He had done it before, but only internally. Now he spoke out loud, and the sound of his own voice vibrating in his body felt vital.
—WILLIAM STEIG

How often do you talk to yourself to give advice, support, encouragement, or praise? Most people rely on others for such things. Yet remaining silent with yourself and dependent on others to recognize and reward times you need to hear positive or soothing sentiments can leave you disappointed when such words aren't forthcoming. And waiting for the voices of others can deprive you of exercising your own voice and becoming a resource of inner strength.

Self-talk can be one of the best stress-reducing techniques. After all, who knows best when you're feeling anxious, under pressure, or overwhelmed? And so it follows that you, too, can be a good resource to help you through such times.

To feel more comfortable with self-talk, you first need to get used to the sound of your voice. To do so, "discuss" a topic with yourself for at least two minutes every day. Over time, you'll find that the two minutes pass quickly and you'll be more at ease with having daily conversations with yourself.

My inner strength doesn't always have to come from external sources. Today, I'll start to learn to trust my voice and rely on it.

Oh, the comfort, the inexpressible comfort of feeling safe with a person, having neither to weigh thoughts nor measure words, but pouring them all right out, just as they are, chaff and grain together . . .
                    —DINAH MARIA MULOCK CRAIK

Many working couples end up discussing in counselors' offices what they're too tired to talk about at home. By trying out some creative communication solutions, however, working partners may be able to find more time for communicating with each other and with their children.

Begin by setting aside a block of time every week to spend just with each other. That may mean you need to reschedule a weekly activity such as golfing with friends or taking a cooking class, but the benefits to your relationship can make the sacrifice worthwhile.

You can also set aside a specific time each day—over lunch, for instance, or after the children have gone to bed—to discuss problems or simply to talk about your day. Some couples arrange to talk on the phone once a day.

You can set aside time to spend with each child alone—going out for pizza, or going to the park—so all your children feel important and have the opportunity to talk with you one-on-one. Finally, you can agree that when an important event in the relationship or with your children is scheduled, you will say, *No, I can't work overtime today.*

Working couples need to work extra hard at their relationships. Today, I'll show my partner and my family their importance to me by sharing special times alone with them.

When you have shut the doors, and darkened your room, remember never to say that you are alone; for God is within . . .

— EPICTETUS

As an adult, you may feel embarrassed about the methods you use to fall asleep at night. You may have a night light in your bedroom, listen to soothing music, or hug a favorite stuffed animal in your arms. Each of these makes you feel safe—and less alone in the times of darkness.

But you can conquer nighttime anxiety by keeping in mind that you're never alone at night, even if you live by yourself. The methods you use to fall asleep may work, but what can work better is remembering that there is always an angel to guard you at night.

This angel is your Higher Power. This power exists during the sunny days as well as the dark and scary nights. Your Higher Power believes in you and in your ability to take care of yourself. It's the gentle, hopeful spirit that reminds you that dawn emerges from night and a new day greets you when you wake up.

By knowing that your angel is there at night to watch over you, you can sleep in peace.

Today, I'll think about my angel throughout the day. Then tonight, I'll know this angel will be there to watch over me.

When I hear somebody sigh, "Life is hard," I am always tempted to ask, "Compared to what?"

—SYDNEY J. HARRIS

Imagine at this moment that a loved one had to undergo life-or-death surgery or that a devastating fire has just ripped through your home and destroyed all your possessions. If you say, *Life is hard* during such moments, you would certainly be justified.

But how many times do you find yourself saying *Life is hard* when things simply don't go your way, when you've had a tiring day, or when you're faced with a minor hassle? Compared to the catastrophes that can happen, such things are minor.

Although it may seem at times that life is difficult, there are some truly wonderful people and things in your life that can be quite fulfilling and shouldn't be overlooked during these times.

Today, rather than feel dejected with the way your life is going, make up your mind not to say, *Life is hard.* Instead, tell yourself, *No matter how bad things go for me each day, I'm going to maintain a positive attitude about my life.*

Have I become conditioned to expect the worst instead of the wondrous? Today, I'll feel good about an event or person in my life.

I never make the mistake of arguing with people for whose opinions I have no respect.

—EDWARD GIBBON

When you say things like, *She just doesn't understand,* or *He doesn't listen to me,* you may be driving yourself crazy trying to change another person's opinion. But no matter how much you may argue or how convincing your argument, you may never be able to change the opinions of others.

Before you become tense and angry, you need to look at the people in whom you're attempting to elicit change. Do you feel as if your parents don't see your point of view? You need to consider whether you really value their opinion or whether you're trying to force their approval. Do you feel as if your boss or coworkers don't understand you? You need to consider whether they're people who really matter to you outside work.

Sometimes you may actually be struggling to change the opinion of those who have never supported you rather than gravitate toward those who have always been there for you. The next time you find yourself trying to force change in another, ask: *Do I respect this person? Do I value his or her opinion?* To distinguish between those who matter and those who don't is the difference between finding disapproval and tension and respect and acceptance.

Am I wasting my time trying to change another's opinion? Today, I'll take a close look at those I talk to and seek the opinions of people I value and trust.

It used to be that, if I had a good working day, I thought I was a wonderful person, but otherwise I thought I was a terrible person.

—BYRON JANIS

Many years ago, Gelett Burgess, the humorist who wrote "I never saw a purple cow," attended a lecture that changed his life. Burgess had been going through a particularly difficult period in his life, but when the speaker asked everyone to laugh at the start of his talk, Burgess looked around the room and saw the faces of smiling people. He couldn't help but smile at the sight. Before he knew it, he was feeling better about his life.

How often are you buoyed up by the successes and achievements in your day, yet feel easily let down on tough days? Too often you may let your mood or attitude from the bad days creep into your assessment of yourself, so they make you feel like you're a "bad person."

No matter what happens in a day—no matter what the victories or defeats—you're still a good person. Resolve today to set a goal for September 1: Not to let what's going on in your life color how you feel about yourself as a person. To help you achieve your goal, whenever you ask the question, *How do I see myself?* respond: *I always see myself as a good person.*

Today, I'll remember that a good day doesn't mean I'm good, just as a bad day doesn't mean I'm bad.

The human organism has only so much energy at its
disposal. If you divert a great deal of it into any one
channel . . . plan to be physically and mentally bank-
rupt. . . .

—LISA ALTHER

In nature, there's a pattern of high energy activity,
followed by dormancy, or a period of low energy. During the time of high energy, bees gather pollen, hawks
hunt for food, and trees burst forth with color. During
the ebb, grass and flower growth slows and animals
hibernate. It's this rhythm that allows for new life and
renewed energy after periods of sleep and rest.

You, too, have periods during the day when your
energy level is the highest. Perhaps you're someone
who rises at daylight and goes for a run, who accom-
plishes much in the afternoon, or who is a "night owl."
You also have periods during the day when your energy flow is low. You may be a late sleeper, crave an
afternoon nap, or crawl into bed soon after dinner.

Identifying your "prime" times and "down" times
can help you tackle the most demanding activities
when you're mentally and physically most capable and
least stressed. Note the time of day when you accomplish the most and when your attitude is the most positive and relaxed. Then strive to work with your prime
and down times.

Today, I'll tackle projects that need mental concentra-
tion and physical energy during my prime times and
save routine or low-demand tasks for my down times.

If we listened to our intellect, we'd never have a love affair. We'd never have a friendship. We'd never go into business . . . Well, that's nonsense. You've got to jump off cliffs all the time and build your wings on the way down.

—RAY BRADBURY

You may often ask yourself the question, *Where am I going in my life?* But do you ever ask yourself, *Where am I growing in my life?* You may move through each day on automatic pilot, doing the same things in the same way—taking the same route to work, eating the same meals, reading the same types of magazines or books, and spending time with the same people.

Although sticking to familiar routines and socializing with the same circle of friends may feel comfortable and stress free, such routines may prevent you from experiencing challenge, excitement, change, and growth. Doing something new every day can help you break out of the rut of your daily grind, give you something new to think or talk about, and help you see your life in a whole new way.

Today, take a new route to work. Stop at a different coffee shop. Strike up a conversation with a colleague or neighbor. Such experiences can spark a new interest in your life and stimulate you into a new way of thinking, feeling, and acting.

The goal of doing something new is awareness, not anxiety. Today, I'll view any new experiences I attempt as a source of challenge, novelty, and excitement.

We should think seriously before we slam doors, before we burn bridges, before we saw off the limb on which we find ourselves sitting.

—RICHARD L. EVANS

Just like everyone else, you have difficult days. People disappoint you. Events or circumstances upset you. Projects can't be completed. Demands far outdistance the time required to address them. Bills accumulate.

Your first response may be to react in anger or frustration toward coworkers, family members, friends, your partner—even total strangers. Unfortunately, acting upon your anger by saying things you may later regret, by making shortsighted decisions, or by abruptly terminating a conversation or slamming a door in someone's face can come back to haunt you. Sometimes a slammed door can't be opened again. Sometimes the people you insult or snap at will eventually distance themselves from you. Some decisions made in anger or haste can't be changed—or may take considerable time and effort to undo.

Angry moments don't have to erupt into fiery volcanoes. If you can learn to sit on your anger until you're calmer and more rational—by counting slowly to ten, for instance—you may be able to avoid shameful, regretful results. Today's anger doesn't need to erupt toward any person, place, or thing.

Today, I'll let the dust settle and tempers cool so time can help me get things back in perspective. Waiting can show wisdom and maturity.

Why do some people always see beautiful skies and grass and lovely flowers and incredible human beings, while others are hard-pressed to find anything or any place that is beautiful?

—LEO BUSCAGLIA

It may be hard to break the habit of seeing or thinking of things solely from a negative perspective. When a stranger smiles at you, you might wonder, *Am I dressed inappropriately?* After listening to someone go on and on about how wonderful things are, you may conclude, *Nobody can be that happy. They must be very shallow.* When someone does something nice for you, you might think, *The only reason they are treating me so nicely is because they want something from me.*

Focusing on the negative may be a habit you learned from growing up in an unhealthy home. Or it may have come from coping with numerous disappointments in adulthood. But no matter what its origin, you may be hard-pressed to see the good in anything or anybody.

But you can use today to think more positively. Instead of focusing on the negative, try to find just one positive thing in your life. Perhaps today is a sunny day. You may be blessed by wonderful friends. You may love your work. Perhaps you have a close relationship with your children. After a while, you'll find yourself coming up with two, three, or even more blessings in your life.

Today, I'll not only try to find positive people and things in my life, but I'll also share these things with others.

One of the most tragic things I know about human nature is that all of us tend to put off living.
—DALE CARNEGIE

Don't you just love to think about all the things you'd like to do! There's the addition to your home you'd like to build, the quilt you'd like to start, the degree you'd like to earn, or the trip you'd like to take.

What's preventing you from doing any of those things? Perhaps you can't find enough time or are waiting for "the right time." Maybe you're afraid you won't be able to complete it. Or you may be intimidated by any number of other factors—your age, your abilities, not being good enough, or what other people might think.

But sometimes fears and excuses are like bricks you use to build a wall that becomes impossible to scale, preventing you from experiencing new, exciting, or interesting things.

To be alive is to break schedules, challenge time constraints, change patterns, and do things out of the ordinary. To be alive is to participate in all the fun, all the travel, all the relationships, and all the activities life has to offer.

Think about one thing you'd really like to do. Then write down how you can accomplish it. This simple act can help remove a few of your "excuse bricks" so it'll be easier to take the first step toward what you want.

Rather than look out over the horizon at the things I keep putting off, I'll focus my energy today on the one thing I can start to do right here and right now.

According to the calendar, this back-to-school, back-to-work week is the time for the ritualistic sharpening of pencils and the shaking of sand out of briefcases. But we all know better. It's actually the week of the Really Serious Exercise Resolutions.

—JUDY FOREMAN

As you drive to work now, you may see high school and college students running along the roadways or practicing team sports on playing fields. Your children may be making plans to try out for a school team. At work, you may notice coworkers going to the health club together.

How can you get gung-ho to begin some sort of exercise program? First, think of all the positive results you'll gain from exercising. You'll lose weight, strengthen your heart, make new friends, and improve your overall health and well-being. Second, set aside exercise time in your schedule. You can get up earlier in the morning, work out during your lunch hour, or unwind through exercise after work. Third, purchase a health club membership or exercise equipment, and comfortable clothing to motivate you to exercise.

With sound reasons to begin an exercise program, time set aside for it, and the right equipment, you can set realistic goals that can help you achieve the results you want.

What kind of activity do I like the most? Today, I'll choose an exercise I'd like to do, not necessarily one I see others doing.

But where was I to start? The world is so vast, I shall start with the country I know best, my own. But my country is so very large. I had better start with my town. But my town, too, is large. I had best start with my street. No, my home. No, my family. Never mind, I shall start with myself.

—ELIE WIESEL

How many times have you tried to change others—a parent, loved one, friend, or boss—rather than change yourself? Sometimes it may seem easier to focus on other people, but the truth is that the only person you can change is yourself.

But you can't change yourself in five-minutes or go to bed one night expecting to wake up the next day the person you've always wanted to be. Changing yourself means getting to know yourself first—your likes and dislikes, goals and desires, skills and abilities, and limits and boundaries.

One way to get to know yourself is to balance your time alone with the time you spend with others. Time alone gives your mind and emotions the space in which to relax, to let go of tensions and irritations, to gain a new perspective, and to rejuvenate. Structure each day to allow for a minimum of fifteen minutes alone. Then go for a walk, take a drive, listen to soothing music, or meditate. The purpose of alone time is to eliminate both interactions and distractions.

Today, I'll give myself a chance to spend some time alone. Such time can provide me with a valuable way of getting to know myself a little better.

You can clutch the past so tightly to your chest that it leaves your arms too full to embrace the present.
                                                    —JAN GLIDEWELL

Do you have an "energy drain" in your life—a person or circumstance from the past that drags you down in the present? Perhaps it's an ex-lover who broke your heart or an error you made on a report that cost you a promotion. Constantly dwelling on this person or circumstance can make you feel imbalanced, out of touch, and exhausted as you transfer your time and energy away from today.

Energy drains are like the barnacles that cling to the hulls of ships. Over time, they will drag you down. So no matter how happy, successful, or satisfied you become in your life, such an energy drain from the past will prevent you from moving full-steam ahead in the present.

The next time you find yourself reflecting on your energy drain, say aloud: *It's over and done with and there's nothing more I can do about it. It's time to move on and concentrate on today.* Then focus your time and attention on a person or activity in the present.

History can never be rewritten. It's time I begin to create new interactions and new experiences for the history that's about to be written.

*I have to laugh at the times I've knocked myself out
over a tough spot only to find out afterwards there was
an easier way through.*
—ROBERT FRANKLIN LESLIE

In your hurry to arrive somewhere on time, have you
ever found yourself pushing in exasperation against a
door, only to have someone behind you tap you on the
shoulder and point to the sign marked PULL? Or in
your desire to come up with the way to resolve a problem, have you spent hours alone mulling over the solution only to have the input of others help you come
up with the answer in minutes?

You don't have to knock yourself out over the difficulties of daily life when others can provide you with
assistance and direction. Sharing your difficulties
rather than hanging on to them is one way to make
your life easier.

Today, try teamwork in your responsibilities. For example, make your household chores events. Shop,
clean, and cook with your housemates or family members. Try to see doing these chores as occasions to
spend time with each other. Or if you need to undertake a major project, such as packing for a move or
painting the exterior of your home, ask others to a
packing or a painting party. This teamwork strategy is
not only creative, but also makes your "tough spots"
less stressful and much more manageable.

*Today, I'll participate in a spirit of community. I'll reach
out to others and ask for help as well as offer my assistance.*

. . . it's not unusual to find 10-year-olds who carry Week-At-A-Glance calendars in their backpacks . . .
—BARBARA F. MELTZ

By second or third grade, a child is usually ready and eager to participate in extracurricular activities. But while it may be hard to impose restrictions or to ask your child to make choices—particularly when he or she responds, *But everyone else is doing it*—it's important to encourage your child to limit the number of activities in order to avoid overscheduling that can lead to stress.

For example, a child who plays soccer, takes piano and tennis lessons, and participates in scouting is going to have very little time in which to relax—to watch a video, read a book, enjoy a hobby, or to spend quality time with you. So you need to limit your child's activities by allowing participation in only one sport each season (soccer *or* basketball) or being a member of just a few organizations (scouting and band, but not scouting, band, *and* the theater production).

While it's okay for your child to be active, it's not okay if he or she is forever in motion. So it's important that you teach him or her how to make choices and limit commitments.

Today, I'll let my child know that free time can be just as enjoyable as time spent in structured activities.

*During World War II my nickname was "Cannonball."
I never walked—I ran. I interrupted people. I got furious waiting in lines. And I always did two things at
once.*

—DR. MEYER FRIEDMAN

After Dr. Friedman suffered a heart attack, he ex-
amined his personality and determined that his "Type
A" behavior had contributed to his ailment. So he set
about finding ways to become less stressed. Today he
lives by his "five-year test." When stressed about an
upcoming event, he asks, *Will I care about this five
years from now?* If he doesn't care, he won't attend a
dinner out, concert, or conference. If he does care, he'll
go. With the five-year test, he's able to weed out the
trivial engagements from the truly important ones.

There are other ways to transform your Type A behavior. You can manage your stress better by gaining
control over the things that irritate you. If you're often
stuck in traffic, install a car phone so you can call ahead
and adjust your schedule. Finally, learn to rate your
difficulties on a scale of one to ten. In that way, rather
than let spilled coffee become a ten—and a catastrophe—you can see it's really a two and not that big a
deal.

*Although there are many hassles in life, my reaction
turns them into stresses. Today, I'll stop sweating the
small stuff and concentrate on much bigger—and more
important—things.*

The most beautiful discovery true friends make is that they can grow separately without growing apart.
                                    —ELISABETH FOLEY

Too often those in close friendships or intimate relationships think they have to be twins—to dress alike, think alike, talk alike, and act alike. Individualism can be threatening to two people who harmonize well with one another, for they may feel that taking separate paths may eventually force them apart or in some way damage the peaceful resonance in their relationship.

Yet time spent apart, with others or alone, is essential to a relationship. Healthy relationships are made of two individuals, not one. And even though the relationship is based on common points of interest, it's important that the individuals maintain a variety of outside friendships and interests. One person can never satisfy all your needs. Be sure to share what you did in the time spent apart from one another so that time apart becomes encouraged, supported, and respected—and not a source of stress.

I won't be upset when my partner spends time with others or joins groups, attends classes, or becomes a member of organizations without me. I'll choose my time apart too so we have new experiences to discuss together.

The bluebird carries the sky on his back.
—HENRY DAVID THOREAU

Do others see you as a Superman or a Wonder Woman? Are you the one your family looks to for organization and leadership? Are you the one with boundless energy, awake and doing things before everyone's up and in bed long after everyone's asleep? Do you have several projects going at one time? Are you the one who always volunteers?

While you may pride yourself on your ability to be there when others need you, do you ever stop to think what would happen if you weren't always rushing in to take charge? What would happen if you took time off for yourself? Would your partner be unable to cook a meal, and therefore starve to death? Would no one else be able to bake for the bake sale and so it would be a disaster? Would your boss be incapable of faxing information to clients, so the business would fail?

Sacrificing your time and energy to do for others what they're often capable of doing for themselves only cheats you. Today, rather than carry the world on your back, let others take some of the burden from you and do for themselves. Then you can do for you.

Today, I'll make it clear that I need time and attention, too. I can do for myself, or even let others do for me for a change!

. . . I think it is safe to say that no day is complete without a good dose or two of irony.

—JOSEPH MEEKER

Life doesn't always give you what you plan for. In fact, you often get the exact opposite of what you expect. You're given a raise, and your rent goes up. You have dental work on a day you're craving caramels. Or you get your hair done, then walk out of the beauty shop into a torrential downpour.

You can view such ironic situations with anger, resentment, or frustration, or you can see such situations as totally out of your control and, in some ways, humorous. Certainly being able to laugh at an ironic situation, particularly when it's as frustrating as having your raise go to your rent, may take time. But when you can convert your setbacks into some form of positive release—by smiling, shrugging your shoulders, or being able to share a laugh with others over the absurdity of it—then you will begin to find it easier to find the humor in a situation.

As you go through your day, see if you can find some ironic incident and try to chuckle at it. As Gahan Wilson says, *Life essentially doesn't work. And that's the basis of endless humor.*

Today, I'll laugh at the ironies in newspaper articles I read, news reports I hear, and the everyday events in my life. I'll find things that prove my life can provide the basis of endless humor.

To be nobody-but-myself—in a world which is doing its best . . . to make you everybody else—means to fight the hardest battle which any human being can fight, and never stop fighting.

—E. E. CUMMINGS

People with a high level of self-esteem are comfortable with themselves. They can accept who they are and how they look. Although judgments and criticisms may hurt them, they try not to let the negative statements of others influence or change how they feel about themselves. Of course, that's not always easy to do!

Oftentimes you may revise the way you think or feel in order to avoid judgment or criticism and gain the approval of others. It may not always be easy to accept who you are and feel good about yourself when there are those around you who will shoot you down, but try this experiment. Write the names of three people whose opinions you respect on one side of a sheet of paper. Then write three judgments or criticisms you've been told on the other side of the paper. Look at the two lists and ask: *Would any of the people listed ever say any of these statements to me?*

The next time judgments or criticisms land in your lap, consider the source and your respect for that person's opinion. Chances are the person—as well as the comments—mean very little to you.

Today, I won't let outside influences dictate how I feel about myself. I'll feel good about myself and enjoy the way I do the things I do.

There is an Indian belief that everyone is a house of four rooms: a physical, a mental, an emotional and a spiritual room. Most of us tend to live in one room most of the time, but unless we go into every room every day, even if only to keep it aired, we are not complete.

—RUMER GODDEN

For most people, serious prayer doesn't usually begin until after age thirty. Then, the illusion of immortality and the control one thinks one has over one's destiny fades and there's a need to rely on a guiding force who can provide "answers." But how do you make space in your "house" for such spiritual contact?

There are many ways to begin communicating with a Higher Power. You may wish to break the ice by using a familiar prayer,—*Our Father, who art in heaven . . . , Now I lay me down to sleep . . .* or *The Lord is my Shepherd, I shall not want . . .* , for instance. Or you may want to write your own prayer, one that addresses the particular areas in which you feel you need spiritual guidance and wisdom. You may even use different prayers at different times, depending on your physical, mental, and emotional states.

But what's most important about communication with a Higher Power is that you do it every day. By making it part of your daily routine, you may discover a more profound—and a much more rewarding—relationship with Him or Her.

Today, I'll find time to pray. It doesn't matter if I pray before I rush off to work, while exercising, or before I go to bed—just so long as I do it.

Death happens because life happens; creatures die because creatures live. It sounds so simple, yet this truth has been somehow sterilized out of . . . life today.
—TONY CHAMBERLAIN

One experience that's particularly stressful to go through is loss: loss of a job or an expected raise or promotion, loss of a close friend or neighbor who moves away, loss of personal possessions through fire or theft, loss of a loved one through separation, divorce, or death. Any loss can leave a vacuum in your life—a space and time that was once pleasantly filled but now feels empty and meaningless. The sadness can be overwhelming. It may be nearly impossible to perform even the simplest routine tasks, concentrate on anything, or accept that life must go on.

Everyone faces loss; some more than others. But as Elbert Hubbard says, *The cure for grief is motion.* You need to grieve your loss, then recommit to life. You must go on and raise your children, find a new relationship or friends, build a new house, or look for a new job.

By forcing yourself back into the swing of living and trusting, you'll eventually feel good again, and you can get through your loss.

How I respond to any loss is the difference between a hopeful attitude and a hopeless one. Today, I'll believe that I can be happy despite the loss I've suffered.

*If you try to study yourself according to another you
will always remain a secondhand human being.*
                                    —J. KRISHNAMURTI

No matter who you are, it can be tempting to look
at others and wonder, *Why can't I be like them?* You
may wish for what others have—straight hair or curly
hair, a perfect body, or a beautiful smile. You may want
what others have achieved—career success, a close-
knit family, or a large bank account.

Oftentimes, it's easier to focus on others rather than
on yourself, particularly when you don't know what you
need or want. But when you do so, you're turning away
from yourself by holding to the belief that others are
better than you.

To raise your self-esteem and your level of self-
acceptance, begin a list titled "Twenty-One Good
Things About Me." Every day for a week, list three
things about yourself that are positive. Try not to compare yourself to others; rather, focus totally on yourself
by recording statements that reflect your abilities *apart*
from others; for example, *I'm a great tennis player,* or
I'm a very good listener.

*Today, I'll work on my ability to focus on myself, not
on others. I'll feel good about finding the good in me.*

The ideal day never comes. Today is ideal for him who makes it so.

—HORATIO DRESSER

What's so good about today? Have you ever begun a day with that challenge? Approaching any day with the attitude that something's bound to go wrong or that it'll be one hell of a day won't allow you to see the good in it. Rather, you'll be so busy focusing on the circumstances that support your negative attitude that it'll be hard to see anything positive.

While today may hold many work demands and difficulties, you can take time to notice the positive things that happen. For instance, maybe for once the copying machine doesn't run out of paper when you use it, a coworker invites you to lunch, or you easily find a parking spot. Your ability to see some of what's good in today can give you a feeling of importance and excitement that you want to recognize and enjoy.

It has been said that *Today is the first day of the rest of your life.* So how do you want to spend it—agonizing over how bad you think it'll be, or appreciating how good it can be?

I'll see today for what it is—fresh, clean, and full of possibilities—and strive to match my attitude to it.

You take yourself too seriously! You are too damn important in your own mind. That must be changed!
—CARLOS CASTANEDA

How can you appreciate the world around you if all you talk or think about are the events in your world—your career, your feelings, your interests, your problems? Like the horse who wears blinders, focusing solely on the things in your life allows you to only see yourself. Such a vision can make you take yourself much too seriously and become overly concerned about your own needs and wants—and not how your needs and wants often interact with those of others.

Losing self-focus means opening your eyes and ears to those around you so you can feel a part of everything else. By truly seeing others who coexist with you, you can learn to accept that your world is a shared space. By listening to others, you can learn that the experiences in your life are really not unique, that everyone goes through what you go through, and that there is a great deal of wisdom to be shared with others that can be mutually beneficial.

Today, try taking your blinders off. Notice the events and people around you. See how you're different from them as well as similar. Then join in with the world around you.

Today, I'll notice the uniqueness in the people around me. What makes each of them special?

You have to leave the city of your comfort and go into the wilderness of your intuition. . . .What you'll discover will be wonderful.

—ALAN ALDA

There are those who see themselves as continually failing or having bad things happen to them. In contrast, there are those who routinely see themselves accomplishing whatever they want to do and who mentally program themselves for success.

The difference between someone who submits to defeat and someone who achieves success has nothing to do with ability. Rather, it's "all in the head"—what their mind believes they're capable of.

How can you activate your mind to be less negative so you can dispel some of the self-limiting beliefs you have about yourself and your abilities? First, list some of your beliefs about your limits. You might write, *I don't stick to getting things done, I can't ask for help when I need it,* and so on. Then, for each belief, write an opposing statement. For example, *I can stick to getting my projects done, I can ask for help from my co-workers,* and so on. Say each new statement aloud and imagine what could happen if it were true. Then, the next time a self-limiting belief comes up, use your new belief to transcend it.

Self-limiting beliefs may be based on my erroneous conclusions about real experiences or can simply be untested assumptions. Today, I'll test the truth of my beliefs.

Whatever your life's work is, do it well....If it falls your lot to be a street sweeper, sweep streets like Michelangelo painted pictures, like Shakespeare wrote poetry, like Beethoven composed music; sweep streets so well that all the hosts of heaven and earth will have to pause and say, "Here lived a great street sweeper, who swept his job well."

—MARTIN LUTHER KING, JR.

Too often people feel worthless in jobs that don't pay a lot of money, require a great deal of schooling, or command the respect or envy of others. As a result, their low opinion of themselves and what they do can cause tension and negativity.

Yet imagine what the world would be like if everyone was a doctor, lawyer, best-selling author, or company president. There would be no one to transport people to doctors or to carry out their orders. There would be no one to record court cases, guard criminals, or file briefs on behalf of attorneys. There would be no typesetters or book binders to put together an author's books and no stores in which to buy them. And there would be no clerical help, manufacturers, or truckers who would keep a company operating.

Today, no matter what your job—from homemaker to home seller—remember that it's not only important, but also something you can be proud of.

Today, I'll strive to do my job so well that no one else could do it better.

Now I look at rough times as an opportunity to put down some roots to help me weather future storms that may come my way.

—JERRY STEMKOSKI

There's the story of the old farmer who stood on his porch, watching another spring rain drench his new crops. A motorist who had stopped for directions commented how good the farmer must feel seeing the rain soak the ground.

But the farmer shook his head. *The plants may only grow roots on the surface. If that happens, a storm could wipe out the crops. It's not good if things are too easy in the beginning. The plants have to put out deep roots to get at the water and nourishment below to become strong. Then they can withstand the storms.*

You may often think how wonderful life would be if things were easier. But think back to a particularly rough time you went through in the past. Maybe it was a difficult childhood, a hurtful relationship, or the loss of a job. Would you be as strong as you are today if it hadn't been for that experience?

When faced with a difficult situation today, try not to think about how great it would be if the solution were easy. Instead, think, *What will getting through this experience teach me? How will this make me stronger?*

Today, I'll remember that I learn and grow more from the harder, not the easier, lessons in life.

There was a period in high school when you had to figure out who you were. You'd think, "Well, I'm not fitting in with this group or that group." And then you'd start to examine your own inventory and wonder, "Is there anything I can do that is going to make me desirable . . . ?"

—DAVID LETTERMAN

Too often you may feel inferior or not good enough because you don't fit into a desirable or prestigious social or business circle. You may even attempt to change or take on unfamiliar or uncomfortable behaviors in order to feel more like you're part of a particular group.

Yet being able to express yourself without pretense or needing to please others means you can be more relaxed. In so doing, you can then be yourself and not an imitation of others.

Since everyone has a talent that makes them unique or sets them apart from others, one way to develop a sense of who you are is to identify a talent you have. What do you do that makes you different from other people you know? Identifying your unique talent puts you one step further toward finding the right circle of friends and acquaintances for you.

Today, I'll nurture my special talent. I'll use my creative abilities, my skill with tools, my expertise with figures and finances, or another talent I possess.

What makes people despair is that they try to find a universal meaning to the whole of life ...
—ANAÏS NIN

The only universal meaning to life that holds true for everyone is that no one's ever going to get out of it alive. So rather than waste your time and energy trying to understand why you're here, where you're going, or why you have to face the trials you do, perhaps the best approach to life is simply to enjoy it for as long as you can.

Would you enjoy your life more if you added a meaningful challenge that would bring adventure, rather than adversity, to your life? Then sign up for a white-water rafting expedition or a high-ropes course. Would you enjoy your life more if you were able to be more playful? Then buy a bag of peanuts and go to the park and feed and be entertained by the squirrels. Would your life be more enjoyable if you had more opportunities to get in touch with yourself? Then look at your calendar and plan to spend a weekend at home alone or make reservations at a peaceful country inn. Would you enjoy spending more time with others? Then plan a dinner party or time to be with friends.

The enjoyment of life can involve many different things. But most importantly, it involves the realization that you're part of something larger than yourself—and you don't have to try to understand it.

Daring to live today—and to enjoy it—can simply be a matter of being disciplined enough to find a new adventure in my life.

Our dilemma is that we hate change, but we love it at the same time. What we want is for things to remain the same but get better.

—SYDNEY J. HARRIS

How often do you complain that you would be able to do something if only something else wasn't preventing you? *I can't look for another job because I don't have time; I can't break up with my lover because I don't have anyone to fall back on;* or *I can't discipline my children because I've never been very good with kids* are only a few of the responses that may prevent you from accomplishing something.

It's important to recognize that saying *I can't* is just another way of saying *I fear,* and if you could take away your fearfulness, just think of all you could do. There would be nothing to prevent you from taking risks, trying new things, going new places, becoming more intimate, changing careers, going back to school, or setting limits with your children.

Today, change your response from *I can't* to *I'll try* in order to take the first step away from your fear. In so doing, you can push aside or even remove the obstacles you've placed in your path and challenge your fears.

If I don't welcome change, it'll be hard to respond to the challenge of a world in flux. Today, I'll attempt a new behavior or use a new way to handle things.

Simply to live is a wonderful privilege in itself....
But to what are you alive? Is it merely to a daily
routine?... How much do you really live outside of
your chosen profession or occupation?

—HENRY WOOD

From the time it's an acorn to the time it grows into
a tree, the mighty oak puts all its energy into becoming
as strong and tall as it can. Moisture, sunlight, and nutrition are gathered in its roots for its leaves, acorns,
branches, and trunk. Yet if the oak tree takes all the
moisture, sunshine, and nutrition for itself, other
nearby trees will be weaker and smaller and unable to
flourish.

You have within you a "forest" that demands attention: a career tree, a family tree, a parent tree, a friendship tree, and a personal tree. But if you spend more
time and attention nourishing just one, the neglected
trees will not be able to grow strong.

That means that every part of your life needs to be
equally important to you—your family and friends as
well as your career and your personal development.
Today, think of everything and everybody in your life
as a tree that needs your "nourishment." By devoting
some time and attention to each tree, you're ensuring
they can all flourish.

Achieving and maintaining balance is my goal today so
I can help develop the full potential of each part of my
life.

It is universally admitted that there is a natural healing power resident in the body....Many people have learned to relax and keep quiet like the animals, giving nature a free opportunity to heal their maladies.
—HORATIO W. DRESSER

Do you know people who rarely get sick, even from the sore throat everyone seems to have? Then there are those you know who always seem to be sick, getting one cold after another or having perpetual headaches.

You may notice that those who rarely get sick make their wellness a priority. They eat well, get plenty of rest, exercise, and strive to maintain a positive outlook. As a result, these people stay physically, emotionally, and spiritually healthy.

To take the first step toward such wellness, strive to reduce or eliminate any self-destructive health habits you may have. Instead of eating something that's been deep fried, heavily salted, or loaded with sugar, eat a fresh garden salad. Stop work when you start to become fatigued—not when you can't see straight or you're ready to drop. And go to bed at a reasonable hour—one that gives you sufficient rest so you can start each day refreshed and invigorated.

I am my own healer. Today, I'll learn to listen to my body and respect its messages.

Lack of something to feel important about is almost the greatest tragedy a man may have.
—ARTHUR E. MORGAN

There are many things you need to stay alive—food, air, shelter, and warmth. But in order to grow and thrive, you need so much more. You need other people for companionship, love, and support. You need to feel important and valued. You need to feel challenged. You need spiritual connection and to feel that your life has meaning and purpose.

Right now, can you identify the needs that are important to you? Perhaps you're feeling open and vulnerable and need the support of others. Or you may be tense and under pressure and need time to meditate or unwind. You may be frustrated and need some sort of activity or a more creative outlook.

Getting in touch with your needs can help you identify them. Once you do, you can then communicate them to others so you can get their support. Or you can pay attention to them yourself so you can meet them on your own. Identifying and meeting your needs can help you to realize that they—and you—are important.

What do I need and how can I get it? Today, I'll focus on the requirements that concern me so I can address them rather than ignore them.

Never accuse others to excuse yourself.

—ANONYMOUS

Have you ever blamed your negative feelings on others—your boss, coworkers, friends, teachers, parents? While it's true that you may feel anger or resentment at the things people say or do, what's not true is that they're the cause of your feelings. You're the sole owner of your emotions.

Since you're the one who owns your feelings, you're also the one who has the choice of holding onto them or releasing them. Holding onto them prolongs their intensity, keeps alive the events that led up to the feelings, and prevents you from experiencing life in the present moment. But releasing them can free you from the hold they have over you so you can move on.

How can you release your feelings? One technique is called the "put-off method." Rather than continue to experience an emotion, you can decide to put it off for a period of time—from fifteen minutes up to an hour. Focus your attention on something else. Then, when the time is up, ask: *Do I still feel the feeling?* Chances are that putting it on the "back burner" of your mind has enabled it to cool off on its own.

All the feelings I have are my own. Today, I'll let go of feelings I don't want and hang onto those that feel good.

Where will I be five years from now? I delight in not knowing. That's one of the greatest things about life—its wonderful surprises.

—MARLO THOMAS

The elderly man who had turned ninety-eight was asked what his next goal was. *To live to tomorrow,* he replied. When was the last time that your only goal was the next twenty-four hours?

Some people set complex goals that require years of hard work before they can be achieved. Others create grandiose goals they feel will "guarantee" them success, happiness, and meaning in their lives. Still others set goal after goal, achieving one goal and then immediately setting another without reflecting on the ground they've gained. And there are those who set goals that put them in the position of burning the candle at both ends as they strive for more and more.

Like the elderly man's desire to live another day, the best goals are simple, uncomplicated, and easy to achieve. You can set a simple goal for yourself today—to read the paper at your lunch hour, write a long-overdue letter to a friend, or take a walk after work—and then simply enjoy reaching your goal for the day.

Today, I'll set a realistic, attainable goal that will be enjoyable to achieve.

Dallas Cowboys defensive tackle Larry Cole, on the reason he went scoreless in the 1970s before scoring a fumble-recovery touchdown in 1980: "Anyone can have an off decade."

—JEFF PARIETTI

When you experience an upset, loss, or disadvantage, are you able to view such adversity with a positive attitude?

Having a good attitude, even when the chips are down, involves the ability to view any situation in a positive light. This means finding the advantage in the disadvantage. By looking for some uplifting aspect—like the silver lining in the cloud—or focusing on what you learned, setbacks can seem less devastating and overcoming problems can be easier.

The important thing to remember in any crisis or difficult situation is that there's *always* an opportunity for something new to be discovered. Or, as a Zen poem states in another way: *Since my house burned down, I now have a better view of the rising moon.*

Think about an upset or setback you're experiencing in your life. Ask, *What is the new door that's been opened for me? How can this make me stronger or wiser?* Then strive to find at least one positive aspect or opportunity.

Today, I'll use humor and insight to get through any problems or difficulties.

We come closest to God at our lowest moments. It's easier to hear God when you are stripped of pride and arrogance, when you have nothing to rely on except God. It's pretty painful to get to that point, but when you do, God's there.

—TERRY ANDERSON

Do you remember the story of the man who thought God had deserted him during a most troubling time because he only saw one set of footprints along the difficult path he had just walked? When he asked God why He wasn't with him when he needed Him the most, God told him that he had only seen one set of footprints because He had been carrying him.

Whether you realize it or not, the seeds of your faith are always with you. All it takes is for you to plant them, tend to them, and let them grow.

To plant your seeds, keep in mind that things will get better. There isn't a problem that can't be solved, a teardrop that won't be dried by a smile, and a weary soul that won't be energized again. Then tend to your seeds—talk to them through prayer or meditation—to strengthen the faith needed to get you through the difficult passages of time.

Today, I'll find a voice within me to help me have faith that all things change, all wounds heal, and all is eased through the passage of time.

*. . . the tortoise is good at nurturing energy, so it can
survive a century without food.*
                                   —CHINESE PROVERB

The ancient Chinese taught that it was wise to emulate the tortoise, who knew when to withdraw into itself to restore energy.

Do you know when to withdraw from conflicts, pressures, and energy drains? Are you able to step back from difficult or painful situations so you can become less confused and more centered?

When you're confused and uncentered, you can project inner conflicts onto the world around you. So rather than resolve situations, you may actually escalate them. But when you're at peace with yourself, you can see more clearly and act more definitively so you can help restore tranquility to your world and the world around you.

Cultivating inner peace can involve deep breathing to slow the mind and restore the body to a relaxed state, periods of silence to reflect quietly without interruption, or listening to a guided-meditation tape.

But no matter what form of spiritual exercise you choose, practice it every day. Establishing regular inner-peace breaks can make restoring your energy during tense times that much easier.

*There's always the potential for inner peace. I'll find my
inner peace today by setting aside a time for breathing
deeply and listening to my inner voice.*

Whoever wants to reach a distant goal must take many small steps.

—HELMUT SCHMIDT

People are often overwhelmed by large projects. Yet when they learn how to divide the work into manageable units, they discover that they can handle it in its entirety after all. As one man commented when asked how he lost 150 pounds after being overweight all his life: *I did it one day—and one pound—at a time.*

Any large project—writing a 300-page doctoral dissertation, planning and preparing for a large dinner party, or starting a new business—can be broken down into smaller steps. The dissertation gets written one chapter at a time, the meal gets prepared one course at a time, and a new business gets started one step at a time.

How can you divide your work into manageable units? Perhaps an outline can help, or a list that details a step-by-step approach. Using a phrase such as *One Step at a Time* or *Take It Nice and Slow* can keep you patient. Or developing a faith in the process through the belief that *a journey of a thousand miles* does *start with a single step* can help you relax when you don't see immediate results.

In life, as in nature, everything has its own cycle. Today, I won't rush the process. I'll take everything one step at a time.

A handful of patience is worth more than a bushel of brains.

—DUTCH PROVERB

Your best work often comes from patient dedication to something designed to last over time. Rome wasn't built in a day, the ceiling of the Sistine Chapel is the result of years of work, barns built centuries ago still stand firm, and the finest and most brilliant gems are the result of hours of study, cutting, and polishing.

The desire to have things done quickly can prevent them from being done thoroughly. For example, those in recovery programs such as Alcoholics Anonymous learn from their first meeting that putting away the bottle won't instantly solve all their problems. They hear the life stories of others, who talk about their years of recovery. They read the Twelve Steps and begin to recognize that the personal work and growth involved will never be accomplished in twelve days.

But, to paraphrase a familiar quote, "Good things can come to those who take their time." To master anything—from a company report to a personal recovery program—requires long hours and dedication. Today, try working on something without setting a deadline. Sometimes eliminating the pressure and time frame to get something done can bring about results that will make you proudest.

Today, I'll work on one thing patiently and thoroughly, knowing the results will be better with time.

With history piling up so fast, almost every day is the anniversary of something awful.
　　　　　　　　　　　　　　　—JOE BRAINARD

Which do you remember: the anniversary of a painful time or the anniversary of something wonderful? You may be more aware of the dates of terrible events in your life—when you got laid off from work or when a parent died—rather than the wonderful events— when you were made a vice-president or when your sister got married. The media often perpetuates remembrance of awful events in history by reminding you of dates like the anniversary of President Kennedy's assassination (instead of his birthday) or the bombing of Pearl Harbor (instead of when the war ended).

Perhaps today you could start to create a calendar of positive anniversaries in your life: the first time you fell in love, a wonderful day spent with a parent, the day you stopped smoking, a romantic time spent with your partner, or a day when your child said, *I love you.*

Keeping such a calendar and adding to it over time can give you a record of wonderful memories you can commemorate each year. Then you'll be able to look at every day as the anniversary of something wonderful rather than something awful.

I'll leave it up to the media to keep track of the terrible events in history. Today, I'll begin a personal history that focuses only on the events I wish to celebrate.

Are you able to accept blows without retaliation?
                              —MARTIN LUTHER KING, JR.

Facing conflict is one way to learn how to deal effectively with people. But you learn nothing when you face conflict with the desire for retaliation rather than resolution. Violent actions, threats, lawsuits, or vengeful acts can't solve problems. But compromise can.

Throughout the years people like Thoreau, Gandhi, and Martin Luther King, Jr., promoted compassion and nonviolent action as a way to achieve resolution. Today, Greenpeace uses the power of the media to raise awareness of the plight of endangered sea creatures. Amnesty International encourages writing letters to political leaders in countries where prisoners of conscience are held. The Quakers conduct an active letter-writing campaign to promote humane politics.

The next time you face a conflict, try not to react with fear or hatred. Instead, attempt to see the conflict with an open mind. First review what the conflict is about from your perspective as well as from the other person's point of view. Then say: *I have the power and the ability to help resolve this. I can be flexible and open to many options in order to reach a happy compromise.* Looking at facts and searching for suggestions can prevent conflicts from turning into combat.

Making enemies keeps me from taking responsibility; making friends helps me seek resolution. Today, I'll look at a conflict objectively and strive to take the first step toward compromise.

Why do so many houses turn into . . . "homework hell" every evening around 7 o'clock?

—Barbara F. Meltz

While doing homework is a child's reponsibility, the child's desire to avoid it or put it off in favor of participating in other activities can create arguments and pressure that can impact on your relaxing time at home. After a long, tiring day, the last thing you may want to do is go to battle with a child who refuses to take responsibility for schoolwork.

The dilemma you face when you try to help your child do homework is that if you don't say anything, chances are the work won't get done. But if you do attempt to set parameters, you end up assuming some of the responsibility that belongs to the child.

How can you ensure your child gets the most out of homework without inhibiting his or her decision-making skills and accountability? Think of yourself as a manager and your child as an employee. Hold a weekly, biweekly, or even daily meeting to discuss "workload" (homework) and "time management" (how to budget the time needed to complete the work). If you can think of yourself as a guide or mentor rather than a disciplinarian or dictator, both you and your child will benefit in the long run.

Today, I'll show my child, through my example, how to get things done in a timely fashion. I'll be a teacher first and a parent later.

Worry often gives a small thing a big shadow.
                                        —SWEDISH PROVERB

Worry does absolutely nothing for your emotional, physical, or spiritual health. It can take a small situation and enlarge it to the proportion of a giant who looms above you and casts a long, dark shadow over your life. Over time, you may become a constant worrier whose life is ruled by fear as you expect the worst to happen all the time.

How important is it? is a good question to ask at times when you're worried, because your answer can help you put your concern into proper perspective. Another question you can ask is: *What can I do about this right now?* By focusing on what you actually can do about something that's bothering you, you may discover that your worry involves something that has already happened or something that hasn't yet happened—both of which you can't change or control.

You have the power within you to continue to make your worries gigantic or to begin today to shrink them to a more manageable size. As you go through the day, try not to waste your time worrying over things left undone or things that have yet to come. You can choose instead to live for right now and to leave your worries where they belong.

I manufacture stress for myself when I worry. Today, I'll walk in the sunshine, not the shadows, so I can see and experience everything as it's happening.

The difficult things of this world must once have been easy; the great things of this world must once have been small. Set about difficult things while they are still easy; do great things while they are still small.

—TAOISM

Very often you may not pay attention to things until they reach a crisis stage. For example, you may put off paying bills—even when you have the money—until you begin receiving past-due notices. Or you may avoid working on communication issues in your relationship until your partner offers an ultimatum of couples counseling or separation.

Handling events before they get out of hand is like practicing preventive medicine. Rather than be rushed to the hospital with a heart attack, it's better to eat right every day, exercise in moderation, and get a yearly checkup. Taking action before things get out of hand can avert future trouble or keep a bad situation from growing worse.

To become a "troubleshooter," list areas of your life that run the risk of reaching a crisis—perhaps your job performance or your finances. Then think of things you can do now to avert a potential future crisis. Arriving to work on time or starting a savings plan can keep things at a low risk so they don't become high-stress situations.

I'd rather handle things effectively than move from one crisis to the next. Today, I'll take care of my personal and professional responsibilities when they're small.

While the right to talk may be the beginning of freedom, the necessity of listening is what makes that right important.

—WALTER LIPPMANN

How many people do you communicate with in an average day? Probably dozens—and hundreds in a week and thousands in a year. But does the quality of your communications improve with the quantity?

Effective communication can only happen when you are willing to hear what others are saying. Good listeners focus on everything a person is saying without jumping in with reactions, retorts, defenses, and justifications. They allow others to express everything they're feeling without lining up responses in their mind.

How can you become an active listener? First, make sure you have the time to listen carefully. If you only have five minutes before a meeting or appointment, make sure this is known. Then listen and keep your mind free of distractions. Put aside your own problems or concerns, unfinished business, or the desire to second-guess what someone's going to say. Active listening means making the time and taking the energy to hear wholly, not partially, what others have to say.

By using active communication, I encourage depth and honesty in the way others relate to me. And by being receptive, I encourage similar attention from others.

Patience is a particular requirement. Without it you can destroy in an hour what it might take you weeks to repair.

—CHARLIE W. SHEDD

Harvesting a sucessful crop of pumpkins this fall reminded one farmer about a lesson she learned years ago in the cost of impatience. One year, she noticed that the long, meandering pumpkin vines were taking over her garden. Since she'd heard that pinching off some of the flowers produced better fruit, she did some pruning. She had nearly finished—and had her mind on her next project—when she mistakenly sliced off the best vine. As she looked at the severed vine and the pumpkins that would never ripen for the fall, she realized how much damage had been done in one instant of impatience.

Everyone loves to finish projects. Projects that are completed can raise self-confidence and bring about recognition and personal reward. But trying to do anything in haste may necessitate hours of revision or result in damage that can't be undone.

Intense passion for closure can lead to carelessness, stubbornness, and unfocused attention. So slowing down is the only antidote to end haste. To do so, enjoy each moment. Progress is guaranteed only when your mind is centered in the present and on only one event at a time.

Patience allows me the power to move forward with purpose. Tomorrow's fruits will be in proportion to today's patience.

I don't like work . . . but what I like is in work—the chance to find yourself.

—JOSEPH CONRAD

People work best when they feel competent and effective at what they do and when those around them validate their value and worth. A work environment that's filled with criticism, backbiting, or blaming others can make you feel powerless, unsupported, and frustrated.

Your central need from your work is not a better salary, being able to move up the corporate ladder, or even fame; rather, it's a high level of self-esteem. When you feel good about who you are and enjoy what you do, then you can be confident and creative. And when you are confident and creative, you're more likely to take risks and make changes for growth and self-discovery.

But how can you attain self-esteem if your work environment devalues you in some way? Rather than look to feeling accepted and valued by others, focus instead on your achievements and act on your personal values. While you can't control how others feel or act, you can control what you achieve and how true you are to ideals that are important to you.

Today, I'll create situations and act in ways that enable me to grow and flourish and encourage my self-esteem.

Anxiety in human life is what squeaking and grinding are in machinery that is not oiled. In life, trust is the oil.

—HENRY WARD BEECHER

Do you see your life as a dance between trust and fear? When your trust level is high, are you more capable of handling a difficulty than you are when you're afraid? Do you sometimes submit to your fear and "flee" from possible confrontation, rather than work through it?

While it would be wonderful if everything you approached could be based on trust, the truth is that everyone experiences some level of fear when they face certain tasks and responsibilities. Even the most confident people can have lingering feelings of doubt and insecurity.

But if you can trust in the belief that everything that comes to you can be handled, then it may be easier to face those things that you need extra courage for. The next time you feel yourself giving in to fears, say: *I trust in the process of being able to work out this situation. I will simply do the best that I can and trust that this will turn out all right.*

Today, I'll recognize that the more trust I have in the people, places, and things in my life, the less stress I'll feel.

Part of having a strong sense of self is to be accountable for one's actions. No matter how much we explore motives or lack of motives, we are what we do.
—JANET GERINGER WOITITZ

What would happen if you started saying "no" to some of the requests of others? How would you feel? Hesitant about not taking care of things? Anxious about letting go and letting another take control? Scared you'd lose love or approval, or open yourself up to criticism?

If you always feel it's a necessity to satisfy the requests of others, then it'll be difficult for you to refuse to do things for them. Yet you know it's impossible to meet everyone's needs all the time. So how can you do for others only when you want to or are able to?

Think about the good things that might occur if you *don't* give to others all the time. Perhaps those people might learn greater responsibility or will be encouraged to make their own decisions. Maybe you'll learn how to feel more comfortable putting your own needs first. Perhaps those people will make mistakes, but will learn and grow from them. Focusing on such positives can give you much needed support for yourself and the decisions you make.

Today, I'll practice saying no to a person I find particularly hard to refuse. In doing so, I'll be protecting my best interests.

Do not lose your inward peace for anything whatsoever, even if your whole world seems upset.
—SAINT FRANCIS DE SALES

Your days may be filled with tense people, hectic schedules, or frustrating events. You may live and interact with a variety of stressful situations. But just because the environment around you is like a battlefield doesn't mean you have to prepare for daily warfare. Whatever is happening outside you is someone else's issue, not yours. What is your issue, however, is how you control your inner peace.

To remain calm in stressful situations, practice a breath-counting meditation. Go to a quiet place, settle in a comfortable sitting position, close your eyes, and begin to breathe slowly and deeply. When you feel yourself relaxing, picture in your mind a series of stairs that leads away from tension to a peaceful place. Begin walking up the stairs. Breathe in and count "one" as you step onto the first stair, then exhale. Breathe in and count "two" as you step onto the second stair, then exhale. Continue counting to ten as you slowly "walk" up the stairs toward your inner peace—and away from outer tension.

I can remain calm and serene in the face of any crisis because of my strong inner peace. Today, I'll believe that all is well with me, and it will be so.

When health is absent, wisdom cannot reveal itself, art cannot manifest, strength cannot fight, wealth becomes useless, and intelligence cannot be applied.
                                                    —HEROPHILUS

You know the "rules" for optimal health: Eat right. Don't smoke. Keep stress to a minimum. Drink moderately. Get regular checkups. But even though the rules make sense, and you may do everything you can to heed them, that doesn't guarantee you won't die young or be diagnosed with a life-threatening disease.

When Lee Remick, the stunning Hollywood actress, fell victim to cancer, the disease drained her physical health, but her mental and spiritual health remained strong and provided a valuable perspective on living. She said that her ordeal taught her to slow down and relax her once-rigid standards. Michael Landon, the actor who died of cancer the day before Remick, expressed similar sentiments. When asked to give his advice on life, he replied, *Live every minute, guys.*

Today, you can appreciate all aspects of your good health—physical, mental, and spiritual—while you have it. You can do the things you've always wanted to do but have avoided because *there's no time.* You can tear up the list of all the things you feel you have to do and spend the day doing what you want to do—bird-watching, going on a picnic, or talking to an old friend.

Today, I'll experience my physical, mental, and spiritual health. I'll appreciate each moment and enjoy my life.

The eternal quest of the individual human being is to shatter his loneliness.

—NORMAN COUSINS

Traveling alone can evoke great feelings of loneliness. It can move you away from loved ones, familiar places, and the things that make you feel secure.

Yet spending time in the company of strangers—on airplanes, in restaurants, or while sightseeing—can be a positive and enjoyable experience when you're able to reach out and start conversations. The easiest way to start a dialogue with a stranger is simply to smile and say hello. By taking the risk of being the first to say something, you send the message: *I'm friendly and interested in communicating if you are, too.*

If the response you receive seems positive, you can then start a conversation. Notice something the stranger is wearing or carrying and ask a question based on it. For example, if you see someone carrying a novel, you can comment, *I haven't read that book yet, but I hear it's good. What do you think of it?* Or if someone is walking a dog, you could ask the dog's name and its breed.

By breaking the ice and finding out more about the other person, you may be able to establish a casual acquaintance that can make your time away from home relaxing and enjoyable.

Today, I have a choice: I can be alone or I can be with others. I can reach out of my loneliness and take the initiative in starting a conversation.

Complaining—bitching, moaning, kvetching, *griping, and carrying on—is a terrific and constructive thing to do. You've just got to learn how to do it* right.

—BARBARA SHER

Even though you may like to say, *I'm not a complainer,* the truth is that it isn't human nature to feel accepting of everything and everybody all the time. From time to time, life is going to make you angry, disappointed, frightened, and confused. So what do you do when you have feelings that aren't directed at any one particular person or thing?

You still need to let the feelings out and keep them from building up inside. How do you do it? You can take a cue from the movie *Network:* Open your car window or a window in your apartment or home and cry out, *I'm mad as hell and I'm not going to take it anymore!* Or you can throw a "paper fit," using writing to replicate crying, yelling, throwing things, or stamping your feet. First write a list of the things that really bug you—you can't stand waiting for utility companies to make service calls, or you're fed up with all the traffic. Then say how each thing makes you feel—frustrated, unhappy, bored, and so on. After you've had your paper fit, tear up the paper, take a deep breath, and focus your attention on less-stressful things.

Today, I'll let go of the things that really bug me so I can be more positive. First I'll gripe, then I'll grin!

I know I am somebody's friend if I think "Oh, isn't it wonderful that such and such a thing should be happening to so and so," and feel happy for him or her.
                              —CARLO MARIA GUILINI

Sharing and experiencing another person's joy is what friendship is all about. Yet do you sometimes feel jealousy and envy over the fortunes of a friend or restrained comfort over a successful friend's small misfortunes?

It may not always be easy to be happy for what others get or are given. A coworker and friend who earns a promotion you wanted, a college buddy who marries into a wealthy family, or a friend who asks someone else to share a vacation can make you feel hurt and resentful. You may let such feelings build until you harbor a secret desire to see your friend fail in some small way.

While such thoughts aren't uncommon—it's only natural to want what others want from time to time— they can impact on a friendship by building a wall of tension between you. So how can you work through such feelings when they occur? Think of how you'd like your friend to react or treat you if the situation were reversed. Then apply that same treatment to others. Remember, to have a friend, you need to be a friend.

Today, I'll strive to treat my friends well and to share in all their successes.

*[Children] refuse to appreciate the gravity of our mon-
umental concerns, while we forget that if we were to
become more like children, our concerns might not be
so monumental.*

—CONRAD HYERS

Comedian Dom DeLuise talks about a time when
nothing made him laugh: *Everything was wrong—life
was hopeless and I was feeling useless.* When his son
asked what he wanted for Christmas, DeLuise replied,
Happiness—and you can't give it to me. But on Christmas day, his son handed him a piece of paper with the
word HAPPINESS printed on it. His son declared:
See, Dad, I can give you happiness!

Children can be a valuable resource when you feel
unhappy or overburdened. They look at the world differently, because to them everything's a game and the
world's one huge playground.

Your burdens can become less weighty when you
can learn how to play, too. Try to look at the world
through a child's eyes. Marvel at the wonders of the
world, both big and small, from the space shuttle to an
anthill to the changing colors of leaves in the fall. Be
with children and play with them, or observe them
playing. See their complete lack of inhibition and self-
criticism. Then find yourself a "buddy"—someone to
have fun with. Play can make your larger upsets seem
smaller, expand your limited picture, and get you to
see more than your problems or pressures.

*Today, I'll keep in mind that play is an activity that has
no purpose other than to relax my mind and body.*

There are people who learn, who are open to what happens around them, who listen, who hear the lessons. . . . The question to ask is not whether you are a success or a failure, but whether you are a learner or a nonlearner.
—CAROLE HYATT AND LINDA GOTTLIEB

Suppose you were walking down the street when someone came up to you and said, *I want you for the U.S.A. Olympic volleyball team,* or *I need a president for the new company I'm starting.* While either one of these offers might represent a dream come true for you, chances are you probably don't have the skills or training to assume such a position immediately.

Expecting to be able to jump into anything—graduate school, a new job, an intimate relationship, or raising a family—and then to handle it with all the grace, skill, and ease of someone who has been doing it for years is highly unrealistic. It takes a great deal of time to develop necessary skills, as well as dedication and perseverance to build confidence.

But you don't have to give up your long-range goals or dreams because of this. Instead, you can become a "sorcerer's apprentice." Hang around with someone who has achieved what you want so you can watch them and help them—and receive a valuable education at the same time.

Today, I'll say to someone: "I've watched your work for a long time, and I'd really like to learn from you." My serious interest and willingness can help me learn from those I admire.

*But just because you haven't led a normal life doesn't
mean you can't lead a healthy life. Just because you
have a . . . handicap . . . doesn't mean that you can't be
happy; it just means that it takes a lot of work to figure
out how to do that.*   —JODIE FOSTER

One day a blind woman with a cane attempted to cross
a busy street. As she stepped off the sidewalk, she
bumped into a car that was parked in the crosswalk. *Who
owns this car?* she demanded. *Get someone here to move
it right away. Can't anyone notice that I'm blind?*

In the midst of her ranting, another blind person
tapped her on the arm. *Excuse me,* he said, *but my dog
and I would be happy to take you across the street.* The
woman shook her head. *I'm waiting until the owner of
this car returns,* she said. *I've got to make this person
realize that this was a wrong thing to do.*

*The man smiled. I agree with you. It was wrong. But
rather than waste your time and get all worked up over
something you can't change, why not just cross the
street safely with us?*

Having a visible or invisible handicap can add a
great deal of stress to living. You have to work extra
hard doing things most people take for granted, such
as crossing the street, watching a movie, or talking on
the phone. Yet rather than bemoan such difficulties,
you can be thankful for the small gifts others are willing
to give—a guiding arm, a door held open, or a seat
offered on a crowded subway.

*Today, I'll be willing to let go of the actions or com-
ments of the insensitive and accept the help of those
who care.*

When you aim for perfection, you discover it's a moving target.

—GEORGE FISHER

Do you believe you must be unfailingly competent and almost perfect in everything you undertake? Do you believe in the existence of perfect love and a perfect relationship? Do you believe that your worth as a person depends on how well you achieve the things you do?

Such perfectionistic thoughts are unrealistic. A more rational assessment of your worth depends on your capacity to be fully alive and human. Belief in the ideal partner and unwavering love often results in unhappiness and resentment in the search for the "perfect fit." And believing you must always be flawless can make you hesitant to try anything for fear of failure.

Promoting realistic thinking involves disputing your previous ideas. Think about one of your beliefs about perfectionism—for example, *I should be able to do everything right.* Then ask yourself: *Is there any rational support for this idea? Does any evidence exist that supports its truth?* Discovering that your previous ideas regarding perfection are of your own creation can help you let go of your need always to hit the mark of perfection—and to hit whatever mark that's right for you.

Today, I'll keep in mind the thought that "All humans are fallible creatures." I'll expect to make mistakes and experience failure from time to time.

Of course there is such a thing as a level or risk that is unacceptable. But in America the threshold of tolerable risk has now been set so low ... If America's new timorousness had prevailed among the Vikings, their ships with the bold prows but frail hulls would have been declared unseaworthy.

—HENRY FAIRLIE

The desire for risk-free living—where you maintain a consistent schedule in a predictable environment—can lead to sterility rather than serenity. Everyone, at one time or another, needs at least one thing in their lives that provides them with a certain degree of stimulation, challenge, and change.

Risk taking is essential to progress, as the phrase *Nothing ventured, nothing gained* espouses. But it may be a lot easier to parrot these words than to participate in actually making the phrase come true.

To overcome the fear of change and disruption in your life caused by taking a risk, begin with small ones—for example, taking one college course rather than enrolling in an entire program, or going to a social event with a friend rather than going alone. As you take each small risk and experience the changes it brings, you'll become more comfortable taking bigger risks that result in bigger changes in your life.

Today, I'll look forward to the excitement and challenge of risk taking to spice up my life and give it flavor and meaning.

Mountains should be climbed with as little effort as possible and without desire....Then, when you're no longer thinking ahead, each footstep isn't just a means to an end but a unique event in itself.
—ROBERT M. PIRSIG

Striving for a goal is like climbing a mountain: while you may think that climbing as quickly as possible will help you reach your goal faster, it often results in fatigue or costly error. So you need to exercise caution in your effort to reach the top.

Rather than push your progress to a goal, you might like to visualize your journey to the goal as a climb up a gorgeous mountain. First you need to pay attention to your reserves of energy. When you're feeling refreshed and restless, speed up your climb. But if you become winded, be ready to slow down.

It's even okay to take a moment to savor your journey to the top. Rather than keep your focus solely on what lies ahead, take time to look around you. Notice the view, breathe deeply of the clean air, and taste the pristine spring waters that flow down the mountainside.

Today, on your quest to achieve an ambitious goal, remember that you can take a break, rest, go for a walk, or do something different for a while. Then return to your journey up the mountainside with renewed energy and insight.

Today, I won't push myself more than I need to on my journey to reach a goal. There's much I can notice and enjoy on my way there.

Not in a perturbed mind does wisdom spring.
                                   —WISDOM OF KAPILA

Although problems constitute a normal part of life, it is possible to solve most problems rather than let them upset you. The key to doing so lies in the way you approach any difficult or perplexing situation. If you believe a problem will get the better of you, it will. But if you believe there's a solution to every problem, then you'll be able to find it.

To become an effective problem solver, don't respond to your problem right away. Ineffective problem solvers tend to be impatient and quick to give up if a solution isn't immediately apparent. Then they become angry when their problem isn't solved after their first ineffectual try.

A good problem solver is first able to identify what the real problem is—perhaps it's not related to a present situation such as being stuck in traffic, but to something else, like the previous night's argument at home.

Once you identify the real problem, think of as many ideas as you can to solve it. The greater the number of solutions, the greater the likelihood of your being able to find the best solution.

The real problem isn't what's done or not done, how it happens, or why it happens—it is how I respond. Today, I'll be a positive, rather than frustrated, problem solver.

Making the simple complicated is commonplace; making the complicated simple, awesomely simple, that's creativity.

—CHARLES MINGUS

Are you often overwhelmed with responsibilities or an impossible work load? If so, you may have so many pressing demands that it may be difficult to rank all your tasks in order of importance and to attend to them in a logical, orderly fashion.

When you're under this kind of pressure, the first thing you need to do is list every one of your priorities. From work to family responsibilities to social obligations to personal needs, compile all the things you need to do in a week. Next, separate your list into those things that are most essential and need to be accomplished right away ("top-drawer priority"), those things that can be put off for a short time, but are still important ("middle-drawer priority"), and those things that can easily be put off for a longer time with no harm done.

Once your lists are prioritized, rank the top-drawer items in the order in which they should be accomplished, from most critical to least critical. Then focus your attention on the top-drawer items and, when they're accomplished, work your way down through the rest of the drawers.

Today, I'll make signs that remind me of my top-drawer priority projects. I'll place them in conspicuous spots around the home or office so I don't neglect them.

Be aware of yourself and validate your experience. Pay attention to your world, what's happening, and why.
                                          —ALEXANDRA G. KAPLAN

Imagine you have the opportunity to take a trip across the country. You can stop wherever you'd like, spend however long you want at any location, and have no set timetable. Are you going to focus solely on your destination and simply drive there? Or are you going to let go of the need to arrive anywhere at any particular time and enjoy the scenery, the people you meet along the way, and the places you linger in?

Every day you have the opportunity to go on a "cross-country" trip—a once-in-a-lifetime, twenty-four-hour adventure that'll never be repeated any other day. How do you wish to spend the time? By enjoying every minute and stopping to savor every unique opportunity, or by simply focusing on your goals and trying to achieve them?

Today, you can reach any destination or any goal you set for yourself. But how you do so will determine how enjoyable and memorable today will be. The runner who only looks down at the road will surely reach her destination, but won't have the same experience as the runner who looks at the road as well as notices the sights, sounds, and smells around her. Today, make an effort to notice one person's face, one facet of nature, or one event on your journey to tomorrow.

Today, I'll take time to notice what's around me instead of just what's ahead of me.

There is no more miserable human being than one in whom nothing is habitual but indecision.
—WILLIAM JAMES

Do you have great difficulty making a decision? Perhaps you were blamed and criticized for choices you made as a child, which may have led you to decide early on to leave decision making to others. But the problem with this is that most people won't know exactly what you want or need. Or perhaps choices you've made have resulted in mistakes or failures you feel will continue if you make other decisions. So you may procrastinate or avoid decision making today. Yet whether you realize it or not, you are making decisions every minute of your life. Even deciding not to decide is a decision.

There are ways to overcome such decision-making paralysis. One is called the "quick pick" method. With quick pick, you use any of the following guidelines to make a relatively unimportant decision instantly: Pick the one that comes first in the alphabet (grocery shopping instead of ironing); pick the one that takes the least amount of time to accomplish (order takeout rather than cook a meal); or pick the one with the most letters (go to a museum rather than a movie). Although the quick pick method of decision making may seem simplistic, it can take away some fears and even motivate you to make more important decisions in your life.

I know that making decisions isn't always easy. But today, I'll try to make at least one.

I can't write a book commensurate with Shakespeare,
but I can write a book by me.
                                                    —SIR WALTER RALEIGH

When you were a child, did you want to emulate
your favorite heroes, wishing you could be as strong,
as beautiful, as smart, or as self-sufficient as they were?
Do you still sometimes put people up on pedestals and
wish you could be just like them?

In striving for imitation of others, you neglect your
own uniqueness. By looking around you at what everyone else has, you ignore what you have. In focusing
your energy and attention on others rather than on
yourself, you hinder your ability to discover your own
skills and talents.

Rather than envy the qualities others possess, why
not discover your own unique qualities and talents that
make you who you are? To find out what they are,
create a "victory list"—a compilation of your successes
and the things you've done in your life that have given
you great satisfaction. A victory could be major, such
as leaving a bad marriage or changing jobs, or it could
be a daily achievement such as making time for yourself. It doesn't matter whether the victories are big or
small or how they compare to what others have done.
What matters is how they make you feel.

I know it's not relaxing to strive to be anyone else but
myself. Today, I'll be more comfortable with who I am
and not stressed about who I'd like to be.

I couldn't wait for success . . . so I went ahead without it.

—JONATHAN WINTERS

You can learn much from people who have consistently conquered stress and achieved the things they wanted to. What these athletes, astronauts, survivors of life-threatening illnesses, managers, world leaders, writers, and performers all have in common is the attitude that they either grow or die. People who successfully manage stress don't stay in one place or do things in the same way. Rather, they strive to grow and be creative in all they do, whether their tasks require physical, mental, or creative skills.

To become more creative at conquering stress, you need to break out of your routine—to do something out of the ordinary so you can add freshness and vitality to your life. How can you do this? Today, think about something you've always wanted to do. You might think big—*I've always dreamed of being an astronaut*—or small—*I'd love to browse in that antique shop I pass on the way to work.* Then do something to help bring you closer to your dream. Spend your lunch hour antiquing or plan to visit Cape Kennedy, NASA, or the National Air and Space Museum of the Smithsonian during your next vacation. By focusing not only on what you have to do in your life but also on what you want to do, you can creatively conquer stress.

Each day, I'll allow time to do things I haven't done before so I can ease the stress of my routine.

When one's thoughts are neither frivolous nor flippant,
when one's thoughts are neither stiff-necked nor stupid,
but rather, are harmonious—they habitually render
physical calm and deep insight.

—HILDEGARDE OF BINGEN

Is your mind often filled with unwanted thoughts
that leave you filled with worry, doubt, or dread? Such
thoughts are often the catalysts for stressful emotional
and physical responses.

Your thoughts may take the form of self-doubt; for
example, *I'll never be able to do this job right.* Or they
may be based on insecurity: *I'm too plain to get a date.*
Or they may revolve around your fears: *Look at this
airplane's wing shake; I bet there's something wrong.*

Stopping such thoughts can help you eliminate many
stressful responses. How do you do so? First, become
aware of how you think in situations that produce negative thoughts. Imagine a situation in which a stressful
thought is likely to occur, such as while you're sitting
in an airplane waiting for takeoff. As you begin to think
stressful thoughts, interrupt them by saying, *Stop!* to
yourself, by snapping your fingers, or by standing up.
Then replace the stressful thought with a more positive
one; for example, *This airline has the safest record in
the industry.* By practicing thought stopping twice a
day for a week, you can begin to think more sensibly
and less stressfully.

*Today, I'll believe in mind over matter. I'll substitute a
positive, relaxing statement for any negative, stressful
thought I have.*

Romance isn't always pretty dresses and guys that don't sweat. Sometimes it's about threat and anxiety and fear and walking through minefields together.
—JAMES WOODS

When difficulties arise in your intimate relationship, are you able to communicate with care and concern? Or are you quick to react in anger and distance yourself from the conflict?

True harmony in relationships doesn't happen without each person being committed to resolving discord. It's not enough to say, *Let's just get along.* You have to be willing to take the next step in order to do more than just keep the peace.

Relationship conflicts are best resolved by using the "three A's"—awareness, acceptance, and action. First, know what it is that you want or need, and then listen to what your partner wants or needs. From this awareness, you can build acceptance by taking the focus off yourself and concentrating on how your partner thinks and feels about the conflict.

Finally, take action to restore harmony. Choose a resolution that gives each person some of what he or she wants or needs so that both of you can benefit from the time and energy that was put into working through the conflict.

Today, I'll remember that conflicts between loved ones are best resolved through positive reactions rather than negative actions.

*Do not confuse notoriety and fame with greatness . . .
greatness can crown the head of a janitor just as readily
as it can come to someone of high rank.*
                                    —SHERMAN G. FINESILVER

The well-known *Peanuts* comic strip often features
Snoopy in a variety of identities that made the canine
feel great about himself, such as a world-famous writer
(*It was a dark and stormy night . . .*), a world-famous
World War I pilot (*Curse you, Red Baron!*), and "Joe
Cool," the big man on campus. Yet in his struggle for
greatness, no role makes him as great as the wonderful
companion he is to all the *Peanuts* gang.

Greatness isn't symbolized by salary, a rank, or a
recognition you receive. So moving up a corporate ladder, raising famous children, operating a successful
business, or chairing a well-regarded organization
won't necessarily make you great.

Greatness is a measure of one's spirit, not a result of
one's rank in human affairs. A four-star general, a president, an athlete, or a renowned musician is no greater
than any other human being; you too can be as heroic.

To see this, identify a passion you have—one that
few see but to which you bring your spirit to learn,
achieve, and reach for greatness. It may be an old car
you're lovingly restoring, delicious meals you prepare,
or beautiful poems you create that are your signs of
greatness.

*Fame and fortune don't necessarily mean greatness. To-
day, I'll focus on my achievements that give me the feeling of greatness.*

All miseries derive from not being able to sit quietly in
a room alone.

—BLAISE PASCAL

When you're alone, what's the first thing you do? Turn on the radio or the TV? Call a friend? Invite someone over? Make plans to go out?

Silence may be an uncomfortable experience for you. So perhaps you fill your rooms with noise so you don't feel alone, or cram your calendar with events so you aren't left with nothing to do and nobody to do it with. But whenever you choose to drown out the sounds of silence or escape from them, what you're really doing is drowning out and running away from another sound—that of your inner self.

You can't learn to think, meditate, write in a journal, or relax with noise constantly bombarding you or with people constantly surrounding you. To learn to sit comfortably alone in silence, you need to try it in small steps. You can start with five minutes, then build to ten, to fifteen, then to a half hour or more. During your time alone, talk to yourself with upbeat, inspirational words rather than lonely, self-pitying messages. By gently easing into quiet moments, you can allow your inner self the time and space in which to grow.

Today, I'll spend time alone in silence. I can create my
own diversions, explore new options, and use the stim-
ulation of my inner self for entertainment.

We're all proud of making little mistakes. It gives us the feeling we don't make any big ones.
                                        —ANDREW A. ROONEY

Do you know that Babe Ruth struck out 1,330 times in his baseball career? But if he had concentrated on his little mistakes—his outs instead of his hits—he would have never set nearly fifty baseball records, many of which still stand today.

Where did you get the idea that you're supposed to be error-free? From parents who were less than perfect? From friends who often made mistakes themselves? From bosses who considered themselves omnipotent?

In a certain sense, making mistakes can be very liberating because they open you up to new possibilities. Mistakes are also great teachers; they can help you learn what doesn't work so you can figure out what does.

To accept your ability to make mistakes is like taking a giant step toward peace of mind. You can take the first step today by creating a more positive outlook when you make a mistake. Think, *This didn't turn out the way I wanted it to. Why? What can I do differently next time?* Then, like Babe Ruth, keep swinging until you succeed.

Today, I'll accept that my mistakes can accelerate my growth. I'll apply the lessons I learn from the errors I make so I can make my next attempt more successful.

Dear World . . . I am leaving because I am bored.
—GEORGE SANDERS

George Sanders was a man who had everything: four wives, more than ninety film appearances, and an Oscar for his performance as a cynical drama critic in *All About Eve.* But all of that wasn't enough to keep him interested. On April 25, 1972, he swallowed five bottles of Nembutal and penned his infamous suicide note as a farewell to a world that bored him to death.

How often are you bored with the people, places, or things in your life? But what do you do about it? Too often people complain that they're bored, but don't do anything more than that.

It's up to you to change your feelings of boredom into feelings of interest. If you're bored sitting in front of the TV, then turn off the TV and pick up a book or go for a walk. If you're bored with your work, then scan the classified ads for a more interesting job or enlist the help of a career counselor. If you're bored in your intimate relationship, then do something out of the ordinary—make reservations at a bed-and-breakfast inn for the weekend or plan a surprise party. Or if you're just bored in general, renew your interest in the arts. Rent a classic film, visit a museum, enroll in a painting class, or reread an old favorite. Rather than be bored to death, you can become more interested in life.

It's my responsibility to overcome the boredom in my life. Today, I'll take the initiative and explore what's available to capture my interest.

*Most of us have very little idea of how we actually
spend our time—and it can be pretty hair-raising to find
out.*

—BARBARA SHER

Do you realize that the way you spend your day is
often the way you spend your life? If you're a procras-
tinator—someone who spends more time worrying,
planning, revising, or renegotiating rather than actually
doing—then chances are you'll spend the rest of your
life wasting time. If you're a Superman or a Wonder
Woman—someone who spends your time doing, doing, doing—then chances are you'll spend the rest of
your life in a constant state of agitated achievement.
But if you're able to balance your planning time with
your doing time, then chances are the rest of your life
will be similarly balanced and enjoyable.

To cease your procrastination or ease your superhuman tendencies, set up a Today-Tomorrow calendar.
Create one large box for each day, then divide them
into thirds for morning, afternoon, and evening. Write
the activities you need to accomplish by today or tomorrow. If you tend to procrastinate, you'll find that
putting things off until tomorrow will make tomorrow's
schedule too full. If you're a doer, you'll discover that
spreading your activities over two days can leave you
with more unstructured time. Either way, you'll benefit!

*Before I can work with the time I have, I have to be
sure where it goes. Then I can make the changes I want
in the time I have.*

*Measure wealth not by the things you have, but by the
things you have for which you would not take money.*
—Anonymous

You may feel a certain sense of security knowing that
if you ever got into a financial bind, you could sell your
house, car, jewelry, or other valuable possessions. Yet
what price would you put on the other things in your
life that also make you feel secure—your relationship,
children, skills, pet, or health? How would you feel if
you lost one of them?

Sometimes it's only when you think about your definition of wealth that you can see the things that are
truly valuable to you. Those things that cost nothing or
are so dear that no amount of money could replace
them comprise a more meaningful measurement of
your wealth.

Imagine what your life would be like if all you had
was money in the bank—and no love and companionship, no photo albums filled with treasured memories,
or no reassuring spiritual belief.

Today, reflect on how wealthy you are—not in terms
of dollars and cents, but in the things that can't be
bought. Just for today, forget about the pursuit of
money and consider instead how enriched your life is
because of something or someone dear to you.

*Today, I won't treat money as the most important thing
in my life. There are so many other things I have to be
grateful for that are more meaningful.*

And remember, we all stumble, every one of us. That's why it's a comfort to go hand in hand.
—EMILY KIMBROUGH

Coping with stress depends not only on your inner resources, but also on the connections you have with people who are part of your life. Just as you need professional support from coworkers and mentors, so too do you need personal relationships from which you can receive emotional support.

The greater the number of people available who can offer help and advice during times of crisis or difficulty, the healthier you're likely to be. Those in self-help groups such as Alcoholics Anonymous and Overeaters Anonymous can attest to this fact; they know the benefit of having people to call when they crave a drink or food, who help them make it through another day sober or without bingeing.

So it's a good idea to build a support network before you need it rather than try to find one when you're in crisis. Now's the time to create your Help Line—a listing of telephone numbers you can use during a time of difficulty. Include your family members, close friends, a partner, a college roommate, and others who act like family. Then keep the numbers handy for future support.

I know I'm not alone. My family and intimate friends take time for me when I need it, and I do the same for them.

Life is, for most of us, a continuous process of getting used to things we hadn't expected.

—ANONYMOUS

The dinner party preparations for the evening were moving along as planned. The hostess dashed frantically about the house and kitchen all morning. By early afternoon, she beamed at the delicious dishes that were cooking, surveyed the well-decorated table, and smiled at her immaculately clean home.

But as the afternoon wore on, snow began to fall. Driving became treacherous, and the dinner guests were delayed. The food went from perfectly done to overcooked. The candles on the table dripped wax as they burned low. And when the guests finally arrived, they tramped snow and dirt all over the glistening floor.

Like the hostess, you may face times when even your best-laid plans go awry—the copying machine breaks down before an important business meeting, a highway accident snarls traffic on your way to an interview, or you lose a sales slip for an item you want to return. How you react to the unexpected can determine how well you cope with the stress of change.

When something out of the ordinary occurs, ask: *Is there anything I could have done to have prevent it?* If there was, then use that information to help things run more smoothly next time. But if not, it's best to let go and just accept the present situation.

Today, I'll remember there are many things out of my control. So I'll do my best to handle what I can control—myself.

Fall seven times, stand up eight.

—JAPANESE PROVERB

In a basketball game, a player who takes one shot and misses doesn't walk off the court and give up. He keeps playing and shooting. Likewise, to be successful in life, no matter what you do, you need to exert a continuous and constant effort.

Perseverance is an effort that comes from the heart. So when you fail or fall short of your expectations or desires, perseverance can give you the stamina to try over and over again until you achieve what you want.

But like the basketball player, you may find that it's easier to persevere when your goal can be shared with others. So why not enlist others for support and encouragement? Ask a dieting friend or a friend who wants to quit smoking to be your "buddy" so you can share your triumphs as well as your setbacks. Form a class study group when you decide to go back to school to make writing papers and studying for exams less intimidating. Ask those who live around you to join you in forming a crime-watch patrol so you can safeguard your neighborhood.

Perseverance doesn't necessarily mean "going it alone." It can mean balancing self-guidance with valuable support.

No one can accomplish everything alone. Today, I'll use material as well as human resources to help me move closer to my goals.

*This morning I woke up to a cold, miserable, rainy day.
So I prayed for the strength to get up, get dressed, and
run five miles. Then I rolled over and went back to
sleep. I had prayed for strength but received wisdom
instead.*   —ANONYMOUS

How much tension and stress can you handle? Is
there a limit on the number of questions you can answer or the quantity of problems you can solve? How
many projects can you juggle and how crowded can
your schedule be? When is enough *enough?*

Determining when you've reached your limit involves two parts. First, you need to know what your
limits are. This can vary on a daily or even hourly basis.
Sometimes you may feel energetic, creative, and capable of handling anything that comes your way. But
other times it may be all you can do to open the mail
or return one phone call. Knowing your limits means
staying aware of how your mind and body are handling
the events of the day and being able to "read" when
you're becoming fatigued or short-tempered or when
you're losing your concentration.

Second, you need to respect your limits. It's one
thing to say, *You know, I think I've about reached my
limit.* But it's another to say, *I've reached my limit, so
I'm going to take a time-out until I feel capable of handling this.* By communicating your limits, you—as well
as others—can accept and respect them.

*Today, I'll be aware of when I've reached my limit.
Then I'll take time to stretch, move around, or focus on
something completely different.*

It does seem so pleasant to talk with an old acquaintance who knows what you know.... Conversation has got to have some root in the past, or else you have to explain every remark you make, and it wears a person out.

—SARAH ORNE JEWETT

In this highly mobile society, where people frequently move from job to job or neighborhood to neighborhood, it can be hard to form close and lasting friendships. Socializing may involve coworkers, neighbors, or those connected by a common purpose rather than those who know who you are. So you may structure activities around events such as movies, parties, or athletics rather than around intimate times created by sharing coffee or taking a walk.

When was the last time you talked with someone who really knew you—a childhood friend, a college roommate, or a coworker from a former job? Remember how wonderful your conversations used to be or how easy it was to spend time together?

You always have the opportunity to reconnect with close friends from the past so you can recapture the intimacy you once shared. They may be only a phone call, letter, or short drive away. Why not make the effort to get back in touch and reminisce about old times?

Today, I'll recall what it was like to talk to or be with someone who really knew me. I'll make it a point to stay in touch with my close friends on a regular basis.

Compassion for myself is the most powerful healer of them all.

— THEODORE ISAAC RUBIN

It may be difficult to learn and practice new habits on your own, especially when the rewards for your efforts may seem minimal at first. Losing a couple of pounds, going a few hours without a cigarette, taking a short walk, or meditating a couple of times in one week may not immediately result in the desired new and improved you. So it may be tempting to resort to an old behavior or habit—even if it's having just one cigarette, eating a tiny sliver of chocolate cake, or going one day without exercising or meditating.

Examine your reasons for wanting to break a good habit. Is smoking one cigarette what you really want to do, or is there something else going on—nervousness over an upcoming work presentation or conflict between you and your partner? Is a piece of cake what you really want, or is it just hard to watch everyone else help themselves to it? Do you really want to forget about going for a walk or meditating, or are you just feeling down in the dumps?

Once you examine your reasons, then you can make your choice whether or not to break your habit—and feel good about it.

Today, when I slack off on a commitment I've made to myself, I'll examine why—and give myself reasons, not excuses.

*If time be of all things most precious, wasting time must
be the greatest prodigality, since lost time is never found
again.*

—BENJAMIN FRANKLIN

Do you feel like you waste a great deal of time each
day—time that takes you away from doing responsible
as well as recreational activities?

Starting today, you can learn to make more time.
First, assess how much time each day you spend
watching the biggest time-killer of all, television. Think
about cutting out a half hour to an hour of television
watching each day or use a videocassette recorder to
record your favorite shows. Then watch them at another time, fast-forwarding through commercials.

Second, throw away all the mail you possibly can by
simply scanning it and then tossing it. Third, incorpo-
rate planning time with time you spend doing other
things. For example, plan dinner while you vacuum, or
organize an important business letter in your mind on
your commute.

Finally, block off the "escape routes" that lead you
to waste time: daydreaming, puttering aimlessly around
the house, socializing on the phone, doing tiny and
unimportant tasks rather than the big and important
ones, or running out for ice cream or other sudden
indulgences instead of facing the things you need to
do.

*Today, I'll make up my mind just to get things done.
I'll stop wasting my time doing mindless or procrastinating activities.*

Death, when it approaches, ought not to take one by surprise. It should be part of the full expectancy of life.
—MURIEL SPARK

At the end of Dostoyevsky's *The Brothers Karamazov*, a young man dies. After the funeral, his friend Alyosha reminds those gathered of the custom of eating pancakes. The purpose is to mix a little sweetness with the bitterness of death.

But when you can only see death as a terrible loss, it will continually cause you pain; when you can only see death as a great sorrow, you'll never be able to experience a little sweetness with the bitterness. In either case, it will be hard for you to accept how much death is part of life.

The process of living includes many dimensions. Some are joyful. Some are not. Yet if you can allow some lighter moments in ceremonies such as funerals or on anniversaries of loss, such events will become a celebration of a life lived rather than just the mourning of a life lost.

Focus on the wonderful memories you have of someone dear, the accomplishments made during that person's life, or a favorite story or humorous anecdote. It is possible to have an attitude of lightness toward everything in life—including death.

Today, I can mix laughter with tears, celebration with suffering, and sweetness with bitterness.

*Flatter me, and I may not believe you. Criticize me, and
I may not like you. Ignore me, and I may not forgive
you. Encourage me, and I will not forget you.*
                                     —WILLIAM ARTHUR WARD

Wouldn't it be nice if every once in a while someone
said, *You did a great job; You're a terrific parent;* or
You're the best friend anyone could have. But you can't
always expect others to give notice or praise. In fact,
waiting for or even depending on words of encouragement can be a waste of time.

If the recognition of others is something you thrive
on, then not getting it can lead you to belittle or con-
demn your efforts with thoughts such as, *See, I must
not have done a good job; otherwise, she would have
said something.* But if you can get into the habit of
using encouraging self-talk, you can provide yourself
with the recognition you deserve. Then you can feel
good about yourself, the things you do, and the decisions you make so when words of praise do come from
others, they're an added bonus.

Whenever you accomplish a task—from a complex
project like designing a year-long marketing plan to a
simple project like baking cookies—tell yourself, *That's
a job well done.* Then point out something you particularly like about what you did and be proud of your
accomplishment.

*Today, I'll believe that I'm an important person—no
matter what others say or don't say—because of the
things I say.*

. . . to have a crisis, and act upon it, is one thing. To dwell in perpetual crisis is another.
—BARBARA GRIZZUTI HARRISON

Every crisis has a negative side and a positive side. The negative side is that sometimes a crisis can seem so big or serious that it can be difficult to ride out or handle. So rather than work through it, you may despair and stay mired in it.

But the positive side is that it can push you out of your fear-based paralysis and motivate you to take action. Then, when you see that you *can* make it through the rough time, you learn to trust that even the most difficult things can be faced.

In addition, a crisis can also present you with unknown opportunities and a chance for change and growth. By recognizing that a crisis is something you can survive as well as something that presents a positive challenge, you will begin to learn to respond to each new crisis promptly and effectively.

The best approach to any crisis is one of rationality, rather than irrationality. Say, *No matter how bad this seems to be, I know I can get through it.* Then think of at least three responses to the question *What can I do about this?* Choose one—and put it into action!

Today, I'll respond calmly and sensibly to any crisis so I can move up and out of the crisis and move ahead to face other challenges.

*The change of one simple behavior can affect other be-
haviors and thus change many things.*

—JEAN BAER

A pebble thrown into a pond changes the pond for
a short time as the ripples circle outward to the surrounding shore. So, too, can a change you make in
yourself ripple outward and impact upon other things
and people in your life.

Imagine what would happen if you set this behavior-
changing goal: *For today, I will not raise my voice—
no matter how angry I get or how much I want to
scream.* How would those around you respond to your
new way of behaving? Your child may accidentally spill
the milk at breakfast and cringe in expectation of your
usual blowup, but would instead be told, *That's okay.
Let me help you clean it up.* Or your partner, who made
plans to work late without telling you, may expect to
face your usual angry tirade. But instead you'd respond, *I wish you'd check with me next time this happens, okay?*

Changes can alter you, as well as your life, in many
positive ways. In addition to making you healthier and
happier, they can bring you closer to others, make you
a more productive worker, and help you use your time
and energy more effectively.

*Today, I'll start making changes in my life. I'll set a
small goal for myself that will bring about a positive
change in me.*

There are no victims, only volunteers.

—ANONYMOUS

Painful situations, hurtful relationships, or memories that pinch your nerve endings don't need to imprison you or prevent you from moving on. However, most people are seldom quick to let go of their emotional pain.

Are you a victim of your own pain? You are if it's something you frequently focus on, find it hard not to talk about, or perpetuate through the choices you make. For example, if you're uncomfortable at a party, do you stay or go? If your boss asks you to work overtime when you have other plans, do you say yes or no? When someone asks you how you are, do you say, *Pretty good* or *Not so good*?

When you become obsessed with your pain, you voluntarily opt to stay in it and continue to feel it. Yet there are actions or choices you can make that can take some of the sting out of it. Rather than stay in an uncomfortable situation, leave. Excuse yourself from working overtime by explaining that you've made other plans. And try to respond positively, rather than negatively, to the inquiries of others.

You no longer need to feel pain, unless you want to. It's up to you to decide to do things that are painful for you or pleasurable.

Today, I'll choose to participate in helpful, positive, and uplifting experiences. These can help me move away from my pain.

Let me listen to me and not to them.
                                    —GERTRUDE STEIN

Does your head sometimes spin with all the advice, criticism, and opinions you receive from others? Your ears may be filled with endless guidance—all well-meaning, of course: *Your hair would look much better longer. Can't you lose some weight? Why are you still stuck in that awful job? If I were you, I'd go back to school. Why are you living in that neighborhood? You're not going to marry that person, are you?*

Perhaps you try to pay attention to all of it, striving to satisfy the desires of family and friends, business associates and social acquaintants, spiritual advisers and therapists, and countless others.

Yet to do so causes conflict and confusion between what you want and need and what others want you to want and need. In striving to think, feel, and do what others want you to do, you avoid your own individuality.

You're unique. And you have an inner voice that tells what you want and need. To choose for yourself means to listen to and respect this voice so you can say, *I do this because I want to, not because others want me to.* Acknowledging who you are means listening to and then taking your own best advice.

I'm an expert on my own life. Today, and every day, I'll be wise enough to consult myself first.

Success is loving your work.

—LIZ SMITH

Some people think of their job solely in terms of what they earn. Others think of their job as a place where their worth is measured by the amount of control they exert over others. In both cases, what they get from their work will eventually result in dissatisfaction, tension, and disappointment.

The work you do is more than just a paycheck or a position of power. Often your work teaches you something about yourself and the world around you. Leaving yourself open to experiencing such lessons can make your job—be it full-time or part-time, paid or volunteer—personally rewarding as well as challenging. For example, even if you dread giving a corporate presentation, you may do well and be given other presentations. Such an experience may help you become more at ease speaking in front of others, build your confidence, and earn you a promotion.

Today, think of at least two things your work teaches you about yourself or the world. By becoming more aware of your relationship with your work, you can better appreciate the greater, positive impact it has upon you.

Today, I'll change and grow along with my work so I can find great happiness and reward from what I do.

*Death and life, failure and success, hunger and thirst,
and many other things—these are the operation of our
appointed lot. . . . But they cannot be allowed to disturb
harmony . . .*

—CONFUCIUS

Life often places us somewhere between happiness
and sadness. Life can't always be ecstatically happy and
free from woe, just as it isn't always miserable or unhappy. Somewhere in the middle is an area where neither smiles nor sobs predominate—and where most
people live and grow.

Living life on its terms means accepting the events
life brings you without overreacting with ecstasy or depression. Experiencing an event or person who brings
you joy doesn't mean that from now on, your life is
going to be forever joyful, just as going through a sad
time doesn't mean that your life will always be this way
either.

Life isn't always a roller-coaster ride, full of incred-
ibly high highs and terribly low lows. Sometimes the
ride is surprisingly smooth and uneventful. Enjoy those
times, for those are the periods in which you are in
balance and harmony with life.

*Having a serenely harmonious area in my life is okay.
It keeps me from bouncing off walls or wailing into a
box of tissues.*

Why are things so terribly, unbearably precious that you can't enjoy them but can only wait breathless in dread....

—ANNE MORROW LINDBERGH

Stress and anxiety are especially dominant before and during the holidays. The upcoming family events, shopping, cooking, preparing for guests, and the scheduling of activities seem to take precedence over everything else in your life. Yet there are ways to seek out peace and serenity amidst all the hustle and bustle.

Instead of focusing on the things that put pressure on you, concentrate instead on the things that are positive and enjoyable. You might think: *I'm looking forward to a great meal; I can hardly wait to have time off from work; It'll be wonderful to see my family again;* or *I especially like watching the parades and the football games.*

You can also set aside time to do the things you want to do. Make plans with friends, pick up a book you've been meaning to read, or sleep late. You can put the stress of the holidays to rest by putting enjoyment first.

I'll have a nice time this holiday by putting positive energy into the events and by focusing my attention on the people and things I enjoy.

What we have to learn to do, we learn by doing.
                                                        —ARISTOTLE

As a boy, Dwight Eisenhower used to play card games with his brothers and his mother. One night, young Dwight complained that he was dealt a less-than-great hand. His mother told him, *This is only a game—and you're at home where you're surrounded by love. After you grow out of this home and go into the tough world, you'll be dealt many bad hands. What are you going to do then? Complain? If you play out the hand courageously—and clearly—you will succeed beyond your dreams.*

Doing the best with what you've got can teach you a lot about yourself. Just when you think the deck is stacked against you and there's no way of getting ahead, you may be able to put together a winning hand. Think of the times when the odds seemed to be against you. You may have had a limited amount of time to accomplish a task, a depleted checking account with mounting bills, or a difficult decision to make. How did you get through the hard time? While part of the solution may have been the result of a lucky draw—a project may have been put on hold, money owed may have been repaid, or circumstances may have dictated one solution—not all your difficulties have been solved by chance.

Playing out your hand courageously means trusting that for every losing hand you're dealt, there will always be a winning one to follow.

Today, I'll look at the cards I've been dealt and view my hand as a challenge that I can play out in a whole new way.

*The [person] who is always having . . . feelings hurt is
about as pleasant a companion as a pebble in a shoe.*
                                        —ELBERT HUBBARD

Are you overly sensitive, afraid of personal criticism,
or find that your feelings are easily hurt? Sometimes it
may seem like no one can say anything to you without
your feeling hurt, rejected, or ashamed.

Feeling overly sensitive from time to time is a normal part of living. Everyone has times when they feel
ready to cry at the drop of a hat, feel terribly defensive,
or are horribly embarrassed.

When you have such feelings, it may be hard to step
back and listen to what's being said or done objectively.
It may be difficult to discern whether someone is being
overly critical or taking out a bad day on you, or if
you're simply being much too sensitive.

But it's important to keep in mind that no matter
what someone else says, and no matter how much you
may hurt, you're still a good and worthwhile person.

The next time you feel attacked by the comments or
criticisms of others, write down what was said. Sometimes reading rather than hearing can dull the desire
to react, cool your emotional response, and help you
not take the words personally.

*Today, I can accept personal criticism and not react.
I'll remember my good qualities and use what I want
from the criticism to make these qualities even better.*

I always distrust people who know so much about what God wants them to do to their fellows.
                                        —SUSAN B. ANTHONY

Do you always strive to be the one in charge, the one who gives orders, the one who makes the decisions?

You may have been forced into the role of controller growing up in a dysfunctional home, where someone had to be in control—and it certainly wasn't your parents. Or you may have gotten into the habit of managing others without realizing it, perhaps from your sound organizational and managerial abilities.

While a certain degree of control in any situation is good, exerting control over others without considering their needs, feelings, or the good of the overall organization or family isn't. Running the lives of your children, dictating rather than delegating work duties to your employees, or supervising rather than serving on a committee can deprive others of the opportunity to make decisions, learn, and grow.

Today, strive to let go of some of your control. Ask others for their help rather than demand it. Listen to the thoughts or feelings of loved ones rather than lecture them. And decide, for at least one time, to follow the lead of another.

Today, I'll respect the rights of others to do things in their own way and in their own time.

You cannot shake hands with a clenched fist.
—INDIRA GANDHI

The guests on a popular talk show were twins who had cut off contact from one another. One guest tearfully related how her brother hadn't talked to her for two years, even though they lived two miles from each other and often passed on the street. On the show, the man told his sister why he hadn't talked to her for so long. *Because I was mad at you,* he said. *I wanted you to apologize to me and you didn't.*

Staying angry at family members, while it may not end the relationship, can severely damage your ability to connect with them. A disinherited son is still your child, but he may never come back through your door and give you a hug. An abusive mother is still your parent, even though you may not be able to let go of your anger over past hurt.

While you can't change the actions or behaviors of others that may have caused your anger, what you can do is strive to reconcile the past with acceptance and forgiveness in the present.

Ask, *What can I do to let go of my anger?* It may be helpful to write a letter you don't mail, in which you vent your feelings. Or identify some of the good qualities of the person you're mad at and recall the good times you had together before you broke apart. Such things can help you release your anger so you can have positive feelings rather than negative.

Today, rather than ask for or expect retribution, I'll strive to extend my hand to another in reconciliation.

Nothing in life is more remarkable than the unnecessary anxiety which we endure, and generally occasion ourselves.

—BENJAMIN DISRAELI

The moment Thanksgiving Day ended, a gun went off to sound the start of the race to the Christmas season. Every newspaper you read is now filled with sales pages, radio announcers count down the shopping days left, TV advertising focuses on gift and party giving, and there are crowds everywhere. So it's not surprising that you may want to scream, *I just wish Christmas was over and done with!*

At times like this, you may feel pressured to accomplish so many things in such a short period of time that you feel like an overloaded circuit. There's not only Christmas shopping and holiday preparations to handle, but also your usual daily activities. You may not even be aware of the fact that you're rushing through your activities aimlessly, giving only half your attention to others, or living more in the days to come than in today.

Now's the time to slow yourself down. Like a swimmer before a race, take a few moments simply to breathe deeply, relax your muscles, and keep in mind the phrase "*Easy does it*" before you plunge into the waters for a hectic race to the finish.

Today, I'll think of phrases or slogans to keep me calm and focused on the present. "Take your time," "One thing at a time," and "Easy does it" are just a few.

The nice thing about football is that you have a score-board to show how you've done. In other things in life, you don't. At least, not that you can see.

—CHUCK NOLL

Competition may have been drummed into you from the time you were a kid and wanted the most marbles, the most ice cream, the best paper route, or the most important position on a team. If you grew up in a dysfunctional home, your competitive drive may be even stronger. It may make you unwilling to give to others because it seems unfair to you. You may think, *Nobody ever gave me anything. I had to fight for what little I got. So there's no way I'm giving up or giving in to anyone.*

Competition may be a hard lesson to unlearn. But there aren't many traits that are so unsuitable—and so personally frustrating—as competitiveness. An unwillingness to let go of who has the biggest office, makes the most money, has the nicest home, takes the greatest vacations, or has the best kids can doom you to a life of unhappiness and inadequacy.

Not always being the winner takes nothing away from you and what it gives back by refreshing the soul, relaxing fears, and easing resentment will bring you closer to others. To stop attempting to be the best in everything, tell yourself, *I am the best at one thing— at being myself.*

Today, I'll realize that someone else's success doesn't signal my failure. My successes enrich me, just as the successes of others enrich them.

*Let each sweep the snow from his own door; let him
not be concerned about the frost on his neighbor's tiles.*
— CHINESE PROVERB

Have you ever walked through your neighborhood
and noticed a rather run-down or neglected home and
wondered, *Why doesn't someone take better care of it?*
But what you may not see is that the people living
there think of their home as warm and filled with love
on the inside so the outside doesn't matter as much to
them.

People can appraise the same situation differently.
Imagine sitting with three other people at a card table.
A letter block with "M" printed on it is in the middle
of the table. Depending on where you're sitting, you'll
see an M, an E, a W, or an angular numeral three. Yet
what you see and what everyone else sees is valid from
their perspective.

Accepting others means learning to let go of the importance you give to where you're "sitting" and how
you view things. Where others are sitting and what
they see is real—and right—for them.

Today, rather than look at the things you think others should change or do differently, focus your attention on yourself and concentrate on the things *you* can
change.

*Today, I'll use the sentiment "Different people see
things differently" as a catalyst for letting go of my need
to control what others should do.*

Enthusiasm is the yeast that makes your hopes rise to the stars. Enthusiasm is the sparkle in your eyes, the swing in your gait, the grip of your hand, the irresistible surge of will and energy to execute your ideas.
—HENRY FORD

For the 6' 9½" Boston Celtics superstar Larry Bird, who made millions playing with an amazing enthusiasm that included buzzer-beater shots and incredible lookaway passes, life hadn't always been easy. When he was eighteen, his father committed suicide. When he played college hoops, his coach told him he wasn't going to make it to the pros, and when he sought a career in professional basketball, he was told that he'd never be able to keep up. He faced countless injuries, operations to remove bone spurs from both heels, and major back surgery. Yet despite it all, Bird remained invincible on the court, a feat he attributed to a combination of enthusiastic physical and spiritual energy that made him feel like he was a champion every game.

What do you put your physical and spiritual energy into that makes you feel equally enthusiastic? Perhaps your work or being a parent does. Maybe it's going for a long run every weekend. Or it could be your skill at a particular sport or hobby. Find what gives you that thrill of being great, and then feel that thrill as much as you can!

I don't have to be a superstar to feel good about something I do. Today, I'll feel the butterflies of excitement when I do something I'm good at.

Hurry up and learn patience.

—WES SMITH

What do you think about while watching a winter storm? Do you think: *Look at all that snow I'll have to shovel. And the roads are going to be treacherous. The children will be home from school today. Oh, how I wish winter would hurry up and be over.*

Thoughts like these prevent you from enjoying the moment. You don't see the beauty of the glistening snow, hear the stillness of sounds muted by the snow, or feel the warmth of your home. You only see what lies ahead.

Imagine how your life could be different if, for every minute that passed, you stayed focused on that particular minute and all the events and people in it. That may sound pretty easy to do, but are you even aware of how often your mind strays from the present? When you're in the grocery store, you may be thinking of the next errand you have to run; in a business meeting with a client, your thoughts may be on the work piling up on your desk; when with a friend, your thoughts may be on your child's schoolwork.

One way to stay in the present is to ask, *What can I do about this right now?* when your thoughts stray. Your response can serve as a reminder to keep your thoughts in the present moment so you can appreciate it more.

Things in life happen one minute at a time. If I don't stay focused on each minute, I may miss some wonderful things.

Have you learned lessons only of those who admired you, and were tender with you, and stood aside for you? Have you not learned great lessons from those who braced themselves against you, and disputed the passage with you?

—WALT WHITMAN

As much as those who earn their living in the arts may hate to admit it, they often read critiques of their work with enthusiasm. While they may not always agree with their critics, what they discover is a more objective review of their work that they might not get from others. They usually value this review, take the advice from it they feel is constructive, and then apply that knowledge to their next work.

While you may love to hear that everything you say and do is wonderful, such an assessment really tells you little about why it's wonderful or whether it can be improved. Hearing only the good things may build your ego, but does little to encourage growth, create challenge, or provide goals. As Ruth Gendler comments: *Sometimes I want to write criticism a letter and tell him to leave me alone. The problem is when I don't see him for a while, I start to miss him.*

Rather than accept kind words, why not ask, *But how do you* really *feel? I really want to know.* By showing you're receptive to hearing a more in-depth critique, you may learn a lot about yourself.

Today, I can use criticism to learn something about myself and to gain experience in making choices about things I might like to change.

*It's funny the things you do under stress. I remember
that when [we were being attacked at Pearl Harbor by
the Japanese] . . . a quarter fell out of my pocket and
started rolling down the floor of my ship. I started to
chase it for a few seconds until I thought: "What am I
doing?"*

—CARL RYAN

When you're under pressure, do you find yourself
doing things that often add to your stress? For instance,
you're late for work and don't even have time for a cup
of instant coffee, yet you begin to cook an egg. Or
you're on your way out the door to make an important
appointment, but rush back in to answer the telephone.
Or you're tired and ready for bed, yet continue to put-
ter aimlessly around the house.

Oftentimes you may do such things because you're
so overwhelmed by your pressing priorities that you
focus your attention on something less important. But
by getting caught up in these other activities, you only
end up increasing the pressure on you.

That's when you need to stop and ask, *What am I
doing?* Then remind yourself of what it is you really
need to do by using the slogan, *First things first.* Then
take care of your first—and most pressing—priority.

Today, I'll ask, What do I need to do right now? *when
I find myself getting farther and farther away from a
matter that needs my attention.*

Everyone has a talent. What is rare is the courage to follow the talent to the dark place where it leads.
                                              —ERICA JONG

A writer knows that a first draft is just a first step toward creating a final manuscript. There's often much polishing and revising that needs to be done before the writer can send the manuscript to a publisher. And even when the writer is willing to share the book with the world, what's then involved is the process of waiting to hear from a publisher, possible rejection letters, or disappointment in needing to do more rewriting.

Every day of your life is like a first draft. It's just a first step you take in working toward the kind of person you'd like to become and the kind of life you'd like to have. Sometimes this can feel bright and exciting, like finishing the final draft of your novel. Other times it can feel dark and depressing, like the hard work and dedication that's involved in believing in your book when others don't.

The writer uses a belief in his or her talents to get through the "dark times" of self-doubt and waiting for a publisher. So, too, can you make it through your dark times by focusing on the skills it has taken to get you to where you are today.

Today, I'll be a "talent scout" to promote an awareness of my own abilities. Then I'll use my abilities to guide me through the darkness before my dreams come true.

I think the purpose of life is to be useful, to be respon-
sible, to be compassionate . . . to count, to stand for
something, to have made some difference that you lived
at all.

—LEO ROSTEN

A student at a preparatory school had just completed
his assignment for a "Death and Dying" class. The assignment was to write an essay detailing how he'd like
his funeral to be structured. A few days later, the young
man was killed in an automobile accident. At his
funeral, his essay was read and his family members,
students, teachers, and members of the community followed his wishes to the letter.

Imagine today that you had to design your own funeral. How would you like to be remembered?
Wouldn't you want others to focus on the good things
you accomplished, the good qualities you had, and the
ways in which you contributed to life?

Today, you can start to live up to those ideals. You
can change your view on the meaning and purpose of
your life from that of a struggle to achieve happiness,
fame, wealth, or material rewards to a life dedicated to
giving, to guiding others, and to promoting good in
your community. How you live your life from now on
can determine how others will remember you.

Today, I'll think about what my life does for others
rather than think only about what my life can do for
me.

To know oneself, one should assert oneself.
                                        —ALBERT CAMUS

While nearly everyone can be assertive in some situations—telling a waiter your steak is underdone or asking someone to hurry up so you're not late for the theater—very rarely are people assertive in every situation. Too often, people talk themselves out of being assertive by equating assertiveness with pushiness, stubbornness, selfishness, or impatience.

If you find it hard to be assertive in any—or many—situations, you may believe you don't have a right to your feelings, beliefs, or opinions. In fact, you may even consciously or unconsciously reject the idea that you're equal to or as important as others.

The first step in changing from such passive behavior to more assertive actions is to become more vocal in "safe situations"—minor interactions with familiar people. For instance, you can say to a friend, *I don't want to see a movie tonight. I'd rather go to the coffee-house.* Or you can tell your parents, *I won't be spending my entire Christmas break at home; I'll also be visiting my friends in the area.* Once you become comfortable standing up for yourself in safe situations, you can become more assertive with those who don't know you as well and in situations that are more meaningful.

Today, I'll strive to make requests that include my wants and needs. Instead of going along with what others want, I can assert myself.

*I've had ma fill of savin' souls. I'd just like to hole up
in some dogpatch and nurse ma own.*
                                    —A SOUTHERN PARSON

A middle-aged housewife and mother could rarely
find time to meditate for even twenty minutes every
day because her housework was never done. She felt
she couldn't take time out for herself or else the pile
of chores would grow into an unassailable mountain.
After years of doing continuous housework with no
time set aside to relax, she became run-down, depressed, anxious, and suffered from migraines and
lower back pain.

What excuses do you use to explain why you don't
have time to develop your inner peace through meditation? Typical reasons include: *I'm too busy; I'm too
tired; Missing once won't hurt; I feel relaxed and
unstressed, so I don't need to bother;* or *So-and-so
needs my help.*

Your excuses are likely to be the same ones you've
used for years. But any excuse is often based on a faulty
premise—like the housewife who believed she couldn't
meditate until her work was done, when the work of a
housewife and mother is never done!

When you place your priorities in the order of *"others first"* and *"me second,"* you prevent yourself from
maintaining mental, physical, and spiritual health. And
there's no excuse for that! So today place you first—
and let others fall in after you.

*I need time to relax and reenergize. Today, I'll set aside
time so that I can come first.*

My philosophy is that not only are you responsible for your life, but doing the best at this moment puts you in the best place for the next moment.

—OPRAH WINFREY

To cope with stress, everyone has different ways of relaxing and unwinding. Some are healthy and pleasurable—taking a walk, having dinner with friends or family, or spending a quiet evening at home. Others, however, use less healthy habits: smoking, drinking, overeating, fighting, using tranquilizers or drugs, or withdrawing from people.

Frequent use of such unhealthy tension-reducing activities can put you in the worst possible condition to handle your current stress. While an occasional drink or infrequent argument are probably not damaging, they can become habits that can undermine your health and, over time, make it hard for you to cope from day to day.

The key is balance. Any habit used to excess can add to your stress and further harm your health. So it's important that you take responsibility now to modify or eliminate frequent unhealthy habits so you can do your best at this moment—and the next.

Today, I'll determine if my bad habits are frequent. Then I'll change my habit by joining a support group, asking for help, or making the change myself.

Experience is what you get when you don't get what you want.

—DAN STANFORD

There's a story about a little boy who always wanted the biggest of everything because he thought it was the best. Once he was invited to dinner at a friend's house. He took the biggest piece of meat, but found it tough and gristly. He took the biggest baked potato, but discovered it was uncooked in the middle. He grabbed the biggest piece of chocolate cake, but it was bitter and stale.

How many times have you longed for something only to discover that it wasn't quite what you expected? Perhaps your transfer to a different department didn't make you like your job any better. Perhaps owning a home required more energy than you thought. Or maybe your hard-earned master's degree didn't increase your earning power in the way you had imagined.

How you react to things that disappoint you or fall short of your expectations will tell you how adaptable you are in dealing with dashed hopes and desires. Today, you can learn from such experiences. Once you find out what doesn't give you what you want, you can then strive to discover what will.

Today, I'll use my experiences to help me discover whether I've found what I want or if I need to continue my search.

If you are distressed by anything external, the pain is not due to the thing itself, but to your estimate of it; and this you have the power to revoke at any moment.
—MARCUS AURELIUS

What goes on outside you can easily become how you feel and think inside. For example, if someone you care for is crying, you may feel unhappy. Or if those around you are anxious, you may feel anxiety.

But you can prevent outside thoughts from becoming inner realities by learning to use your imagination to visualize an interaction between your pain and the peace you'd like to achieve.

First, close your eyes and breathe deeply. Be aware of your pain. Then give pain a symbol. For example, you might imagine a headache as a red-hot coal. Then give your peace a symbol. This could be a mountain stream filled with sparkling, clear, cool water. Now imagine drawing the two symbols together so they interact with one another in a way that removes the pain—your peaceful mountain stream rushes over the painful glowing coal and extinguishes it.

Such visualization can give you the power to eliminate many of your stress-related aches and pains or any negative thoughts brought about by external pressures.

Today, I'll make an audiotape of a visualization that can help me ease or even heal a chronic stress-related problem in the future.

Happy families are all alike; every unhappy family is unhappy in its own way.

—LEO TOLSTOY

Holidays focus on families. Because of this, it may be hard to escape from old hurts or unhappy childhood memories when you interact with your parents. It may be hard not to want to try once more to get from them the love, attention, or support you may not have gotten when you were growing up.

It may be futile, however, to try to get from your parents today what you didn't get when you were growing up. But that doesn't mean you can't strive to reconnect with them today so you can have a good relationship from now on.

To do so, keep in mind that your relationship today isn't parent to child—it's adult to adult. Instead of making demands on aging and perhaps still dysfunctional parents, expect less from them. Rather than carry old grudges and hurts with you when you go home for the holidays or when your parents visit you, sit down beforehand and think about all the things you do appreciate about your parents. Even though it may be hard to find things that are wonderful and warm, at least there may be little things they've done for you that you may discover mean a lot to you today.

Today, I'll anticipate some of the anxiety and tension I might feel at Christmas. I'll focus on the ways my parents have helped me instead of how they've hurt me.

What is more cheerful . . . than an open woodfire? Do you hear those little chirps and twitters coming out of that piece of apple-wood? Those are the ghosts of the robins and bluebirds that sang upon the bough when it was in blossom last spring.
—THOMAS BAILEY ALDRICH

There's a story of a religious teacher whose daily sermons were wonderful and inspiring, and he often spent hours preparing them. He thought that someday he might collect them into a book and seek a publisher or even appear on his own television show. With these thoughts in the back of his mind, he was about to begin a sermon when a little bird came and sat on the windowsill. It began to sing away with a full heart. Then it stopped and flew away. The teacher thought for a moment, folded the pages to his prepared sermon, and announced, *The sermon for this morning is over.*

While many things can be sought after, worked hard for, or struggled over, some things simply exist—and exist well. Appreciating nature at any time of year and being able to "connect" with it in some way—by cross-country skiing through a still pine forest or watching birds flock to a feeder—can help you forget your work-related goals or aspirations for a moment and show you the wonder of greater things.

Today, I'll notice how natural beauty can be spectacular—the brilliance of sunlight on pristine snow, the striking colors of winter birds, and the stately sight of bare trees against a winter sky.

Anxiety is a thin stream of fear trickling through the mind. If encouraged, it cuts a channel into which all other thoughts are drained.

—ARTHUR SOMERS ROCHE

A woman who worked at a rape crisis center began to fear the possibility of a sexual assault happening to her. After all, she had seen it happen to so many other women. But even though the woman took intelligent precautions, she couldn't shake her fear. Soon she grew so frightened she was afraid to leave her home.

While some amount of fear is good because it can make you cautious and conscious of your safety, too much fear can undermine your physical, emotional, and spiritual health. Living *in* fear—rather than living *with* fear—puts your physical senses on constant alert, encourages suspicion and mistrust, and leads you away from the faith that good exists in the universe.

To change this, create a "fear map"—a drawing that shows your work environment, home, the space between work and home, and other people, places, and things that make up your life. Identify those areas that evoke the greatest fear, then ask what it is you fear about each one. Confront your fears, then think of ways to "reroute" them—by taking a safer route home from work, by not spending time with an anxious friend, by meditating on a regular basis, or by reading literature that's relaxing or entertaining.

To live a more peaceful life involves facing my fears, learning to distinguish whether the fear is real or imaginary, and then taking appropriate action.

*This, like all times, is a very good one if we but know
what to do with it.*

—RALPH WALDO EMERSON

There's a classic story about two brothers with opposing attitudes—one an incurable optimist and the
other a diehard pessimist. Both brothers ask for a pony
for Christmas. Christmas morning comes, and they
both run excitedly to the barn. They fling open the
doors but find nothing except an enormous pile of manure. Disappointed, the pessimistic brother runs back
to the house in tears. The optimistic one, however,
picks up a shovel and starts to dig. *With this much
manure,* he thinks, *there's got to be a pony in here
somewhere.*

Fostering a positive attitude doesn't necessarily
guarantee that everything will turn out exactly the way
you want it to. But it can help you temper troubling
times or difficult situations by opening your eyes to a
different way of seeing things.

Rather than start today by reading the front page of
the newspaper—with headlines that focus on blood-
shed, poverty, and loss—turn to the comics. Focusing
on humorous and pleasant happenings can remind you
that there are joyous things in the world, too.

*Even in negative times, there's always something posi-
tive. Today, I'll try to find one thing I can feel good
about in my life or the world around me.*

He who cannot dance puts the blame on the floor.
                                    —HINDU PROVERB

Anyone can blame other people or things for their own personal faults, weaknesses, or mistakes. But when you can avoid blaming others, you make your behavior your responsibility—not theirs. In so doing, you remain connected with others, but have an opportunity to be open and honest with them at the same time.

It takes a courageous person to admit faults of their own making, their own deficits, or inappropriate actions. While blame is often used to take an easy way out, honesty can help you realistically confront something you may be afraid or hesitant to admit to others.

The simplest way to stop blame is to use statements that begin with *I.* Instead of saying, *It makes me mad,* say *I get mad;* instead of saying, *We all make mistakes,* say *I make mistakes;* and instead of saying, *This music isn't right for the way I dance,* say *I'm really not a very good dancer.* Even reading these statements aloud can help you hear how effective honest, blameless communication can be.

Blaming others only results in defensiveness. Today, I'll accept my feelings as mine and communicate them in that way.

. . . there comes a time when rituals have to be modified
to fit present circumstances.
—MARCIA LASSWELL

The season of joy and sharing can turn into a time
of anger and rigidity when people aren't willing to
compromise on traditions or let go of their expectations
about how the holiday should be celebrated. Disagreements over the size and type of tree, how to decorate
it, the type of foods that will be prepared, the number
of gifts that will be exchanged, and many other details
can send couples into separate rooms, evoke shouting
matches between parents and their children, or create
animosity between friends and roommates.

Such holiday battles aren't usually over simple differences of opinion or matters of taste or preference.
Rather, years of comfortable and familiar holiday
traditions are at stake. If your partner grew up in a
home where a wreath on the front door and a spotlight
were the only outside decorations, while you grew up
in a home that consistently won a prize for the most
elaborately decorated home, then you'll be at odds with
one another when it comes time to trim your house.

The key is to compromise. You and your partner can
take turns each year decorating the outside of your
home, or you can each have what you want for a part
of the month of December. By compromising, you can
ease the annual holiday tension and foster good feelings
of the season.

I like the holidays, but sometimes I want to orchestrate
things the way I want. Today, I'll be willing to com-
promise on one of my traditions.

. . . it's December twenty-first. Do you know what that means? . . . That means that every day from here we get more light. Every day there's a little more.
                                    —WILLIAM E. COLES, JR.

Do you get "blue" or feel down in the dumps in the dead of winter? Some people suffer from Seasonal Affective Disorder, which results from long periods of darkness and infrequent exposure to bright sunlight. But you don't have to have S.A.D. to suffer from the winter blues. When dipping wind chills and icy conditions keep you cooped up in the house, you may feel like all you do is get up, go to work, and come home.

While it's true that the cycles of nature designate winter as a time of natural hibernation—you store up food for needed fuel and become less active to save your energy for survival—your cycle of living doesn't have to slow down. Starting today, the periods of greatest darkness for the winter season are behind you. From now on, the period of light each day will become longer and you'll move steadily toward the spring thaw.

Rather than sit around and wait for spring to come, you can become more active. Join a health club. Invite friends over for an evening of charades or board games. Have a "Hot December" party where you serve summer foods to guests dressed in summer clothes. Rouse yourself out of a winter hibernation and into fun, energizing activities, and you won't be blue anymore!

Today, I'll stop grumbling about winter. Through rain, hail, sleet, or snow, I can think of ways to get up and go!

*Love is a great thing, a good above all others, which
alone maketh every burden light.*

—THOMAS À KEMPIS

Times such as holidays, which emphasize family, relationships, closeness, and emotional connection, can
sometimes leave you feeling empty and alone. When
your parents are no longer around or you're single, you
may feel as if everyone but you has a comforting place
to visit.

But love doesn't always have to come from family or
a partner. Love can come from those who share a big
part of your life. A circle of caring friends can help you
feel like you're part of a family. A close friend who
understands you, accepts you, and who's always there
for you can help you feel as cared for as an intimate
partner.

And there are many other sources of love, too. The
people you work with, the children you teach or care
for, those you give to through volunteer service, members of groups you belong to—even a pet—can help
you feel loved and connected.

Rather than bemoan the love you've lost or don't
have, you can feel the love you do have. By showing
others that you love them and accept the love they give
you, you can begin to see that your life is full—not
empty—of love.

*Today, I'll accept that love will never be truly gone from
my life. I'll open my heart to feeling the love from those
around me.*

Don't look for one right answer. This keeps you from seeking less-obvious alternatives that might provide more creative solutions.   —ANONYMOUS

There's the story of a man who wore himself ragged every December 23 doing last-minute holiday shopping and gift wrapping. Then, one year, he came up with an idea to alleviate the stress of his usual last-minute preparations. He decided to shop early and have the department stores do all the gift wrapping. So on December 23, the man proudly showed his roommate the pile of ready and wrapped gifts. The roommate peered closely at the presents. *But how do you know whose presents they are?* he asked. *There aren't any gift tags on them.*

Shocked, the man glanced through the packages and saw his roommate was right. In despair, he prepared to dash out to buy paper to rewrap all the presents. But his roommate stopped him. *Why don't you give a double gift this year?* he suggested. *A gift and a surprise at the same time?*

On Christmas, the man's family roared with laughter as each opened a "surprise"—the grandmother found a pair of hockey skates, while the teenage boy got a nightie; the baby was given a set of wrenches, while the uncle received a teething ring!

Awakening your creativity can take you down interesting paths. All it takes is letting go of the obvious and thinking, *What if . . . ?*

Today, I'll recognize that any problem can have many solutions. When I'm stuck, I'll ask others what they'd do so I can get creative and helpful suggestions.

Intimacy happens in moments. The mistake we make is in wanting it all the time.

—JoAnn Magdoff

Wouldn't it be nice if the warm glow, loving feelings, and laughter and lightness you feel with your loved ones today was like a match struck to an eternal flame? So, from this moment on, no matter what circumstances occur, how difficult times become, or how much time passes, the flame of intimacy would always burn bright.

But when you look around at your loved ones tonight and see them gathered together in peace and harmony, try to keep in mind, *This is what the holidays are all about.* This doesn't mean that from now on, conflicts will be easier to handle or loving feelings will predominate. What it means is that for right now, there's a respite from the tension of the day-to-day struggle to get along. And that respite should be enjoyed for as long as it lasts and then released, without a struggle, when it ends.

You can delight in the shared laughter, relax with the ease of casual chatter, and be excited by a physical touch or embrace. But rather than strive to light an eternal flame, seek out the glow of a simple candle. Although from time to time the flame may be extinguished, it can always be relit.

Today, I'll remember that those I love have lives as complex and difficult as mine. So I can enjoy a happy holiday with them and then let each day that follows happen the way it needs to.

[To] take something from yourself, to give to another, that is humane and gentle and never takes away as much comfort as it brings again.

—SIR THOMAS MORE

Perhaps the most wondrous gift is the one given to a child so young that it only knows the pure joy of receiving. The child isn't bothered by knowing who gave the gift, why it was given, or whether something needs to be given in return.

But in adulthood, gift giving can take on a different meaning. When adults exchange gifts, their pleasure may be tinged with anxiety—*Did I give more than I got? Did I get more than I gave?* Or there may be the expressed or unexpressed implication of getting something in return, like gratitude, respect, or love—*He'll like me more now that I gave him the shirt he wanted,* or *She owes me something now for that expensive jacket.*

While the gifts you give to others may reflect many things—prosperity, a desire for approval, or recognition of another's likes—the best gifts you can give today are the ones that bring *you* pleasure in their giving.

This Christmas, perhaps your greatest gift can be volunteering, giving blood, or contributing to a charity. Such a gift may evoke the greatest joy.

Today, I'll know that a gift of myself can be a gift to myself.

Nothing can keep an argument going like two persons who aren't sure what they're arguing about.

—O. A. BATTISTA

Is there a member of your family with whom you can't seem to get along, no matter what you do? It may seem that everything you say becomes the topic of a heated debate, any comment you make is misconstrued as a criticism, and all of your facial expressions are interpreted as silent judgments.

Don't you often wish you could ask, *Why don't we get along?* and receive an answer that would help you understand the cause of the friction so you could smooth it out? Yet sometimes the reasons why disagreements and disconnections between family members go on for years and years is that no one quite knows the reasons why.

In the movie *On Golden Pond*, the daughter discovers that her long-standing rift with her father started when she was a child, when he didn't have the time or interest to watch her execute a dive into the lake. Once she realizes why she's had such problems with him, she's able to let go of her anger and embrace him.

While you may never be able to get to the bottom of the friction between you and a family member, you can try. Today, why not simply say, *I really wish we could get along better. Is there anything I can do to help?*

I want to knock down the barriers that exist between me and a family member. Today, I'll try to talk to this person and share how I feel.

Life is tough. It takes up a lot of your time, all your weekends, and what do you get at the end of it? . . . Death, a great reward.

—MARK TWAIN

Have you ever thought, *If I only knew back then what I know now?* Imagine how you would've handled hard times in high school. Today, you might think, *So what if I wasn't the greatest athlete, the brightest student, or the most popular kid in the class? I did okay.* Or think about where you might be in your life now if you could've used today's knowledge to help you years ago. Would you still want to marry when you did? Would you have opted for a degree instead of a job? Would you have chosen another profession?

Mark Twain once composed an essay that proposed that the life cycle is backward. You should . . . *die first, get it out of the way, then live twenty years in an old age home. You get kicked out when you're too young, you get a gold watch, you go to work. You work forty years until you're young enough to enjoy your retirement.*

Today, you don't have to despair over yesterday's decisions. Although the past is gone, you have the power to change your life. You can go back to school, take the vacation you always dreamed of, or try something you never did before. Even though time marches on, you can determine what direction you'll take.

There are some things I'd like to do that I never had a chance to do before. Today, I'll make an opportunity happen and enjoy it for the first time.

We do not love people because they are beautiful, but because they seem beautiful to us because we love them.
—RUSSIAN PROVERB

How would you write "I love you" to someone you love in twenty-five words or less? There's just one catch. You can't use the words "I love you."

Love is not always an easy emotion to feel. It may be easier to say those three words than to try to put into words why you feel them. Sometimes it can be difficult to look at the qualities, gifts, and uniqueness of someone you love. You may wind up making comparisons—*He's more successful than I am,* or *She's much better with the kids*—and, when confronted by your weaknesses, question why someone would love you. You may be a negative thinker who has a hard time focusing on the positive. Or you may be a rational person who has a tendency to think about emotions rather than feel them.

But love doesn't necessarily have to be thought about or expressed in grandiose ways. Love can simply be seeing and accepting someone for who he or she is.

Today, try to write your "I love you" essay. What you may discover is that you love someone simply because that person is beautiful to you.

Today, I'll focus on all the good qualities of the one person I love and think about how nice our love feels.

When one door of happiness closes, another opens; but often we look so long at the closed door that we do not see the one which has been opened for us.
                                                    —HELEN KELLER

Have there been certain events in your life that made you feel quite happy—events you looked forward to and enjoyed? Perhaps it was your high school prom, your college graduation, the delivery of a new car, purchasing your first home, being promoted, or going on a vacation abroad. But how did you feel once the event was over? Were you still happy?

Times that make us feel happy are often fleeting. A dance will always draw to a close, the initial excitement over a promotion will eventually wear off, and the day of your move to a new house will finally arrive. But there will always be another dance, another work success, and the possibility of other exciting moves.

True happiness isn't a feeling; it comes from within. It's a belief that good things can happen and that difficult times won't last forever. When you can think of things in your life that give you an ongoing sense of contentment, peace, or joy, then you won't pay much attention when one door of happiness closes.

Today, I'll think about the things that bring me peace and contentment, and not those whose joy is fleeting.

It is good to have an end to journey towards; but it is the journey that matters, in the end.
—URSULA K. LEGUIN

Your goals lend direction to your life. Without them you might flounder, uncertain of who you are and where you're going. Goals can provide you with a source of confidence, motivate you, and give you something to look forward to.

Yet at some point, you need to sit back and simply enjoy what you've accomplished. After all, what's the good of losing weight if you can't buy new clothes and show your new body off? What's the point of learning how to ski if you can't take off on a long weekend to a ski resort to enjoy your new skill? What fun is saving your money unless you can spend some of it on something you've always wanted?

It may be easier to continue to set more goals rather than to take time out to appreciate a goal's end. Goal setting and achieving can keep you so occupied and active that you may feel that the process—not the end result—is what gives your life true meaning.

Setting your sights on a goal's end is a way of accomplishing it. But looking around you at the sights you reach is a way of giving your life meaning. Appreciating a journey's end, as much as the journey itself, is what really matters.

Today, I'll remember this lesson: A goal is never really accomplished until it's fully appreciated. I won't be able to grasp the full joy of living if my sights are glued to my next goal.

In three words, I can sum up everything I've learned about life: It goes on.

—ROBERT FROST

Have you ever dug into an ants' nest? Their first reaction to your unintended destruction is to do everything possible to save their lives, their nest, and its contents. So the ants immediately act. They scurry around, moving the larvae into a safer underground chamber. Exposed contents of the nest are relocated to unseen passages. The hill of grains of dirt is rebuilt. In a matter of minutes, the ants are again safely underground and ready to resume the normal flow of their daily routines.

How do you react when some catastrophe or unplanned event occurs? Do you want to crawl under the covers, or are you as resilient as the ants? Instead of moaning over postponed plans or the loss of something in your life, you can try to be like the ants and learn how to best work *with* the circumstances that come your way.

Life doesn't stop or give you time simply to lick your wounds. Hours pass, you grow older, and nature continues. Every event is part of life's cycle. So you must meet each event head-on, adjust to its ebb and flow, and keep going on.

Today, I'll look at an unplanned event in my life as simply part of life's cycle. Then I'll trust that life will go on.

Index

About the Author

AMY E. DEAN is the author of *Proud to Be*, a meditational for lesbians and gay men, *Pleasant Dreams: Nighttime Meditations for Peace of Mind*, and the best-selling meditational *Night Light*, which has sold over 500,000 copies. In addition, she has written four books of nonfiction, two novels, and is currently at work on her fifth meditational, *Facing Life's Difficulties: Daily Meditations for Overcoming Depression, Grief, and the Blues*. She lectures nationally and lives in Maynard, Massachusetts.